THE WAR
THAT FORGED
A NATION

THE WAR
THAT FORGED
A NATION

Why the Civil War Still Matters

JAMES McPHERSON

OXFORD
UNIVERSITY PRESS

OXFORD

UNIVERSITY PRESS

Oxford University Press is a department of the
University of Oxford. It furthers the University's objective
of excellence in research, scholarship, and education
by publishing worldwide.

Oxford   New York

Auckland   Cape Town   Dar es Salaam   Hong Kong   Karachi
Kuala Lumpur   Madrid   Melbourne   Mexico City   Nairobi
New Delhi   Shanghai   Taipei   Toronto

With offices in

Argentina   Austria   Brazil   Chile   Czech Republic   France   Greece
Guatemala   Hungary   Italy   Japan   Poland   Portugal   Singapore
South Korea   Switzerland   Thailand   Turkey   Ukraine   Vietnam

Oxford is a registered trade mark of Oxford University Press
in the UK and in certain other countries.

Published in the United States of America by
Oxford University Press
198 Madison Avenue, New York, NY 10016

Title page image: The Hawkins Brothers, Captain Charles A. (born 1841) and
Sergeant John M. (born 1843), Co. E., 38th Reg't Georgia Vol. Infantry.
Ambrotype by unknown photographer. David Wynn Vaughan Collection.

Library of Congress Cataloging-in-Publication Data
McPherson, James M.
The war that forged a nation : why the Civil War still matters / James McPherson.
pages   cm
Includes bibliographical references and index.
ISBN 978-0-19-937577-6 (hardback)
1. United States—History—Civil War, 1861–1865—Influence.
2. United States—History—Civil War, 1861–1865—Psychological aspects.
3. United States—History—Civil War, 1861–1865—Social aspects.
4. War and society—United States—History.
5. Social change—United States—History.
6. National characteristics, American—History.   I. Title.
E468.9.M19   2015
973.7'1—dc23   2014018008

1   3   5   7   9   8   6   4   2
Printed in the United States of America
on acid-free paper

CONTENTS

PREFACE

More than 140 years ago, Mark Twain observed that the Civil War, which had recently ended, "uprooted institutions that were centuries old, changed the politics of a people, transformed the social life of half the country, and wrought so profoundly upon the entire national character that the influence cannot be measured short of two or three generations."

Five generations have passed, and we are still trying to measure that influence. The long shadow cast by the Civil War continues to affect us today. More Americans died in that conflict than in all the other wars this country has fought combined, right through the latest casualty reports from Afghanistan. Several new books about Abraham Lincoln and Jefferson Davis, and the movie *Lincoln*, have offered important insights about presidential leadership in a time of crisis and have raised questions about the political and constitutional constraints on executive powers. The film *Twelve Years a Slave* powerfully dramatized the pain and cruelty of an institution that lay at the root of American society and brought on the war. The close relationship between the abolition of slavery and the subsequent evolution of race relations in the United States has received a great deal of attention, especially since the election of Barack Obama as president.

Since the publication of my first book fifty years ago, I have sought to dissect the Civil War's impact at several levels and in several dimensions.

The twelve chapters in this volume represent a continuation of that effort. One of the essays is published here for the first time (chapter 1). The others have appeared in various venues and formats during the past eight years, but several have been substantially revised and updated. Each chapter is complete in itself and can be read independently of the others, but I have also tried to fit them together in a cohesive pattern so that they can be read consecutively from beginning to end. Although the essays are grounded in many years of reading and research, they are more interpretive than monographic, and I have therefore confined the endnotes mainly to citations for quotations. My interpretations are sometimes stated strongly, and some of them may disagree with the reader's own judgments. I welcome disagreement and dialogue, for that is how scholarship and understanding advance.

James McPherson
Princeton, New Jersey

PROVENANCE OF THE CONTENTS

Chapter 1 has not been previously published. Chapters 2, 3, 4, 7, and 8 are adapted from review essays that first appeared in the *New York Review of Books*. I own the copyright to these essays, and I am grateful to the NYRB for giving me carte blanche to use them in this changed format, and to Robert Silvers for his invitations to review the books that provided the basis for my analyses of several important Civil War issues. Chapter 5, to which I also own the copyright, was initially published in *Dixie Redux: Essays in Honor of Sheldon Hackey*, edited by Raymond Arsenault and Orville Vernon Burton (Montgomery, Ala.: New South Books, 2013). Chapter 6 first appeared in the October 2014 issue of the *Journal of Military History*. I am indebted to the Society for Military History for permission to publish it herein. Chapter 9, to which I own the copyright, was first included in *Our Lincoln: New Perspectives on Lincoln and His World*, edited by Eric Foner (New York: W. W. Norton, 2008). Chapter 10 was originally titled "My Enemies Are Crushed: Lincoln and McClellan" and appeared in *Wars within a War: Controversy and Conflict over the American Civil War*, edited by Joan Waugh and Gary W. Gallagher (Chapel Hill: University of North Carolina Press, 2009). Chapter 11 initially appeared in *Lincoln Lessons: Reflections on America's Greatest Leader*, edited by Frank J. Williams and William D. Peterson (Carbondale: Southern Illinois

University Press, 2009). Chapter 12 was first published in *The Making of Peace: Rulers, States, and the Aftermath of War*, edited by Williamson Murray and Jim Lacey (Cambridge: Cambridge University Press, 2009). I am grateful to these three publishers for permission to reprint these essays.

THE WAR
THAT FORGED
A NATION

CHAPTER 1

Why the Civil War Still Matters

Even before the many conferences, commemorations, books, exhibits, and other public events associated with the bicentennial of Abraham Lincoln's birth in 2009 and the sesquicentennial of the Civil War from 2011 to 2015, that war was the most popular historical subject in many parts of the United States. In 1987 the historian at the Vicksburg National Military Park declared that "Americans just can't get enough of the Civil War." A bookstore owner in Falls Church, Virginia, said a year or so later that "for the last two years Civil War books have been flying out of here. It's not [just] the buffs who buy; it's the general public, from high school kids to retired people." In 1990 some thirty million viewers watched the eleven hours of television documentary produced by Ken Burns, and rebroadcasts in the past two decades have lifted that number to at least fifty million in the United States and abroad. Civil War books are the leading sellers for the History Book Club. An estimated two hundred Civil War Round Tables meet monthly to listen to lectures and discuss the war. Thousands of Americans (and even some foreigners) are Civil War reenactors who fight mock battles every year before thousands of spectators at or near where they took place 150 years ago.[1]

What accounts for this intense interest in the fratricidal conflict that almost tore the country apart? First, perhaps, was the sheer size of that conflict, fought not in some foreign land, as most American wars have been, but on battlefields from Pennsylvania to New Mexico and from Florida to Kansas, hallowed ground that Americans can visit today. Then there is the drama and tragedy of the war's human cost—some 750,000 soldiers plus an unknown number of civilians who lost their lives in the war, according to the latest research.[2] To illustrate the immensity of that figure, it equals 2.4 percent of the American population in 1860. If 2.4 percent of Americans were to be killed in a war fought today, the number of war dead would be almost 7.5 million. Or to take another statistic: 23,000 Union and Confederate soldiers were killed, wounded, or missing in a single day, at the Battle of Antietam on September 17, 1862. This figure was nearly four times the number of American casualties on D-day, June 6, 1944. The human cost of the Civil War cast a long shadow forward in our history, and continues to horrify us but also solemnly to impress us 150 years later.

Then there are the larger-than-life, near-mythical individuals on both sides, whose lives and careers continue to fascinate us today: Abraham Lincoln and Robert E. Lee and Ulysses S. Grant and Stonewall Jackson and William Tecumseh Sherman and Clara Barton—and on and on. There is a kind of romance and glory, as well as tragedy, surrounding these people and their times that is hard to resist.

This drama and romance and tragedy help explain why the Civil War remains such a popular subject, but they do not entirely explain why that war still matters so deeply to us today, 150 years later. To start getting at that question, I hope the reader will forgive a little autobiography, to account for how and why I became interested in the Civil War when I was in graduate school more than a half century ago—because it was for many of the same reasons why the war still matters to all of us today.

Unlike many of my friends and colleagues, I did not have a youthful fascination with the Civil War. When I arrived in Baltimore in 1958 for graduate study at Johns Hopkins University, I had not read anything specifically on the subject except perhaps a couple of books by the journalist and popular historian Bruce Catton. I had not taken a college course on the Civil War because my small college in Minnesota did not offer such a course.

I had a vague and rather naive interest in the history of the South, in part because, having been born in North Dakota and brought up in Minnesota, I found the South exotic and mysterious. During my senior year in college, nine black students integrated Little Rock Central High School in Arkansas under the protection of the U.S. Army. I was well enough acquainted with history and current events to know that the constitutional basis for these students' presence at Central High was the Fourteenth Amendment, one of the most important products of the Civil War and of the Reconstruction period that followed it. In retrospect it seems likely that this awareness planted the seeds of my interest in the Civil War era.

That seed germinated within days of my arrival at Johns Hopkins when, like other incoming graduate students, I met with a prospective academic adviser. Mine was Professor C. Vann Woodward, the foremost historian of the American South, whose book *The Strange Career of Jim Crow* (1955) became almost the bible of the civil rights movement. My appointment was postponed for a day because Woodward had been called to Washington to testify before a congressional committee about potential problems in Little Rock as a second year of school desegregation got under way. Here was a revelation: a historian offering counsel on the most important domestic issue of the day. If I had not seen the connection between the Civil War and my own times before, I certainly discovered it then.

That consciousness grew during my four years in Baltimore, the last two of which included the opening phases of the commemoration of the Civil War centennial. But these events made little impression on me until an episode in Charleston, South Carolina, in April 1961, when a black delegate from New Jersey's centennial commission was denied a room at the Francis Marion Hotel. In protest, several Northern delegations walked out of the commemorative ceremonies, boycotting them until President John F. Kennedy offered the integrated facilities at the Charleston Naval Base. This offer in turn provoked the Southern delegates to secede from the national commission and hold their own activities at the hotel. It all seemed like déjà vu.

The civil rights movement eclipsed the centennial observations during the first half of the 1960s. Those were the years of sit-ins and freedom rides in the South, of Southern political leaders vowing what they called "massive resistance" to national laws and court decisions, of federal marshals and troops trying to protect civil rights demonstrators, of conflict and violence, of the March on Washington in August 1963, when Martin Luther King Jr. stood before the Lincoln Memorial and began his "I have a dream" speech with the words "Five score years ago, a great American, in whose symbolic shadow we stand today, signed the Emancipation Proclamation. This momentous decree came as a great beacon light of hope to millions of Negro slaves who had been scarred in the flame of withering injustice."[3] These were also the years of the Civil Rights Act of 1964 and the Voting Rights Act of 1965, which derived their constitutional bases from the Fourteenth and Fifteenth Amendments adopted a century earlier. The creation of the Freedmen's Bureau by the federal government in 1865, to aid the transition of four million former slaves to freedom, was the first large-scale intervention by the government in the field of social welfare.

These parallels between the 1960s and 1860s, and the roots of events in my own time in events of exactly a century earlier, propelled me to become a historian of the Civil War and Reconstruction. I became convinced that I could not fully understand the issues of my own time unless I learned about their roots in the era of the Civil War: slavery and its abolition; the conflict between North and South; the struggle between state sovereignty and the federal government; the role of government in social change and resistance to both government and social change. Those issues are as salient and controversial today as they were in the 1960s, not to mention the 1860s.

In 2015 we have an African American president of the United States, which would not have been possible without the civil rights movement of a half century ago, which in turn would not have been possible without the events of the Civil War and Reconstruction era. Many of the issues over which the Civil War was fought still resonate today: matters of race and citizenship; regional rivalries; the relative powers and responsibilities of federal, state, and local governments. The first section of the Fourteenth Amendment, which among other things conferred American citizenship on anyone born in the United States, has become controversial today because of concern about illegal immigration. As the Southern novelist William Faulkner once said: "The past is not dead; it is not even past."

Let us take a closer look at some of those aspects of the Civil War that are neither dead nor past. At first glance, it appeared that Northern victory in the war resolved two fundamental, festering issues that had been left unresolved by the Revolution of 1776 that had given birth to the nation: first, whether this fragile republican experiment called the *United* States would survive as one nation, indivisible; and second, whether that nation would continue to endure half slave and half free. Both of these issues had remained open questions until 1865. Many Americans in the early decades of the country's history feared that the nation might break apart; many European conservatives predicted its demise; some Americans had advocated the right of secession and periodically threatened to invoke it; eleven states did invoke it in 1861. But since 1865 no state or region has *seriously* threatened secession. To be sure, some fringe groups assert the theoretical right of secession, but none has really tried to carry it out. That question seems settled.

By the 1850s the United States, which had been founded on a charter that declared all men created equal with an equal title to liberty, had become the largest slaveholding country in the world, making a mockery of this country's professions of freedom and equal rights. Lincoln and many other antislavery leaders pulled no punches in their denunciations of both the "injustice" and "hypocrisy" of these professions.[4] With the Emancipation Proclamation in 1863 and the Thirteenth Amendment to the Constitution in 1865, that particular "monstrous injustice" and "hypocrisy" has existed no more. Yet the legacy of slavery in the form of racial discrimination and prejudice long plagued the United States, and has not entirely disappeared a century and a half later.

In the process of preserving the Union of 1776 while purging it of slavery, the Civil War also transformed it. Before 1861 "United States" was a plural noun: The United States *have* a republican form of government. Since 1865 "United States" is a singular noun: The United States *is* a world power. The North went to war to preserve the *Union*; it ended by creating a *nation*. This transformation can be traced in Lincoln's most important wartime addresses. His first inaugural address, in 1861, contained the word "Union" twenty times and the word "nation" not once. In Lincoln's first message to Congress, on July 4, 1861, he used the word "Union" thirty-two times and "nation" only three times. In his famous public letter to Horace Greeley of August 22, 1862, concerning slavery and the war, Lincoln spoke of the Union eight times and the nation not at all. But in the brief Gettysburg Address fifteen months later, he did not refer to the Union at all but used the word "nation" five times. And in the second inaugural address, looking back over the trauma of the past four years, Lincoln spoke of one side seeking to dissolve the Union in 1861 and the other side accepting the challenge of war to preserve the "nation."

The decentralized antebellum republic, in which the post office was the only agency of national government that touched the average citizen, was transformed by the crucible of war into a centralized polity that taxed people directly and created an internal revenue bureau to collect the taxes, expanded the jurisdiction of federal courts, created a national currency and a federally chartered banking system, drafted men into the army, and created the Freedmen's Bureau as the first national agency for social welfare. Eleven of the first twelve amendments to the Constitution had limited the powers of the national government; most of them contained some form of the statement that the federal government "shall not" have certain powers. Most of the next fifteen constitutional amendments, starting with the Thirteenth Amendment in 1865, say that the federal government "shall have the power" to enforce these provisions. The first three of the post–Civil War constitutional amendments transformed four million slaves into citizens and voters within five years, the most rapid and fundamental social transformation in American history—even if the nation did backslide on part of this commitment for three generations after 1877.

A Southern slaveholder had been president of the United States two-thirds of the years between 1789 and 1861, and two-thirds of the Speakers of the House and presidents pro tem of the Senate had also been Southerners. Twenty of the thirty-five Supreme Court justices during that period had been from slave states, which always had a majority on the Court before 1861. After the Civil War a century passed before another resident of a Southern state was elected president—Lyndon Johnson in 1964. For half a century after the war only one Southerner served as Speaker of the House and none as president pro tem of the Senate. Only five of the twenty-six Supreme Court justices appointed during that half century were Southerners. The institutions and ideology of a plantation society and a slave system that had dominated half of the country and sought to dominate more went down with a great crash in 1865 and were replaced by the institutions and ideology of free-labor entrepreneurial capitalism. For better or for worse, the flames of Civil War forged the framework of modern America.

That last point requires some elaboration. Before 1865 two distinct socioeconomic and cultural systems competed for dominance within the body politic of the United States. Although in retrospect the triumph of free-labor capitalism seems to have been inevitable, that was by no means clear for most of the antebellum generation. Not only did the institutions and ideology of the rural, agricultural, plantation South, based on slave labor, dominate the U.S. government during most of that time, but the territory of the slave states also considerably exceeded that of the free states before 1859, and the Southern drive for further territorial expansion seemed more aggressive than that of the North. Most of the slave states seceded from the United States in 1861 not only because they feared the potential threat to the long-term survival of slavery posed by Lincoln's election but also because they looked forward to the expansion of a dynamic, independent slave-holding polity into new territory by the acquisition of Cuba and perhaps more of Mexico and Central America. If the Confederacy had prevailed in the 1860s, it is quite possible that the emergence of the United States as the world's leading industrial as well as agricultural producer by the end of the nineteenth century and as the world's most powerful nation in the twentieth century might never have happened. That it did happen is certainly one of the most important legacies of the Civil War—not only for America but also for the world.

The explosive growth of industrial capitalism in the post–Civil War generations was not an unmixed blessing. Labor strife and exploitation of workers became endemic. Violence characterized many strikes and efforts by management to break the strikes. Degradation of the environment by air and water pollution and the ravaging of natural resources became endemic. At the same time, the Civil War had left the South impoverished, its agricultural economy in shambles, and the freed slaves in a limbo of second-class citizenship after the failure of Reconstruction in the 1870s to fulfill the promise of civil and political equality embodied in the Fourteenth and Fifteenth Amendments to the Constitution.

Those amendments remained in the Constitution, however, and the legacy of national unity, a strong national government, and a war for freedom inherited from the triumph of the 1860s was revived again in the civil rights movement of the 1960s, which finally began the momentous process of making good on the promises of a century earlier. Though many white Southerners for generations elegized the cause they had lost in 1865—indeed, mourned the world they had lost, a world they sometimes romanticized into a vision of moonlight and magnolias—white as well as black Southerners are today probably better off because they lost that war than they would have been if they had won it. Some of them might even admit as much.

No single word better expresses what Americans believe their country has stood for from 1776 right down to the present than "liberty." The tragic irony of the Civil War is that both sides professed to fight for the heritage of liberty bequeathed to them by the Founding Fathers. North and South alike in 1861 wrapped themselves in the mantle of 1776. But the two sides interpreted this heritage in opposite ways—and at first neither side included the slaves in the vision of liberty for which they fought. But the slaves did; and by the time of Lincoln's Gettysburg Address in 1863 the North fought not merely for the liberty bequeathed by the Founders but also for "a new birth of freedom." These multiple and varying meanings of liberty, and how they dissolved and re-formed in kaleidoscopic patterns during the war, provide the central meaning of the war for the American experience.

Southern states invoked the example of their forebears of 1776, who seceded from the British Empire in the name of liberty to govern themselves. Southern secessionists proclaimed in 1861 that "the same spirit of freedom and independence that impelled our Fathers to the separation from the British Government" would impel the "liberty loving people of the South" to separation from the United States. From "the high and solemn motive of defending and protecting the rights which our fathers bequeathed to us," declared Jefferson Davis in 1861, let us "renew such sacrifices as our fathers made to the holy cause of constitutional liberty."[5]

One of the liberties for which Southern whites contended, Lincoln had said sarcastically back in 1854, was "the liberty of making slaves of other people." In 1861 many Northerners also ridiculed the Confederacy's profession to be fighting for the same ideals of liberty as their forefathers of 1776. That was "a libel upon the whole character and conduct of the men of '76," said the antislavery poet and journalist William Cullen Bryant. Ignoring the fact that many of the Founding Fathers owned slaves, Bryant claimed that the Founders had fought the Revolution "to establish the rights of man...and principles of universal liberty," while the South in 1861 seceded "not in the interest of general humanity, but of a domestic despotism....Their motto is not liberty, but slavery."[6]

In 1864 Lincoln used a parable to make an important point, as he often did, in this case a point about the multiple meanings of liberty. He did so in a speech at Baltimore, in a slave state that had remained in the Union and even then was engaged in bitter debates about a state constitutional amendment to abolish slavery in Maryland (which narrowly passed later that year). "The world has never had a good definition of the word liberty, and the American people, just now, are much in want of one," said Lincoln on this occasion. "We all declare for liberty; but in using the same *word* we do not all mean the same *thing*. With some the word liberty may mean for each man to do as he pleases with himself, and the product of his labor; while with others the same word may mean for some men to do as they please with other men, and the product of other men's labor. Here are two, not only different, but incompatible things, called by the same name—liberty." Lincoln went on to illustrate his point with a parable about animals. "The shepherd drives the wolf from the sheep's throat," he said, "for which the sheep thanks the shepherd as a liberator, while the wolf denounces him for the same act as the destroyer of liberty, especially as the sheep is a black one. Plainly the sheep and the wolf are not agreed upon a definition of the word liberty; and precisely the same difference prevails today among us human creatures, even in the North, and all professing to love liberty. Hence we behold the processes by which thousands are daily passing from under the yoke of bondage, hailed by some as the advance of liberty, and bewailed by others as the destruction of all liberty."[7]

The shepherd in this fable was, of course, Lincoln himself; the black sheep was the slave, and the wolf his owner. As commander in chief of an army of a million men in 1864, Lincoln wielded a great deal of power, and by this stage of the war that power was being used not only to defeat the Confederacy and preserve the Union but also to abolish slavery. Traditionally in American ideology, however, power was the enemy of liberty. Americans had fought their revolution to get free from the power of the British crown. "There is a tendency in all Governments to an augmentation of power at the expense of liberty," wrote James Madison. To curb this tendency, framers of the Constitution devised a series of checks and balances that divided power among three branches of the national government, between two houses of Congress, and between the state and federal governments as, in Madison's words, an "essential precaution in favor of liberty."[8] Madison also drafted the first ten amendments to the Constitution as a Bill of Rights that limited the powers of the national government in the name of liberty. Nearly all of these amendments apply some form of the phrase "shall not" to the federal government.

Through most of early American history, those who feared the potential of power to undermine liberty remained eternally vigilant against this threat. When Dorothea Dix, the famous reformer of the treatment of the mentally ill, persuaded Congress to pass a bill granting public lands to the states to subsidize mental hospitals in 1854, President Franklin Pierce vetoed it in the name of preserving liberty. For if Congress could do this, warned Pierce, "it has the same power to provide for the indigent who are not insane, and thus . . . the whole field of public beneficence is thrown open to the care and culture of the Federal Government." This would mean, continued Pierce's veto message, "all sovereignty vested in an absolute consolidated central power, against which the spirit of liberty has so often and in so many countries struggled in vain." The bill for mental hospitals, therefore, would be "the beginning of the end . . . of our blessed inheritance of representative liberty."[9]

Proslavery Southerners like John C. Calhoun insisted on keeping the national government weak, as insurance against a possible antislavery majority in Congress at some future time that might try to abolish or weaken slavery. State sovereignty, or state rights, was a bulwark against this potential antislavery majority. The most extreme manifestation of state sovereignty, of course, was secession in the name of the liberty of Southern states and Southern people to reject the federal government and form their own proslavery nation. If this version of liberty was to be used to destroy the United States, concluded most Northerners during the Civil War, then it was time to take another look at the meaning of liberty.

To help us understand this change in attitude toward the meaning of liberty, we can turn to the definitions offered by the famous twentieth-century British philosopher Isaiah Berlin in an essay titled "Two Concepts of Liberty."[10] The two concepts are negative liberty and positive liberty. The idea of negative liberty is perhaps more familiar. It can be defined as the absence of restraint, a freedom from interference by outside authority with individual thought or behavior. Laws requiring automobile passengers to wear seat belts or motorcyclists to wear helmets would be, under this definition, to prevent them from enjoying the liberty to choose not to wear seat belts or helmets. Negative liberty, therefore, can be described as freedom *from*.

Positive liberty, by contrast, can best be understood as freedom *to*. It is not necessarily incompatible with negative liberty but has a different focus or emphasis. Freedom of the press is generally viewed as a negative liberty—freedom from interference with what a writer writes or a reader reads. But an illiterate person suffers from a denial of positive liberty; he is unable to enjoy the freedom to write or read whatever he pleases not because some authority prevents him from doing so but because he cannot read or write anything. He suffers not the absence of a negative liberty (freedom from) but of a positive liberty (freedom *to* read and write). The remedy lies not in removal of restraint but in achievement of the capacity to read and write.

The Civil War accomplished a historic shift in American values in the direction of positive liberty. The change from all those "shall nots" in the first ten amendments to the Constitution to the phrase "Congress shall have the power to enforce" this provision in most of the post–Civil War amendments is indicative of that shift—especially the Thirteenth Amendment, which liberated four million slaves, and the Fourteenth and Fifteenth, which guaranteed them equal civil and political rights.

Abraham Lincoln played a crucial role in this historic change toward positive liberty. Let us return to Lincoln's parable of the shepherd, the wolf, and the black sheep. "The shepherd drives the wolf from the sheep's throat, for which the sheep thanks the shepherd as a liberator." Here is Lincoln the shepherd using the power of government and the army to achieve a positive liberty for the sheep. But the wolf was a believer in negative liberty, for to him the shepherd was "the destroyer of liberty, especially as the sheep was a black one."

Positive liberty is an open-ended concept. It has the capacity to expand toward notions of equity, justice, social welfare, equality of opportunity. For how much liberty does a starving person enjoy, except the liberty to starve? How much freedom of the press can exist in a society of illiterate people? How free is a motorcyclist who is paralyzed for life by a head injury that might have been prevented if he had worn a helmet?

With the "new birth of freedom" invoked by Lincoln in the Gettysburg Address, he helped move the nation toward an expanded concept of positive liberty. "On the side of the Union," Lincoln said on another occasion, this war "is a struggle for maintaining in the world, that form, and substance of government, whose leading object is, to elevate the condition of men—to lift artificial weights from all shoulders—to clear the paths of laudable pursuit for all, to afford all, an unfettered start, and a fair chance, in the race of life."[11]

The tension between negative and positive liberty did not come to an end with the Civil War, of course. That tension has remained a constant in American political and social philosophy. In recent years, with the rise of small-government or antigovernment movements in our politics, there has been a revival of negative liberty. The presidential election of 2012 pitted the concepts of positive and negative liberty against each other more clearly than any other recent election. The shifting balance between positive and negative liberty seems likely to continue as a central feature of our political culture, as it was in the Civil War era. The need to understand and manage this balance offers another example of why the Civil War still matters.

CHAPTER 2

Mexico, California, and the Coming
of the Civil War

"I do not think there was ever a more wicked war than that waged by the United States on Mexico," said Ulysses S. Grant in 1879, more than thirty years after he had fought in that war as a young lieutenant. As he was dying of cancer in 1885, Grant reasserted that the American war against Mexico was "one of the most unjust ever waged by a stronger against a weaker nation."[1] Like the adventure in Iraq more than a century later, it was a war of choice, not of necessity, a war of aggression that expanded the size of the United States by nearly one-quarter and reduced that of Mexico by half. And in a striking example of unintended consequences, the issue of slavery in this new American territory set in motion a series of events that would produce a much bigger war fifteen years later that nearly tore apart the United States.

Two principal forces impelled Americans toward what General Grant considered a wicked war. The first was the annexation of Texas by the United States in 1845. Soon after Mexico had won its independence from Spain in 1821, the new government offered American settlers large land grants to settle in its sparsely populated northern province of Tejas. The Mexican government soon had reason to regret this policy. The Americans brought slaves in defiance of a Mexican law abolishing the institution. They also defied Mexican efforts to regulate land claims and political activities.

Despite Mexican attempts to ban further immigration, by 1835 30,000 Americans lived in Texas, where they outnumbered native Mexicans (*tejanos*) by six to one. Determined to establish their own government, the American Texans met at a village appropriately named Washington in 1836 and declared their independence. After suffering the slaughter of all 187 defenders of the mission in San Antonio called the Alamo and another massacre of more than three hundred captives at the city of Goliad, the Texans defeated a larger Mexican army at San Jacinto on April 21, 1836. The Texans captured the Mexican commander, Antonio López de Santa Anna, and forced him to sign a treaty recognizing the independent republic of Texas.

Although the Mexican Congress repudiated this treaty, the Texans managed to maintain their independence for almost a decade even as they petitioned repeatedly for annexation by the United States. These petitions, however, ran into a snag in Washington, where the growing controversy over the extension of slavery temporarily derailed the drive for annexation. So did the opposition of most members of the Whig Party to the idea of continual territorial expansion, which was embraced by the "Young America" faction that increasingly dominated the Democratic Party and generated the second impulse toward the Mexican War. The "Manifest Destiny" of the United States was to possess the whole of North America, proclaimed John L. O'Sullivan of the *Democratic Review* in 1845. "Yes, more, more, more! . . . till our national destiny is fulfilled and . . . the whole boundless continent is ours."[2]

Set against this demand for expansion of territory was the Whig philosophy of "internal improvements" by building up the infrastructure of transportation, education, and economic development within the existing borders of the United States. "Opposed to the instinct of boundless acquisition stands that of Internal Improvement," wrote the Whig journalist Horace Greeley. "A nation cannot simultaneously devote its energies to the absorption of others' territories and improvement of its own."[3]

The foremost exponent of this Whig position was Henry Clay, a three-time loser as a presidential candidate who nevertheless was an immensely influential political figure in the first half of the nineteenth century. His third try for the nation's highest office came in 1844, when he was defeated by the crosscurrents of Manifest Destiny and the antislavery opposition to the annexation of Texas. Clay's presumptive Democratic opponent in this election was Martin Van Buren, also making his third bid for the presidency after winning in 1836 and losing four years later. Both Clay and Van Buren came out against annexation of Texas in letters published simultaneously on April 27, 1844. As matters turned out, however, these letters sealed their fate. The proannexation current ran so strongly in the Democratic Party that it nominated the dark-horse candidate James K. Polk of Tennessee on a platform that endorsed the acquisition not only of Texas but also of Oregon Territory up to the border of Russian Alaska above the 54th parallel.

Despite the slogan "Fifty-four forty or fight!" that seemingly courted war with Britain over possession of British Columbia, it was the Texas issue that caught fire with the electorate. Annexation sentiment was especially strong in the South, which welcomed the prospect of a huge new slave state. To stem the stampede of many Southern Whigs to Polk on this issue, Clay published two more letters in July explaining that while he still opposed annexation if it would mean war with Mexico, he would acquiesce if it could be accomplished without war and with consensus support of Americans. This waffling probably cost him the election. Enough antislavery Whig voters in New York abandoned Clay and cast their ballots for the tiny Liberty Party to give that state—and therefore the presidency—to Polk by a margin of five thousand votes.

In the three years after his inauguration on March 4, 1845, Polk presided over the acquisition of more territory than any other president. He moved quickly to complete the annexation of Texas, which came in as the twenty-eighth state (and fifteenth slave state) in 1845.

Polk then compromised with Britain to establish the northern border of Oregon Territory at the 49th parallel. Having pledged to fight for a border of 54°40′, Polk angered many Northern Democrats by refusing to risk war with Britain while being willing to provoke war with Mexico by annexing Texas and insisting on a border at the Rio Grande River instead of the old Mexican border at the Nueces River, which effectively doubled the size of Texas now claimed by the United States.

The new president sent an envoy to Mexico City to try to intimidate the unstable government into accepting the Rio Grande border and selling New Mexico and California to the United States. Meeting refusal, Polk ordered General Zachary Taylor to lead a contingent of American soldiers (which included Lieutenant Ulysses S. Grant) to the Rio Grande. Polk hoped this move would provoke an incident that would enable the United States to declare war and seize the territory that Mexico refused to sell. If not, Polk intended to ask Congress for a declaration of war anyway. In the event, the Mexican commander on the south bank of the Rio Grande created an incident by sending troops across the river to attack an American patrol, killing eleven of them.

Even before this news reached Washington on May 9, Polk's cabinet had decided to request a declaration of war. Now the president had his casus belli. He sent a message to Congress asking not for a declaration of war as such but for a resolution asserting that war already existed because Mexico had "invaded our territory and shed American blood upon the American soil." As the historian Amy Greenberg notes, "None of it was true—but Polk didn't consider it lies." He believed that "a greater truth" was at stake: "As war exists, and notwithstanding all our efforts to avoid it, exists by the act of Mexico herself, we are called upon by every consideration of duty and patriotism to vindicate with decision the honor, the rights, and the interest of our country."[4]

Most Democrats were enthusiastic proponents of this war; most Whigs were opposed, branding it "Mr. Polk's War." Congressional

Democrats attached the declaration that war existed by the act of Mexico as a preamble to a bill to authorize funds and supplies for American soldiers who were now in harm's way. This was a cynical ploy to force Whigs to vote yes or be forever tainted by a refusal to support the troops. It worked. Only two Whigs in the Senate and fourteen in the House (including former president John Quincy Adams) voted against the declaration.

For the same reason that most Whig congressmen felt compelled to vote yes, many other Whigs volunteered to fight in a war they deplored in order to prove their patriotism. Two of the most prominent were Henry Clay Jr., son of the statesman, and John J. Hardin, a colleague of Abraham Lincoln in Illinois Whig politics who preceded Lincoln as a congressman from the Springfield district. Clay and Hardin became colonels respectively of Kentucky and Illinois regiments. Hardin was a charismatic politician who believed in Manifest Destiny despite his Whig allegiance. When war came in 1846, he was the first man from Illinois to enlist. Henry Clay Jr. was considerably less enthusiastic but no less determined. His departure from home and family was poignant and painful. "How bitter it was," writes Amy Greenberg, "that Henry Junior was risking death for a president his father detested and a conflict he despised."[5]

Death came to both Clay and Hardin at the Battle of Buena Vista in northern Mexico in February 1847. This battle was the most remarkable of American victories in the war, fought against odds of more than three to one. American armies boasted a long string of military successes that gave the United States control of New Mexico and California and captured Mexico City itself by September 1847. Nevertheless, the growing list of casualties and reports of atrocities by American soldiers against Mexican civilians and of savage attacks by Mexican "rancheros" (guerrillas) on American soldiers intensified antiwar sentiment in the United States. Total American deaths of 13,283 (seven-eighths of them from disease) constituted 17 percent of all American soldiers, the highest rate for any war except the Civil War.[6]

Poorly disciplined volunteer soldiers occupying Mexican cities "committed atrocities against Mexican civilians that would come to shock Americans back home," notes Greenberg. Lieutenant Grant wrote to his fiancée, Julia Dent, from Monterrey that "some of the volunteers and about all of the Texans seem to think it perfectly right...to murder them where the act can be covered by the dark....I would not pretend to guess the number of murders that have been committed upon the persons of poor Mexicans and the soldiers, since we have been here, but the number would startle you." By the summer of 1847, according to Greenberg, even journalists employed by prowar newspapers "found themselves forced to report on and condemn American atrocities that left them questioning their assumptions about American morality."[7]

Although most voters in Western and Southern states supported the war, as the months went by and no end appeared in sight, antiwar sentiment increased even though American arms experienced nothing but victory. The slavery issue compounded the controversy. Much antiwar opinion was fueled by the suspicion that the principal purpose of the conflict was to acquire more territory for slavery. As early as August 1846 a Pennsylvania congressman named David Wilmot introduced an amendment to an appropriations bill for the war stating that "as an express and fundamental condition to the acquisition of any territory from the Republic of Mexico...neither slavery nor involuntary servitude shall ever exist in any part of said territory."[8]

This famous Wilmot Proviso framed the national debate on slavery for the next fifteen years. Nearly all Northern Democrats joined all Northern Whigs in the majority that passed the proviso, while Southern Democrats and Southern Whigs voted against it. In the Senate, greater Southern strength defeated it. This outcome, which was repeated several times in the next two Congresses, marked an ominous wrenching of the *party* division between Whigs and Democrats into a *sectional* division between free and slave states that foreshadowed the political breakdown that led to secession and war in 1861.

As the war dragged on despite American conquest of a huge swath of Mexico, Polk wanted to negotiate peace and complete the accomplishment of his territorial goals before he lost control of events. At this point Nicholas Trist entered the story. Obscure today, Trist was prominent in his time. A protégé of the elderly Thomas Jefferson, who supervised his legal education and made him his private secretary, Trist also married Jefferson's granddaughter. Later he served as Andrew Jackson's personal secretary for a time, and in 1845 Jackson persuaded Polk to appoint Trist as chief clerk of the State Department—the equivalent of assistant secretary of state.

Fluent in Spanish, and a Democrat and expansionist, Trist seemed the ideal person to negotiate a peace with Mexico that would force its government to yield half its country to the United States. Polk appointed him as a special envoy to accompany General Winfield Scott's army, which was closing in on Mexico City. Trist was authorized to offer Mexico up to $20 million in return for the Rio Grande boundary of Texas plus California and New Mexico (embracing the present-day states of California, Nevada, and Utah, most of Arizona and New Mexico, and part of Colorado). If Mexico would also throw in Baja California, Trist could pay up to $30 million.

During Trist's sojourn in Mexico, a number of things happened that set up a dramatic confrontation between the envoy and the president who sent him there. Scott's army captured Mexico City in September 1847 and drove President Santa Anna and his army away to Guadalupe Hidalgo, where Santa Anna refused to capitulate or to negotiate despite the hopelessness of his cause. American military success whetted the appetite of some Manifest Destiny expansionists for more of Mexico than Polk had initially contemplated, perhaps even "all Mexico."

Polk also began to think that he should demand more territory. But Trist found himself questioning the justice and morality of American policy. His dispatches indicated a growing softness toward Mexico and an unwillingness to go beyond the original territorial goals. In

October 1847 Polk decided to recall Trist and send a new envoy to extract harsher terms. Trist ignored the recall order, at the risk of his career, and in February 1848 he negotiated the Treaty of Guadalupe Hidalgo with Santa Anna's successor, which carried out Polk's initial goals (minus Baja California).

The arrival of this treaty in Washington presented Polk with a dilemma. He was furious with Trist and tempted to repudiate his treaty in order to force greater concessions from Mexico. But since the autumn of 1847 a growing antiwar movement had begun to threaten to crush Polk between the upper and nether millstones of Democrats' "all Mexico" clamor and Whig pressures for "no Mexico." In November Henry Clay, still mourning the death of his son, broke his silence on the Mexican War with a powerful antiwar speech in Lexington, Kentucky, that received national publicity.

Among others, Clay's speech solemnly affected Abraham Lincoln, who happened to be in Lexington visiting his in-laws while on his way to Washington to take the congressional seat to which he had been elected in 1846. Lincoln heard Clay denounce an "unnecessary" war of "offensive aggression" that had produced "sacrifice of human life … waste of human treasure … mangled bodies … death, and … desolation" in a conflict "actuated by a spirit of rapacity, and an inordinate desire for territorial aggrandizement." Clay also endorsed the Wilmot Proviso and insisted that the United States must not "acquire any foreign territory whatever, for the purpose of introducing slavery into it."[9]

Clay's speech inspired many antiwar meetings around the country and emboldened Whigs to speak out more vigorously against Mr. Polk's War in the congressional session that began in December. One of those Whigs was Lincoln. The freshman congressman achieved national exposure with his "spot resolutions" and speeches in the House advocating these resolutions in December 1847 and January 1848. The resolutions demanded from Polk a description of the exact "spot" where Mexican soldiers shed American blood to start the war, suggesting instead that American soldiers shed Mexican blood on Mexican soil.[10]

The political turmoil surrounding the debates about responsibility for the war forced Polk to conclude that he should get the controversy behind him by submitting Trist's treaty to the Senate for approval rather than try to negotiate a new treaty. In the Senate, seven Democrats who wanted more Mexican territory and seven Whigs who wanted none voted against ratification. But enough senators of both parties voted in favor to pass the treaty with four votes to spare. Polk fired Trist from his job in the State Department and even withheld his pay for the extra time he remained in Mexico. Clay forfeited any chance for another presidential run in 1848 by jettisoning his political base in the South and West, where the war and conquest remained popular. And the Whigs lost Lincoln's congressional district in 1848, in part because of the unpopularity there of his antiwar speeches.

But the biggest fallout from this "wicked war" was the controversy over slavery in the territories acquired from Mexico. This altercation was all so unnecessary, according to historians whose interpretation of the Civil War's causes once prevailed. With the expansion of the cotton frontier into eastern Texas in the 1830s, they maintained, slavery had reached the "natural limits" of its growth and could spread no farther into the arid and inhospitable Southwest.[11] This Natural Limits thesis sustained an argument that the Civil War was a needless war, a "repressible conflict" brought on by self-serving Northern politicians who seized on the artificial issue of slavery's expansion to vault into power by scaring Northern voters with false alarms about an aggressive "Slave Power." Their self-righteous, anti-Southern rhetoric finally goaded slave states into secession when Abraham Lincoln won the presidency in 1860.[12]

The Natural Limits thesis echoed the voices of antebellum politicians exasperated by antislavery claims that slaveholders intended to expand their "peculiar institution" into the territory taken from Mexico. This whole matter, insisted one Southern congressman, "related to an imaginary negro in an impossible place." President Polk wrote in his diary that the agitation about slavery's expansion was "not only mischievous but wicked" because "there is no probability that any territory will ever be acquired from Mexico in which slavery could ever exist."[13] Senator Daniel Webster insisted that the arid climate would keep slavery out of those territories, so why insult the South by the Wilmot Proviso legislating exclusion? "I would not take pains to reaffirm an ordinance of nature," said Webster, "nor to reenact the will of God." Governor John J. Crittenden of Kentucky maintained in 1848 that "the right to carry slaves to New Mexico or California is no very great matter ... the more especially when it seems to be agreed that no sensible man would carry his slaves there if he could."[14]

It comes as something of a surprise, therefore, to discover that the territories of Utah and New Mexico (which included also the future states of Nevada and Arizona) legalized slavery in 1852 and 1859 respectively, that slaveholding settlers in California made strenuous and partly successful efforts to infiltrate bondage into that state, and that California's representatives and senators in Congress voted mainly with the proslavery South in the 1850s. The distinguished historian Leonard L. Richards, who was born and raised in California, learned nothing of this history from his teachers and textbooks there. "Somehow I had gone through the California schools from kindergarten through graduate school," he writes, and never heard or read that several of the state's early political leaders "might as well have been representing Mississippi or Alabama in national affairs." One reason that he wrote *The California Gold Rush and the Coming of the Civil War* (2007), he explains in the book's introduction, was "to bring myself up to speed—to learn material that I should have learned forty or fifty years ago."[15]

About the same time in early 1848 that the Treaty of Guadalupe Hidalgo transferred California from Mexico to the United States, workers building a sawmill on the American River near Sacramento discovered flecks of gold in the riverbed. Word of this find leaked out despite efforts to keep it secret. Rumors reached the eastern United States in August 1848, where a public surfeited with tall tales out of the West initially proved skeptical. Lieutenant William Tecumseh Sherman, aide to the military governor of California, persuaded his commander to send a tea caddy containing more than two hundred ounces of pure gold to Washington. It arrived in December 1848, two days after President Polk confirmed the "extraordinary" discovery of gold. All doubts vanished. By the spring of 1849 tens of thousands of men from all over the United States as well as Chile, China, Mexico, Australia, France, and other countries were on their way to California. So many arrived that by the fall of 1849 the region had as large a population as Delaware and Florida, which were already states.

These men (and they were nearly all men) in San Francisco and the mining camps needed law and order, courts, land and water laws, mail service, and other institutions of government. The U.S. House of Representatives with its Northern majority passed legislation to organize California as a free territory. Southern strength in the Senate blocked this move. Settlers in California soon took matters into their own hands. In October 1849 they drew up a state constitution and petitioned Congress for admission. The Whig administration of President Zachary Taylor (elected in 1848) supported statehood as a way of circumventing the troublesome issue of slavery in California as a territory.

But there was a problem: The proposed state constitution (modeled on Iowa's) banned slavery. Most of the Forty-Niners wanted to keep that institution out of California, not because of moral principle but because they did not want to compete with slave labor. Several slaveowners had in fact brought their bondsmen with them to work in the mines. "There is no vocation in the world in which slavery can be more useful and profitable than in mining," declared one of the South's leading newspapers, the *Charleston Mercury*. Another journal, the *Southern Quarterly*, declared that "California is by nature peculiarly a slaveholding State." If it were not for the agitation to exclude slavery, "thousands of young, intelligent active men ... would have been in that region, having each carried with them from one to five slaves."[16]

Senator Jefferson Davis of Mississippi pointed out that "it was to work the gold mines on this continent that the Spaniards first brought

Africans to the country." Although Davis had never been to California, he insisted that "the European races now engaged in working the mines of California sink under the burning heat and sudden changes of climate, to which the African race are altogether adapted." (He seems to have confused Northern California's climate with Mississippi's.) Davis denounced California's free-state constitution as having been written by "a few adventurers uniting with a herd as various in color and nearly as ignorant of our government, as Jacob's cattle."[17]

Underlying this rhetoric was the Southern fear that admission of California as the sixteenth free state would tip the balance of power against slave states in the Senate and set a precedent for additional free states from the Mexican cession. "For the first time," warned Davis, "we are about permanently to destroy the balance of power between the sections." This was nothing less than a "plan of concealing the Wilmot Proviso under a so-called state constitution." Other Southern leaders described the exclusion of slavery from California as an unconstitutional violation of property rights and political equity that would justify a drastic response. "If by your legislation you seek to drive us from the territories of California and New Mexico," thundered Representative Robert Toombs of Georgia, a rich slaveholder, "*I am for disunion.*"[18]

Several Southerners echoed Toombs's threat. Secession and perhaps war in 1850 over the admission of California seemed a real possibility. Into this crisis strode Senator Henry Clay with a compromise proposal, as he had done twice before, in 1820 and 1833. Clay's compromise would offset the admission of California as a free state and the abolition of slave trading in the District of Columbia (an international embarrassment) by the creation of New Mexico and Utah Territories without restrictions on slavery, by a guarantee of slavery itself in the District of Columbia against federal interference, and by a powerful new fugitive slave law to be enforced by federal marshals, commissioners, and if necessary the army to return slaves who had escaped to free states. One by one these measures became law during a long and contentious session of Congress in 1850. Many Southerners continued to protest the admission of California, but just enough voted for it (or abstained) to get it through Congress. And just enough Northerners in return supported the quid pro quo measures favoring the South.

The fears expressed by Jefferson Davis and others that California would tip the balance against the South in Congress proved baseless. The state could scarcely have given the South more aid and comfort in national politics if it had been a slave state. The Democratic Party dominated California politics through the 1850s. And the California party in turn was dominated by a coalition of Southern-born politicians that became known as the "Chivalry." Most of them continued to own slaves in the states from which they had emigrated. The foremost "Chiv" was William Gwin, a Mississippi planter who arrived in California in 1849 and served as one of its senators for most of the next decade. Gwin controlled federal patronage in the state during the Democratic administrations of Presidents Franklin Pierce and James Buchanan. The other California senator from 1851 to 1857 was, in the political lexicon of the time, a "doughface"—a Northern man with Southern principles. Together these senators voted for every proslavery measure demanded by Southern Democrats, most notably the Kansas-Nebraska Act of 1854, which repealed the earlier ban on slavery in Louisiana Purchase territory north of 36°30´, and the notorious pro-slavery Lecompton state constitution by which Buchanan tried (but failed) to bring Kansas into the Union as a slave state in 1858. Both former California senators supported the Confederacy during the Civil War.

William Gwin's chief challenger for control of California's Democratic Party was David Broderick, a New Yorker who opposed the Chivalry's proslavery tilt. Broderick was a hardened political fighter who had learned his trade in the rough politics of New York City before migrating to California. But he proved no match for the Chivs, who outmaneuvered him to gain the support and patronage of the Buchanan administration even though Broderick managed to get himself elected to the Senate in 1857. His tenure there was short-lived. In 1859 a political mudslinging match between Broderick and David Terry, a Texan who had arrived in California in 1849 and became a prominent Chiv, led to a duel. Terry resigned from his post as chief justice of the California Supreme Court in order to challenge Broderick. Winning the coin toss for choice of weapons, Terry selected pistols with hair triggers that he had brought with him. Unaccustomed to these weapons, Broderick fired too soon and wildly, whereupon Terry took careful aim and shot him dead. This was the third duel in California during the 1850s in which a Chiv Democrat killed a member of the anti-Chiv faction of the party.

In addition to killing off the opposition, the Chivs made repeated efforts to infiltrate slavery into California—or at least into part of it. In 1852 the legislature enacted a law that permitted a slaveowner to "sojourn" indefinitely in California with his human property, and the two justices on the state supreme court who hailed from slave states upheld it. The law was renewed in 1853 and 1854 before finally lapsing the following year. By then the proslavery forces had come up with a new idea: to divide the state in two, with the southern portion reverting to territorial status and open to slavery like New Mexico and Utah.

All of the gold mines were in the northern part of the state, so there was no more talk of slavery's adaptability to mining. Instead, according to the Chivs, slaves in southern California could grow "Cotton, Rice, & Sugar." By "this peculiar labor," they said, California's "valuable soils" could be "rendered productive."[19] In 1859 the state legislature enacted a bill providing for splitting off southern California at approximately the latitude of San Luis Obispo, subject to a two-thirds majority vote in a referendum in the affected counties. They voted for it by almost three to one, but when the measure reached Congress at the end of 1859 it died a quiet death in the House, where the Republicans were now the largest party. For better or worse, California remained one state.

California's admission as a free state gave an impetus to one of the more bizarre phenomena of the 1850s—"filibustering," after the Spanish word *filibustero*, a freebooter or pirate. A new slave state was needed to offset California. The leaders of the Polk administration had not been satisfied with the acquisition of Texas and the Southwest. They wanted Cuba as well, where planters restive under Spanish colonial rule looked to the Americanos. Several Southern politicians were strongly drawn to the prospect of adding Cuba with its almost four hundred thousand slaves to the United States. Spain refused to sell, however, so a private army of American filibusterers led by the Venezuela-born Cuban soldier of fortune Narciso López invaded the island twice, in 1850 and 1851. The first time Spanish soldiers drove them back to their ships; the second time they killed two hundred of the invaders and captured the rest. They garrotted López in Havana's public square and killed fifty-one American prisoners by firing squad, including William Crittenden, nephew of the attorney general.

This experience put a damper on filibustering expeditions to Cuba. The scene shifted three thousand miles west to California itself. In 1857 Henry Crabb, who had migrated to California from Mississippi and had joined the Chivalry wing of the Democratic Party, led a filibustering invasion of the Sonoran province of Mexico. Mexican troops ambushed them, killed or wounded twenty-one filibusterers, and executed fifty-nine others, including Crabb. The all-time filibuster champion was William Walker, a Tennessee native who also turned up in California in 1849. A failed invasion of Baja California in 1853 did not discourage him. In 1855 Walker led an army of two thousand American filibusterers into Nicaragua, where in alliance with local rebels he gained control of the government in 1856, named himself president, and reinstated slavery. But a coalition army from other Central American countries overthrew his regime. After several attempts to return, he was captured and executed by Honduran troops in 1860.[20]

All of the filibuster efforts to organize another slave state to offset California came to grief. They did succeed, however, in exacerbating the controversy over the expansion of slavery. Meanwhile, Minnesota and Oregon came in as free states in 1858 and 1859. By the latter year the South had also lost its campaign to make Kansas a slave state. The balance of power permanently tipped against the South, which strengthened the influence of those who clamored for disunion. This process, which had begun with the loss of California to freedom in 1849, is the implicit theme of Richards's *The California Gold Rush and the Coming of the Civil War*. Richards does not make the theme explicit, however. The central thread of his narrative is the colorful and violent history of internal California politics in the 1850s.

If Richards had made his title theme explicit, the argument would have gone something like this: The discovery of gold in California produced a mass migration there in which settlers who wanted to exclude slavery prevailed. Their application for statehood provoked a polarizing sectional debate in Congress that generated threats of secession if the South did not get its way. The Compromise of 1850 papered over these divisions temporarily, but tensions continued to simmer and burst into flame again with the Kansas-Nebraska Act in 1854. That crisis might not have occurred, at least so soon, without the perceived need for a railroad to connect California with the Mississippi Valley.

Repeal of the ban on slavery north of 36°30′ was the price that Senator Stephen Douglas had to pay for Southern support of the territorial organization of Kansas and Nebraska, through which the railroad would be built. The dominance of the Chivalry faction in California politics invigorated the proslavery element in the national Democratic Party, whose overweening grasp for power in the effort to make Kansas a slave state alienated Northern voters and strengthened the antislavery Republican Party. So did the filibustering expeditions, several of which originated in California. Of course, tensions between North and South had existed before California became part of the United States and would probably have intensified in the 1850s even if gold had never been discovered there. But the precise shape of the sectional conflict that led to secession and war in 1861 was surely influenced by the California story.

Within California itself, perhaps the first shot of the Civil War came from David Terry's hair-trigger pistol that killed David Broderick in

September 1859. The backlash against what many Californians saw as a political assassination weakened the Chivs and redounded to the advantage of the state Republican Party, which had never previously gotten more than 23 percent of the vote. In 1860 Abraham Lincoln won a plurality of 32 percent of California's votes in the four-party contest and came away with the state's four electoral votes. During the Civil War most Californians remained loyal to the United States, and the state's shipments of gold helped finance the Union war effort.

Several prominent Chivs, however, went South. One of them was David Terry, who had suffered no legal punishment for his killing of Broderick. He fought with the 8th Texas Cavalry and was wounded at Chickamauga in September 1863. He returned to California in 1868 to practice law and dabble again in politics. In 1889, exactly thirty years after he had killed a U.S. senator, Terry became embroiled in a dispute with another California political rival from the 1850s. This time it was Stephen J. Field, whom Lincoln had appointed as an associate justice of the United States Supreme Court in 1863. In 1888 Field, as senior justice of the California circuit court, presided over a lawsuit by Terry's second wife against her former husband, a Nevada senator. When Field jailed Terry and his wife for contempt because of their behavior during the trial, Terry vowed revenge. The U.S. Marshal assigned a bodyguard for Field. The following year Terry encountered Field in a railroad station near Stockton and slapped his face (as a challenge to a duel, presumably). The bodyguard shot Terry dead. Perhaps that was truly the last shot of the Civil War.

CHAPTER 3

A Just War?

"War is hell," said General William T. Sherman fifteen years after the end of a war in which he perhaps did more than anyone else to confirm that description. "War is cruelty, and you cannot refine it," Sherman wrote on another occasion.

Harry Stout certainly agrees. The Jonathan Edwards Professor of American Religious History at Yale University and a leading scholar of early American religion, Stout regards the Civil War as the "fulcrum" of American history. The members of the generation that fought the war came of age during the era of the Second Great Awakening in American Protestantism. An understanding of their religious values and ideology, therefore, is necessary to appreciate the way in which that fulcrum worked. Stout decided not to write a "religious history" of the war that would focus "exclusively on chaplains and ministers," however, but rather a "moral history" that "raises moral issues of right and wrong as seen from the vantage points of both the participants and the historian, who, after painstaking study, applies normative judgments."[1]

The starting points for such a judgment of "the rightness or wrongness of war" are theological definitions of "just war" going back to Saint Augustine of Hippo in the fourth century and Saint Thomas Aquinas in the thirteenth. Just-war theory is divided into two principal categories: rationales for going to war (*jus ad bellum*) and principles governing the conduct of war once it has begun (*jus in bello*). The only just reason for going to war is self-defense; therefore "just wars are always *defensive* wars," and unprovoked aggression "is always wrong."[2]

On the question of *jus ad bellum*, Northerners in 1861 had no trouble making such a moral judgment: Confederates started the war by firing on Fort Sumter, an unprovoked act of aggression that forced the United States to fight a defensive war to preserve its existence as one nation. Abraham Lincoln put it this way in his second inaugural address: "Both parties deprecated war; but one of them would *make* war rather than let the nation survive; and the other would *accept* war rather than let it perish."[3]

Southerners, on the other hand, had no doubt that Lincoln's government was the aggressor because it refused to bow to Confederate demands for the peaceful surrender of Fort Sumter to the secessionist government, thereby provoking the Confederacy to open fire. As Jefferson Davis expressed it: "He who makes the assault is not necessarily he that strikes the first blow or fires the first gun." Lincoln's attempt to resupply the fort's garrison with food, said Davis, made "the reduction of Fort Sumter" a "measure of defense rendered absolutely and immediately necessary."[4]

Stout's expressed intention to offer "moral judgments" and a "determination of right or wrong" might cause the reader of *Upon the Altar of the Nation: A Moral History of the Civil War* (2006) to expect such a judgment on this crucial question of *jus ad bellum*. But the reader will be disappointed. "In civil wars," Stout writes, "it often becomes difficult to discern with finality who is the unjust aggressor and who the just defender." Really? He had convinced us that it is the duty of the moral historian to make such a "determination of right or wrong," difficult or not. But because in the American Civil War "each side joined the battle convinced that its cause was just," the moral historian is somehow absolved from the responsibility of determining right and wrong.[5] In what war, we might ask, did one side or the other *not* consider its cause just?

In any event, Stout's book concentrates on the second part of just-war theory, the conduct of war (*jus in bello*), and on the justification of each side's conduct by the principal moral arbiters of the time, the Protestant clergy. Most nations recognize limitations on the savagery of warfare defined by "rules of engagement" and "laws of war." The Geneva Conventions, international treaties, and domestic legislation spell out these limitations. They rest on two basic precepts of just-war theory: proportionality and discrimination. Proportionality requires that the means be appropriate to the end—a nuclear bomb must not be dropped on a city to destroy a single weapons factory. Discrimination separates combatants from noncombatants—the former are a legitimate target but the latter are not, except in the case of "collateral damage," in which noncombatants are unintentionally killed or wounded or their property destroyed.

Measured by these criteria, the conduct of the Civil War was just in its initial stages because it was a limited conflict between uniformed soldiers whose goals were either Confederate independence or restoration of the Union. But the war grew increasingly unjust, according to Stout, as it escalated to what he calls a "total war" by the North to destroy the social and economic infrastructure of the Old South (including slavery) and to build a New South on its ruins. Commander in Chief Lincoln and his generals, therefore, bore the main responsibility for what became an unjust war.

In his proclamation of April 15, 1861, calling state militias into federal service to suppress the insurrection started by the firing on Fort Sumter, Lincoln enjoined these troops to avoid "any devastation, any destruction of, or interference with, property, or any disturbance of peaceful citizens." Eight months later, in a message to Congress, Lincoln reiterated his concern that "in considering the policy to be adopted for suppressing the insurrection, I have been anxious and careful that the inevitable conflict for this purpose shall not degenerate into a remorseless revolutionary struggle."[6] Even General Sherman, at this stage of the war, did his best to instill in soldiers "a common sense of decency...to respect [civilian] life and property," or "we ought never to hope for any friends in Virginia." As late as July 1862 the North's senior general at the time, George B. McClellan, insisted that the war "should not be, at all, a war upon population; but against armed forces....Neither confiscation of property...[n]or forcible abolition of slavery should be contemplated for a moment."[7]

So far so good; official Union policy was consistent with just-war principles of proportionality and discrimination. This policy of a sword for enemy armies and an olive branch for Southern civilians proceeded from an assumption that a residual Unionism would bring the South back into the United States when Confederate armies were defeated. By the summer of 1862, however, that faith in Southern Unionism was wearing thin. So was the distinction between combatants and noncombatants in the parts of the Confederacy and border states occupied by Union forces. The crops and livestock of Southern civilians were feeding and clothing Confederate armies. Their slaves were the principal labor force in the Confederate war economy. Thousands of Southern civilians became guerrillas who roamed behind Union lines destroying supplies and ambushing unarmed as well as armed Unionists. Little more than a year after his reference to respecting Southern property in order to win friends, Sherman had become convinced, as he wrote in a letter to Henry Halleck in 1864, that "all in the South *are* enemies of all in the North....The whole country is full of guerrilla bands....The entire South, man, woman, and child, is against us, armed and determined....We are not only fighting hostile armies, but a hostile people, and must make [them] feel the hard hand of war."[8]

Lincoln did not put it as starkly as Sherman, but by midsummer 1862 he was moving toward similar conclusions. "Lincoln came to understand," writes Stout, "that if his aim of preserving the Union was to be achieved, the war would have to be escalated to a total war on both citizens and soldiers."[9] The newly appointed commander of Union forces in northern Virginia, General John Pope, issued a series of orders authorizing his troops to "subsist upon the country," to hold civilians responsible for shooting at Union soldiers from their houses, to execute captured guerrillas who fired on Union troops, to expel from occupied territory any civilians who refused to take an oath of allegiance to the United States, and to treat them as spies if they returned. Lincoln approved these orders as well as an order by the War Department authorizing commanders "to seize and use any property, real or personal," that would help the war effort.[10] To professed Southern Unionists who protested such actions, Lincoln responded bluntly: "What would you do in my position? Would you...prosecute [the war] in future with elder-stalk squirts, charged with rose-water?...Would you give up the contest, leaving any available means unapplied?"[11]

For Stout, these actions and words should be seen as the beginning of a slide down a slippery slope to the barbarism of an unjust war. Lincoln's "taste for blood," he writes, bore "a large portion of the responsibility for unimaginable suffering and death" and for "campaigns of such unmitigated violence, slaughter, and civilian suffering." In the end this policy may have won the war—but at an immoral cost. "Lincoln's war strategy was and remains genius. That does not make it right."[12]

In Stout's view, the only redeeming feature of this obscenity of total war was the abolition of slavery. "The justness of abolition and the freedom of four million," he writes, "dictates that any moral history of slavery unconditionally conclude that the right side won, no matter what the casualties and sacrifices."[13] Stout is uncomfortably aware that emancipation was an integral and essential part of the escalation to total war. Slaves were property owned by enemy civilians; their confiscation and emancipation and the ultimate abolition of slavery by the Thirteenth Amendment represented the destruction of the largest single category of Southern property. In practical terms, Stout acknowledges, "emancipation was necessary as a means to total war." But it also gave the war "an unprecedented moral stature, allowing the Northern public to fasten on the 'good' of emancipation without ever inquiring into the 'bad' of unjust conduct in a total war."[14]

For all of his forcefulness in praising abolition and his indignation in damning an unjust war against Southern civilians, and his awkward admission that the latter was necessary to achieve the former, Stout never makes clear which he regards as the greater evil: slavery or total war. Instead, he resorts to what can only be labeled an evasion: "But this book is not a moral history of slavery. It is a moral history of a war, where questions of proportionality and discrimination continue to remain in play."[15]

By a twist of logic difficult to follow, Stout considers black soldiers fighting for freedom to have been engaged in a just war even as white soldiers fighting for the same cause were not. "If anyone had a 'cause' that could meet all the moral scruples of a just war, it was the slaves and freedmen," he believes. "The willingness of black soldiers to fight and die helped to transform the moral meaning of the Civil War from a war for Union to a 'crusade' for freedom."[16]

The Union army's organization of black regiments in the second half of the war produced retaliatory actions that undermined any claim the South made to be fighting a just defensive war. The Confederacy refused to exchange captured black prisoners of war under the agreement negotiated in 1862, thus bringing a halt to exchanges; this led to the deaths of thousands of POWs, both Union and Confederate, in fetid and overcrowded prison camps. Even more heinous was the cold-blooded murder by Confederate soldiers of captured black troops on a half-dozen battlefields after they had surrendered. The most notorious such case occurred at Fort Pillow on the Mississippi River on April 12, 1864, when Confederate troopers commanded by General Nathan Bedford Forrest shot at least a hundred black captives.

More lethal, perhaps, but less publicized was the Battle of the Crater at Petersburg, Virginia, on July 30, 1864, when a Confederate counterattack captured several hundred black prisoners, many of whom were shot as they were led, disarmed, to the rear. General Robert E. Lee, writes Stout, "observed the carnage from only five hundred yards away and obviously knew of the murders taking place. In yet another searing enactment of the inhumane racial civil war within the Civil War, he made no comment, then or later."[17]

Curiously, in Stout's account Forrest receives no stronger censure than Lee because Forrest "neither ordered nor condoned the massacre" but, like Lee, merely did nothing to stop it. Recent scholarship on Fort Pillow, however, challenges the notion that Forrest did not condone it.[18] But even if he—like Lee—only failed to restrain his men, "it was a lesson in moral avoidance that Northern generals would also learn perfectly."[19]

What does Stout mean by this last sentence? He is drawing a parallel between Confederate commanders who did not prevent the murder of black prisoners and Union commanders who did not prevent their soldiers from burning and pillaging civilian property. Whether there was in fact a moral equivalency between these actions is a question largely unexamined in Stout's book. He implies, however, that one was as bad as the other. On the last page of the book, he suggests that the top officials and commanders on both sides were equally culpable for terrible deeds in this unjust war. "Americans don't want to concede the unforgivable wrongs committed by the likes of Lincoln, Grant, Sherman, Sheridan, Lee, Forrest, Early, and Davis."[20]

What, then, is one to make of Stout's dedication of his book to the memory of his father, "a warrior sailor in a just war"—World War II? The chief ground on which Stout condemns the Civil War as unjust is its increasing failure to discriminate between combatants and noncombatants (including disarmed prisoners). But all nations in World War II did this on a scale a hundredfold greater than either side in the Civil War. Sherman's "bummers" wantonly destroyed much civilian property on their marches through Georgia and especially South Carolina, but Allied bombers in World War II destroyed not only property but hundreds of thousands of civilian lives as well.

Through carelessness or misrepresentation, Stout grossly inflates the number of civilian casualties directly caused by military action in the Civil War. Lincoln and his generals, he claims, "deliberately targeted civilian farms, cities, and—in at least fifty thousand instances—civilian lives."[21] His cited source for this information is my own estimate in *Battle Cry of Freedom*. But I made clear that this estimate referred to *indirect* consequences of the war in the South: the inevitable results of transportation disruptions, the loss of crops and livestock from army operations by both sides, the overcrowding of refugees fleeing from war zones, and the like, which caused shortages and fatigue and malnutrition that in turn lowered resistance to disease. The highest civilian mortality rate actually occurred among slaves who fled their owners for freedom and crowded into "contraband camps" behind Union lines, where they became prey to diseases and sometimes to murderous raids by Confederate guerrillas.

Except for guerrilla raids, none of the civilian casualties was "deliberately targeted." And in fact, civilian casualties in the American Civil War were far fewer than in large-scale European wars from the seventeenth through the twentieth centuries. These included the Thirty Years' War, the Napoleonic Wars, and of course World Wars I and II (including the influenza pandemic of 1918–19), in which civilian deaths, direct and indirect, were twice to several times greater than soldier deaths. In the Civil War, even if my estimate of fifty thousand civilian deaths is accurate, that was one-fifteenth of the 750,000 soldiers who are estimated to have died.[22]

Another example of misrepresentation occurs in Stout's discussion of Sherman's siege of Atlanta in August 1864. Atlanta was a heavily fortified city defended by an army of forty thousand men and containing important war industries and railroad facilities. Sherman's shelling of the city was quite legitimate according to the laws of war, though Stout implies otherwise. Many houses as well as warehouses and factories were damaged or destroyed by the shelling. But civilian casualties in Atlanta were remarkably low. Stout, however, cites an alleged letter from Sherman to Confederate General John Bell Hood in which Sherman, according to Stout, "estimated that five hundred 'rebel' civilians were killed and twenty-five hundred wounded. Given the source, one can assume these figures are significantly understated." Stout's cited source, however, mentions neither a letter from Sherman nor five hundred civilian dead and twenty-five hundred wounded. But another page of the same source notes a total of twenty documented civilian deaths from the shelling.[23] So far as I am aware, no historian of the Atlanta campaign and no Sherman biographer has ever heard of this supposed letter. One of them wrote to me: "Stout has a good imagination."

* * *

As a historian of American religion, Stout is particularly concerned with the function of churches and their pastors as moral arbiters in what he portrays as an increasingly immoral war. They mostly flunked their assignments. In both North and South they preached that God was on their own side and that the Godless enemy's cause was evil. The clergy became "virtually cheerleaders all," which prevented them from expressing "moral criticism directed at one's own cause" or addressing "the question of what constitutes a just war, and what limitations ought to be observed in the unpleasant event of war." They "fell victim to the sheer power of patriotism" and "privilege[d] patriotism over spirituality." Believing in "the absolute moral right on each side…America's clerical arbiters supported the war without any real qualifications." Along with secular molders of public opinion, the clergy, especially in the North, provided "moral justification and endorsement" of the descent into total war, which "goes a long way to explain how military destruction and civilian suffering reached the levels they did."[24]

Most secular as well as religious leaders subscribed to the "God is on our side" moral absolutism, according to Stout. One who did not, for which he earns the author's praise, was Abraham Lincoln. He was "one of the few principals in the war capable of transcending the prevailing rhetoric of absolute right and wrong" and who could "perceive right and wrong on both sides."[25] In his remarkable second inaugural address, Lincoln noted that each side in the war "invokes [God's] aid against the other." Both could not be right; in fact neither was right, for

40

"the Almighty has His own purposes," which Lincoln suggested might include the punishment of both for the sin of slavery, of which North and South were equally guilty.[26] On this issue Stout considers Lincoln sound both in theology and morality. But what about the author's repeated censures of Lincoln's "taste for blood," his "responsibility for unimaginable suffering and death"? These were the result of pragmatic military strategy, Stout claims, not of moral absolutism.

Some readers might find it difficult to reconcile these two views of Lincoln. And Stout's ambivalence toward the man he describes on one occasion as "a Christ-like messiah for the reconstituted American nation" extends to the matter of civil religion. This typically American phenomenon is a "religion" of patriotism in which icons like the flag and other symbols of nationalism are objects of reverence. "Many Americans," writes Stout, "equate dying for their country with dying for their faith." The "sheer blood sacrifice" of soldiers "on the national altar" was a "baptism of blood" that "would incarnate the national faith."[27] In the South this sacrifice was most notably associated with the death of Stonewall Jackson, "by which a Confederate civil religion was incarnated through a violent atonement." The "Christian heroism" of generals like Jackson and Lee "effectively fus[ed] patriotism with the same Christian legitimation that prevailed in the North. By August 1863 the war had created and consecrated two American civil religions, mortally opposed, but both Christian and both 'American.' "[28]

The Southern civil religion persisted even after defeat in the form of "Lost Cause" reverence for the Confederate battle flag and the men who carried it through four years of blood sacrifice in a doomed but noble cause. The dominant American civil religion, however, was bequeathed by the nationalism of Lincoln's Gettysburg Address, which expressed a "mystical reverence for the Union as itself something sacred and worthy of sacrificial worship." The "sacralization of this particular battlefield," Stout maintains, "would mark it forever after as the preeminent sacred ground of the Civil War—and American wars thereafter." And at the moment of victory, Lincoln's martyrdom by assassination (on Good Friday) transformed him "from the prophet of America's civil religion to its messiah."[29]

For Stout, therefore, "the incarnation of a national American civil religion may have been the final great legacy of the Civil War." But this legacy, he writes, might be more curse than blessing. It reinforced America's sense of its "messianic 'mission' to be a 'redeemer nation' " that "identifies Providence with the 'idealistic conception of American destiny.' " By "linking emancipation and the 'crusade' [a word Lincoln never used] against slavery to total war and a 'crusade' against the Confederacy, Lincoln's administration watered the seeds of an American-led Christian imperialism that was not without costs in later American history."[30]

It was this type of messianic crusade that brought on this "cruel and senseless war" in the first place, according to David Goldfield's sweeping narrative of the Civil War era, *America Aflame*.[31] Goldfield places his interpretation in the tradition known as "revisionism" after a school of historians in the 1930s and 1940s. The revisionists denied that sectional differences between North and South were genuinely divisive. Disparities that existed did not have to lead to war; they could have, and should have, been accommodated peacefully within the political system. But self-serving politicians—a "blundering generation," as one revisionist historian described them—whipped up passions in North and South for partisan purposes. By 1861 these passions grew out of control and erupted in a "needless war."[32]

Although not as stark in his presentation of a similar thesis, Goldfield makes clear his conviction that the war should have been avoided. His villains, however, are not self-serving and blundering politicians; rather, the culprit is "the invasion of evangelical Christianity into the political debate as an especially toxic factor in limiting the options of political leaders." The "elevation of political issues into moral causes," especially antislavery, "poisoned the democratic process."[33]

Goldfield never defines precisely what he means by "evangelical Christianity." He mainly refers to social reform movements like temperance and abolitionism generated by the Second Great Awakening among

Protestant denominations that injected moral fervor into politics, "especially in the Republican Party."[34] His use of evangelicalism, however, tends to be loose and expansive. He tries to connect Lincoln with this tradition, but it is an uphill battle. Lincoln's House Divided speech in 1858 "reflected a growing messianic sentiment" in his views, Goldfield maintains, because the metaphor was taken from a biblical passage in Matthew 12:25. "Lincoln not only identified the Republican Party with the forces of liberty and freedom all over the world," writes Goldfield, "but also framed the debate as a contest between good and evil." "As I view the contest," he has Lincoln say, "it is not less than a contest for the advancement of the kingdom of Heaven or the kingdom of Satan."[35] These words were not Lincoln's, however; they were written *to* Lincoln by an antislavery farmer.[36] Another example of careless attribution of evangelicalism concerns the "Secret Six" abolitionists who supported John Brown's raid in 1859 and their "close ties to evangelical Protestantism."[37] To the contrary, four of the six were Unitarians.

Goldfield is not consistent in his revisionist position. Summarizing what he considers the trumped-up debates over slavery's expansion in the 1840s and 1850s, he asserts that all too often "reality fled." In the controversy over the Kansas-Nebraska Act of 1854, which opened Kansas Territory to slavery, "reality, a rare commodity since the introduction of the Wilmot Proviso, became ever more elusive....Most of the issues worked little harm or benefit to either side," but "the reality, again, no longer mattered. In this atmosphere, demagogues prospered, and moderates faltered."[38]

In a change of tune, however, he declares that the secession crisis of 1861 was concerned with "the core of the sectional problem," slavery. "It had always been thus." The war that ensued abolished slavery. "There may have been other ways to achieve that noble end," Goldfield writes in what amounts to wishful thinking, for while noting that all of the slaves could have been purchased and freed for half the cost of the war, he acknowledges that there were almost no willing sellers in the slave states. And "a new and stronger nation emerged from the fire of war," he writes, a "nation energized and inspired by the war's ideals.... The war unleashed an economic revolution, unparalleled innovation and a degree of affluence across a broader segment of society than any Western nation had known."[39] Perhaps the Civil War was not so cruel and senseless after all.

Many Americans—perhaps most of them, according to George Rable's *God's Almost Chosen Peoples: A Religious History of the American Civil War*—would have seen the bad as well as the good accomplished by the war as God's will. "Men, women, and children, free and slave, Protestants, a growing number of Catholics, Mormons, and even the small number of Jews... shared a providential outlook on life" and "saw God's hand in the war's origins, course, and outcome."[40]

Most clergymen as well as their parishioners in both North and South viewed the war as a holy cause. With little or no debt to St. Augustine, they came up with their own just-war theology. Unionists and Confederates alike believed that they stood at Armageddon and battled for the Lord. Devout Confederate commanders like Stonewall Jackson and Robert E. Lee, and similarly committed Union generals like William S. Rosecrans and Oliver O. Howard gave credit to the Lord for their victories. Defeats were God's judgment on the sins of His people in order to humble and discipline them to greater devotion and effort. Victories brought forth presidential proclamations for days of thanksgiving; defeats elicited decrees for days of fasting, humiliation, and prayer. People in both North and South became more religious as the war went on and on, the toll of death and destruction mounted, and God's will for His almost chosen peoples became more inscrutable. Soldiers facing death or maiming experienced religious conversions; many revivals occurred in the armies, especially in the Confederacy. Jefferson Davis was baptized in May 1862 and joined St. Paul's Episcopal Church in Richmond. Two years later, Confederate general Leonidas Polk, who was also an Episcopal bishop, baptized Joseph E. Johnston, John Bell Hood, and several other Confederate generals in the Army of Tennessee.

Abraham Lincoln also became more religious under the stresses of war. He occasionally attended the New York Avenue Presbyterian Church in Washington, but he never joined a church. He did meditate more profoundly on the will of God in this war, however, than almost anyone else. "It is quite possible that God's purpose is something different from the purpose of either party," Lincoln mused in an undated memorandum, probably sometime in 1864. He could have "saved or destroyed the Union without war," but He had not. And "he could give the final victory to either side any day. Yet the contest proceeds."[41]

In his second inaugural address on March 4, 1865, with the war near its victorious conclusion, Lincoln expanded this idea. "Both [parties] read the same Bible, and pray to the same God; and each invokes His aid against the other.... The prayers of both could not be answered," he said. "The Almighty has His own purposes," Lincoln continued.

> Let us suppose that American Slavery is one of those offenses which, in the providence of God, must needs come, but which, having continued through His appointed time, He now wills to remove, and that He gives to both North and South, this terrible war, as the woe due to those by whom the offence came.... Fondly do we hope, fervently do we pray—that this mighty scourge of war may speedily pass away. Yet, if God wills that it continue, until all the wealth piled by the bond-man's two hundred and fifty years of unrequited toil shall be sunk, and until every drop of blood drawn with the lash, shall be paid by another drawn with the sword, as was said three thousand years ago, so still it must be said "the judgments of the Lord, are true and righteous altogether."[42]

If Lincoln was right, the abolition of slavery was not the self-congratulatory triumph of the "messianic mission" of a "redeemer nation," as Harry Stout would have it, but God's will after He had purged a guilty nation of the sin of enslaving an entire people by the cleansing agency of a terrible war.

CHAPTER 4

Death and Destruction in the Civil War

In 1992 Mark E. Neely Jr. won the Pulitzer Prize in History for his book *The Fate of Liberty: Abraham Lincoln and Civil Liberties.*[1] In the same year that the book came out, he published an influential article in the journal *Civil War History* titled "Was the Civil War a Total War?"[2] His answer to that question was no. The concept of "total war" first arose as a way of describing the horrifying destruction of lives and resources in World War I and achieved even more widespread use to categorize the Armageddon of World War II. The generation of historians who experienced the latter cataclysm used this phrase to describe the American Civil War as well. That conflict cost far more American lives than World War II, even though the United States in 1861 had less than one-quarter the population of 1941, and it left large portions of the South looking like bombed-out cities of Europe and Japan.

The Civil War mobilized human and economic resources in the Confederacy and the Union on a scale unmatched by any other event in American history except perhaps World War II. For actual combat duty, the war of 1861–65 mustered a larger proportion of American manpower than that of 1941–45. And in another comparison with that global conflagration, the victorious power in the Civil War did all it could to devastate the enemy's economy as well as the morale of its home-front population. The Civil War wiped out two-thirds of the assessed value of wealth in Confederate states, two-fifths of the South's livestock, and more than half of its farm machinery—not to mention at least one-quarter of the Confederacy's white men of military age. While Northern wealth increased by 50 percent from 1860 to 1870, Southern wealth decreased by 60 percent.[3]

Such devastation might seem to merit the description "total war." But Neely's article challenged that notion. He maintained that true total war—or, in the words of the Prussian military theorist Carl von Clausewitz, "absolute war"—makes no distinction between taking the lives of enemy soldiers and those of enemy civilians. It is war "without any scruples or limitations," war in which combatants give no quarter and take no prisoners. World War II approached this totality. Germany deliberately murdered millions of civilians in Europe and bombed cities in England; Allied strategic bombing killed hundreds of thousands of German and Japanese civilians; and both sides sometimes refused to take prisoners or killed them after they had surrendered. In that sense of totality, the Civil War was not a total war. Although suffering and death from disease were common among prisoners of war, and Confederates sometimes murdered captured black soldiers, there was no systematic effort to kill prisoners. And while soldiers on both sides in the Civil War pillaged civilian property and several Union commanders systematized this destruction into a policy, they did not deliberately kill civilians. "The essential aspect of any definition of total war," wrote Neely in 1991, "asserts that it breaks down the distinction between soldiers and civilians, combatants and noncombatants, and this no one in the Civil War did systematically."[4]

Neely's article had great influence. Few historians now describe the Civil War as a total war. Perhaps Harry Stout was the last to do so, in 2006.[5] In the nine years that separated the second and third editions of my textbook on the Civil War and Reconstruction, I changed my occasional use of the phrase "total war" to "hard war."[6] This terminology is now as ubiquitous as "total war" once was. It is derived from Mark Grimsley's 1995 book *The Hard Hand of War: Union Military Policy toward Southern Civilians, 1861–1865*. Grimsley takes his title from

Sherman's quote in that letter to Henry Halleck in 1864 about making the South "feel the hard hand of war."[7]

Sherman was the chief practitioner of this prescription. But his armies did not kill civilians. They did not even commit the "wanton pillage" of Southern legend. They destroyed a great deal of civilian property in their campaigns through Mississippi, Georgia, and South Carolina. But most of this destruction, according to Neely and Grimsley, was limited to resources that supported or could support the Confederate war effort. It was a policy of "directed severity" that struck a "balance between severity and restraint" and was "discriminate and roughly proportionate to legitimate needs." Compared with the scorched-earth policies of Philip II of Spain against the Dutch, with those of the British in Ireland in the seventeenth century, or with all armies in Germany in the Thirty Years' War—not to mention World War II—"the restraint of Union armies in the Civil War acquires fresh salience."[8]

The old total-war thesis focused on the radical transformation of the Southern socioeconomic order as well as on the destruction caused by the conflict. The Civil War liberated four million slaves and elevated them to equal citizenship with other Americans—on paper at least. It destroyed the wealth and national political power of the Southern planter class. As Mark Twain wrote in 1873, the war "uprooted institutions that were centuries old, changed the politics of a people...and wrought so profoundly upon the national character that the influence cannot be measured short of two or three generations."[9] To those who lived through this transformation, it seemed total.

Neely returned to the theme of the limited nature of destruction in the Civil War in a book published in 2007. "The American Civil War was, if anything, remarkable for its traditional restraint," he writes. "The relative absence of atrocity from the Civil War remains to this day one of its most remarkable qualities."[10] But can one really characterize a war in which at least 620,000 soldiers—and perhaps as many as 750,000—lost their lives and billions of dollars' worth of property was destroyed as one that was characterized by "remarkable restraint"?

Neely compares the Civil War with three other nineteenth-century conflicts: the Mexican-American War, the French intervention in the Mexican civil war, and the Indian wars on the American frontier. American volunteers in the Mexican War, according to their own commander, General Winfield Scott, "committed atrocities—horrors—in Mexico....Murder, robbery, & rape on mothers & daughters, in the presence of the tied up males of the families, have been common all along the Rio Grande."[11] American soldiers perceived Mexicans as belonging to "another race, and one with a parasitic religion," writes Neely, and treated them accordingly. "Racial constructs help explain the unrestrained passions or the unfeeling contempt exemplified by the American volunteer in Mexico, and racial constructs likewise explain the restraint of white Civil War soldiers fighting other white soldiers."[12]

But what about white Confederate soldiers fighting black Union soldiers? Neely acknowledges the atrocity at Fort Pillow, Tennessee, in which Confederates murdered more than a hundred black soldiers after they had surrendered, and mentions in passing other and almost equally notorious such cases. But these were exceptions, he maintains; the norm was restrained combat between white soldiers.

"Nor was revenge a significant factor in explaining the behavior of most Civil War troops," Neely claims, in contrast with American soldiers in Mexico, especially Texans, who were motivated by a desire for vengeance against the army that had killed Texans in cold blood at the Alamo and Goliad a decade earlier.[13] To minimize the revenge motive among Civil War soldiers, however, is to ignore a great deal of evidence of just such a motive and the behavior it produced. The letters and diaries of Confederate soldiers bristled with stereotypes of the "thieving hordes of Lincoln" who were the "lowest and most contemptible race upon the face of the earth." Southerners constructed a "Yankee race" to substitute for the "mongrel race" of Mexicans they had fought in the earlier war. One Confederate captain told his wife to teach their children "a bitter and unrelenting hatred to the Yankee race" that had "invaded our country and devastated it...[and] murdered our best citizens....If any luckless Yank should unfortunately come into my way he need not petition for mercy. If he does I'll give him lead." A Missouri Confederate vowed that when the Confederate army regained his state, "*vengeance* will be our motto." An officer in the Army of Northern Virginia, grandson of Benjamin Latrobe (who had helped design the Capitol and White House), directed artillery fire against Union attackers at the Battle of Fredericksburg. Afterward he rode over the battlefield and "enjoyed the sight of hundreds of dead Yankees. Saw much of the work I had done in the way of severed limbs, decapitated bodies, and mutilated remains of all kinds. Doing my soul good. Would that the whole Northern Army were as such & I had my hand in it."[14]

Even if Neely is wrong about the lack of significant motives of revenge among Confederate soldiers, is he right about Union soldiers? Not for Unionists from East Tennessee or other regions in the Confederacy where savage internecine warfare took place. An Ohio captain serving with West Virginia soldiers was astonished by "this passion, this desire for revenge....Hate rankled in their breasts." An East Tennessee Union soldier vowed that "if I live, I will be revenged" on the Confederates occupying his homeland. "Yes I will draw their blood and mutilate their dead bodies and help send their souls to hell."[15]

As for black soldiers, many went into action after the Fort Pillow massacre shouting, "Remember Fort Pillow!" "The darkies fought ferociously," wrote Captain Charles Francis Adams Jr. after an attack by a black division at Petersburg, Virginia. "If they murder prisoners, as I hear they did...they can hardly be blamed."[16]

It was not only black soldiers who exacted revenge for Fort Pillow. A white Wisconsin soldier wrote to his fiancée in May 1864 that when his regiment assaulted Confederate defenses at Resaca, Georgia, "twenty-three of the rebs surrendered but our boys asked if they remembered Fort Pillow and killed all of them. Where there is no officer with us, we take no prisoners....We want revenge for our brother soldiers and will have it....Some of the [rebels] say they will fight as long as there is one of them left. We tell them that is what we want. We want to kill them all off and cleanse the country."[17] The more one learns about such attitudes and incidents—and they were not the rare exceptions that Neely implies—the more one questions his assertion that "Civil War soldiers behaved differently toward the enemy" than American soldiers in Mexico.

Neely is on firmer ground in his contrast of the Civil War with the "unrestrained ferocity and destructiveness" of warfare against Indians. In a chapter on the Sand Creek massacre of Cheyenne and Arapaho Indians by white Colorado militia in 1864, Neely correctly concludes that even in the savage guerrilla conflict in Missouri, soldiers and guerrillas did not cross "the barriers to slaughter of women and children perpetrated at Sand Creek"—and, for that matter, on other occasions. By comparison, Civil War soldiers perhaps did show considerable restraint.[18]

The same may be true with respect to a comparison with the thirty-five thousand French soldiers whom Emperor Napoleon III sent to Mexico to install Austrian Archduke Ferdinand Maximilian as emperor of that strife-torn country in 1864. These soldiers carried out Maximilian's "Black Decree" of execution of any captured Mexican soldiers who had fought against his rule. Thousands of them were in fact "killed in cold blood by French and imperial forces," writes Neely. Even the "record of the U.S. army in Mexico in 1846–1848" did not "come close in brutality to the record of the French and imperialists in Mexico twenty years later."[19]

What did come close in brutality, if not in scope, to the French and Mexican case was guerrilla warfare in the Civil War, especially in Missouri. That state experienced a civil war within the Civil War, a war of neighbor against neighbor, an armed conflict along the Kansas border that went back to 1854 and had never really stopped, ugly, vicious, no-holds-barred bushwhacking that came close to total war.

Bands of Confederate guerrillas led by the notorious William Clarke Quantrill, "Bloody Bill" Anderson, and other pathological killers, including such desperadoes as the James and Younger brothers, murdered and burned out Missouri Unionists. Kansas "Jayhawkers" and Union militia retaliated in kind. In contrapuntal disharmony the guerrillas and Jayhawkers plundered and pillaged their way across the state, taking no prisoners, killing in cold blood, terrorizing the civilian population, and leaving large parts of Missouri a scorched earth. In August 1863 Quantrill's band rode into Lawrence, Kansas, and killed all the adult males they found there—more than 150 in all. A year later Bloody Bill Anderson's gang took twenty-four unarmed Union soldiers traveling home on furlough from a train, shot them in the head, then turned on a posse of pursuing militia and slaughtered 127 of them, including the wounded and captured.[20]

Neely acknowledges the barbarity of guerrilla and counterguerrilla warfare in Missouri. "But such savage tactics were an exception," he maintains. "Missouri was itself an exception."[21] He gives virtually no attention to guerrilla warfare elsewhere in Confederate and border states, which was almost as savage as in Missouri. In East Tennessee it was "war at every door," as the title of a book about that region describes it, an "uncivil war," according to the title of another.[22] Neely dismisses the irregular warfare in these places as "sideshows" to the real war of conventional armies facing each other on battlefields like Shiloh and Antietam and Gettysburg and Chickamauga and Spotsylvania. But much recent scholarship argues otherwise. "Confederate irregular forces were intended to be an adjunct to the conventional field armies," writes one historian. They "developed into a powerful tool for the Confederate war effort" and forced the Union army to develop "an extensive counterinsurgency program wherever it faced Confederate unconventional forces."[23]

By 1864 the Union response to both conventional and irregular Confederate warfare included the "hard war" destruction of Confederate resources practiced by Sherman's army in Georgia and South Carolina and by General Philip H. Sheridan's army in its Shenandoah Valley campaign. In his report on the march through Georgia, Sherman estimated the damage "at $100,000,000; at least $20,000,000 of which has inured to our advantage, and the remainder was simple waste and destruction." The devastation in South Carolina was far greater, for Union soldiers considered that state the fount of secession. "The whole army is burning with an insatiable desire to wreak vengeance upon South Carolina," wrote Sherman. "I almost tremble at her fate, but feel that she deserves all that seems in store for her." The Union chief of staff, General Henry W. Halleck, had written Sherman that if he captured Charleston, "I hope that by some accident the place may be destroyed, and if a little salt should be sown upon its site it may prevent the growth of future crops of nullification and secession."[24]

Sherman's army did not get to Charleston, but Confederate troops themselves burned much of that city when they evacuated it. Union soldiers burned plenty of other places in South Carolina, including the town of Barnwell, which they renamed "Burnwell." The Pennsylvania soldiers in Sherman's army felt a grim sense of satisfaction in retaliating for the burning of Chambersburg in their state by Confederate cavalry.

Neely briefly acknowledges the destructiveness of Sherman's march through Georgia, but insists that "it provided a notable exception to the rule of the Civil War in regard to the private property of the enemy."[25] He barely mentions the march through South Carolina, but presumably would describe it as another exception. By the time Neely gets to Sheridan's Shenandoah Valley campaign, to which he devotes an entire chapter, he apparently senses that the reader has grown skeptical of the claim that all of these exceptions prove the rule of "remarkable restraint." Instead, Neely seeks to minimize the extent of devastation in the Shenandoah Valley. He neglects to cite Sheridan's own report of October 7, 1864. "I have destroyed over 2,000 barns filled with wheat, hay, and farming implements," Sheridan wrote, and "over seventy mills filled with flour and wheat; have driven in front of the army over 4,000 head of stock, and have killed and issued to the troops not less than 3,000 sheep." This was just the beginning. By the time he was done, wrote Sheridan, "the Valley, from Winchester up to Staunton, ninety-two miles, will have but little in it for man or beast."[26]

Neely does quote reports by other Union officers, in which he somehow finds evidence that the destruction was not so bad after all. The valley, wrote one, "has been left in such a condition as to barely leave subsistence for the inhabitants." Another noted that "nothing is left where we have been but corn and not much of that. Barns and mills are destroyed. Hay and grain has been given to the flames." The point here, writes Neely, is that Union soldiers did leave enough corn for "the subsistence of the inhabitants." How they were to grind it when all the mills were burned is not made clear.[27]

Neely's final chapter addresses the question of casualty figures in the Civil War. He does not challenge the data that at least 620,000 soldiers died in the war. (The new estimate of 750,000 deaths, based on careful statistical analysis of census data, was not yet available when Neely wrote.)[28] Rather, he questions the interpretation of these data. The figure of 620,000 dead amounted to 2 percent of the American population in 1861. If 2 percent of Americans were to die in a war fought today, the number of American war dead would be more than 6 million. The new figure of 750,000 deaths would increase the relative toll for today to almost 7.5 million. This startling toll—whether 6 million or 7.5 million—might call into question the conclusion that the Civil War was "remarkable for its traditional restraint." So these figures must somehow be sanitized. The figure of 620,000 "lumps the dead from both sides together and calls them all 'Americans,' " Neely points out. "Such a mixing of opponents is rarely done in studying other American wars. . . . If we consider the Civil War casualties one 'country' at a time, then the 360,000 Union dead do not equal even the 407,000 Americans killed in World War II," and "the 260,000 Confederate dead constitute but 64 percent of the 407,000 Americans killed in World War II."[29]

This argument is more than a little misleading. The 360,000 Union war dead were 1.6 percent of the population of Union states. An equivalent

American death toll in World War II would have been 2.1 million and would today be 4.9 million. The 260,000 Southern dead constituted 2.9 percent of the Confederate population (including slaves), which would translate into 3.9 million of the 1940s population and 8.8 million today. (These figures would be higher if the new estimate of Civil War dead is correct.) If we disaggregate the Union and Confederate tolls, as Neely wants us to do, the proportionate casualty rate for the Union is almost as large as when they are lumped together, and the Confederate rate is far greater—and each is several times more catastrophic than for any other war, including World War II. These figures demonstrate the opposite of what Neely wants them to prove.

The same is true of the numbers game Neely plays with a comparison of the American Civil War and the Crimean War of a few years earlier, between 1854 and 1856. The death toll for all nations involved in that conflict was 640,000, which slightly exceeded the most conservative estimate for the American Civil War, as Neely notes. What he does not tell the reader, however, is that the combined population of the four principal nations that fought the Crimean War (Russia versus Turkey, Britain, and France) was about 130 million, four times the 32 million in the Union and Confederacy. In the Crimean War, fewer than 10 percent of soldier deaths occurred in combat; the rest were caused by disease and exposure. By contrast, 35 percent of soldier deaths in the Civil War resulted from combat wounds. On a per capita basis, combat mortality in the Civil War was at least fifteen times greater than in the Crimean War. This reality underscores the irony of Neely's statement that "the true significance of the Civil War casualty figures is quite the opposite of what has been asserted routinely about them in the past."[30] In fact, what has been "asserted routinely" is exactly right, and its "true significance" undermines much of Neely's argument.

Although death on the massive scale of the Civil War was a new experience for Americans, they were no strangers to death on a more personal and individual level. Life expectancy at birth was forty years, largely because of an infant and child mortality rate nearly ten times greater than today. Most parents had buried at least one child; few young people reached adulthood without the loss of siblings or cousins. Many husbands grieved for wives who died in childbirth. Fearful epidemics of cholera, yellow fever, and other diseases periodically carried off thousands in the antebellum era. The scourge of "consumption"— tuberculosis—blighted the existence of many in middle age as well as those who had managed to live beyond it.

The ever-present reality or prospect of death created what the historian Mark Schantz calls a "culture of death" to help Americans cope with that reality. No best-selling novel was complete without deathbed scenes that were often deeply sentimental and accompanied by assurances that Christian redemption would transport the departed to heaven. The death of Little Eva in Harriet Beecher Stowe's *Uncle Tom's Cabin* is the most famous example of this genre.

Poetry seemed even more obsessed with the poignancy of death. "Gathering momentum after the publication of William Cullen Bryant's classic work 'Thanatopsis' in 1821," writes Schantz, "the subject of death became the coin of the realm in the antebellum poetic imagination." Emily Dickinson "accorded death a prominent place" in hundreds of her poems, including the opening lines in one of her most famous: "Because I could not stop for Death / He kindly stopped for me." The cemetery movement that followed the successful model of Mount Auburn Cemetery outside of Boston turned traditional graveyards into beautifully landscaped parks where mourners and visitors could contemplate the bliss of eternity. If modern America is, as many critics have noted, "a death-denying culture" that tries to hide the inconvenient fact of dying, according to Schantz, "nineteenth-century America was a death-embracing culture."[31]

Drew Gilpin Faust would not go that far, although in *This Republic of Suffering: Death and the American Civil War* (2008), she does contrast the preoccupation of antebellum Americans with death to our discomfort with the subject today. But while Schantz believes that "antebellum Americans could face death with resignation and even joy because they carried in their hearts and heads a comforting and compelling vision of eternal life,"[32] Faust portrays death, however frequent, as a heart-wrenching experience for both the dying and their surviving loved ones. If there was a "culture of death," it consisted of rituals to cushion the numbing shock of loss. Faust labels the most important ritual "the concept of the Good Death." Such a death occurred at home in bed surrounded by family and friends who provided every comfort during the last hours of life. The dying person spoke last words assuring everyone that she or he was ready to depart in peace and to meet again in the afterlife where the strife and hardships of earthly toil were unknown. "By the 1860s," Faust writes, "many elements of the Good Death" had been largely "separated from their explicitly theological roots." Assumptions about "the way to die" had "spread beyond formal religion to become part of more general systems of belief held across the nation about life's meaning and life's appropriate end."[33]

While the differences between these two books on the same subject are sometimes distinct and sometimes subtle, together they offer a richer understanding of the impact on American society of widespread death during the Civil War than either does alone. One difference concerns the theme expressed by Schantz's title, *Awaiting the Heavenly Country*. His most important chapter analyzes the central tenet of the American culture of death: a widespread belief that "a heavenly eternity of transcendent beauty awaited them beyond the grave." For many Americans this resurrection would include bodies as well as souls; they would literally be able to recognize and be recognized by their friends and relatives in the next world. "That those who fought the Civil War marched off to battle with robust notions of the literal bodily restoration planted firmly in their cultural universe," writes Schantz, "is a matter of deep significance." He does not mean to suggest that soldiers deliberately courted a martyr's death and immediate ascension to heaven as, for example, a Muslim suicide bomber is said to do. Rather, the literal belief in eternal life "may help to explain how and why Americans on all sides were able to endure such grisly conflict."[34]

Schantz is onto something important here. In my own research on the beliefs and motivations of Civil War soldiers, I have also encountered the conviction that "religion is what makes brave soldiers." A Mississippi private said that "Christians make the best soldiers, as they would not fear the consequences after death as others would." Some soldiers expressed sentiments that come close to justifying Schantz's assertion that Americans could face death with resignation and even joy. An Illinois cavalryman wrote to his wife that death was merely "the destruction of a gross, material body....A soldier's death is not a fate to be avoided, but rather almost to be gloried in," while a Georgia officer found "something solemn, mysterious, sublime at the thought of entering into eternity."[35]

Faust also discusses the belief in salvation as a factor in nerving soldiers to face death with equanimity and as a source of comfort to their families. She cites the funeral sermon for a Massachusetts officer killed at Petersburg, in which the clergyman defined death as "the middle point between two lives." But she seems inclined at times to view this conviction as the equivalent of grasping at straws—or, to change the metaphor, of whistling past the graveyard. Instead of a deeply held belief, it was for many soldiers and their families, she writes, the product of "distress and desire" to make tolerable the intolerable prospect of death. She also suggests the provocative idea that the vision of death as the middle point between two lives was a nineteenth-century version of a death-denying culture.[36]

The same Christian theology that offered the solace of salvation also included the commandment "Thou shalt not kill." "How can a soldier be a Christian?" asked an Indiana officer whose regiment saw a great deal of action. "Read all Christ's teaching, and then tell me whether *one engaged in maiming and butchering men...can be saved* under the Gospel." He had not resolved this question when he was killed at the Battle of Resaca in May 1864.[37] Faust discovered that many Civil War soldiers found it harder to learn to kill than to face the possibility of death. Although few soldiers had read Saint Augustine or

Hugo Grotius on the theory of "just war," they eventually developed their own version of this doctrine as applied to "Yankee vandals" or "Rebel traitors." A variety of beliefs helped soldiers overcome the sixth commandment, among them ideas of duty and self-defense (kill or be killed), a desire for revenge against a demonized enemy who had killed their comrades, the murderous hatred of Confederate soldiers toward black Union soldiers, and the latter's retaliation for the massacres of captured black soldiers. Veteran soldiers became hardened to death. They were, in Faust's words, "never quite the same again after seeing fields of slaughtered bodies destroyed by men just like themselves."[38]

Both Schantz and Faust maintain that however omnipresent death had been before 1861, the Civil War experience was unique, whether the total number of soldier deaths was 620,000 or the new estimate of 750,000. And these figures do not include the unknown (and unknowable) number of Southern civilian deaths indirectly caused by the ravages of disease, exposure, malnutrition, and other inevitable disruptions of a war that was fought mostly in the South and destroyed much of the Southern infrastructure.

Whether or not Americans possessed a "culture of death" in 1861, they were unprepared for mortality on this scale. Faust portrays the shock of death in the war as a matter of quality as well as quantity. A Good Death was impossible for soldiers shot through the head or lungs or guts and dying in agony in no-man's-land between the lines far from home, or suffering from typhoid fever or dysentery in an army hospital hundreds of miles from loved ones and buried unceremoniously in an often anonymous grave. "Sudden death represented a profound threat to fundamental assumptions about the correct way to die," Faust points out. "One of the Civil War's greatest horrors was that it denied so many soldiers" the chance for a Good Death "by killing them suddenly, obliterating them on the battlefield and depriving them of the chance for the life-defining deathbed experience."[39]

Soldiers and civilians did what they could to create a semblance of the Good Death. Some soldiers wrote anticipatory letters home before going into battle or while lying dangerously wounded or ill. These letters substituted for last words at home. They assured loved ones of a readiness to die and to meet them in the next world. Chaplains and hospital nurses sometimes wrote such letters for the dying.

Neither the Union nor Confederate army had an official procedure for notifying next of kin of soldier deaths. This task fell to company officers or chaplains or army buddies, but the process was hit or miss. Mothers or wives or fathers at home often endured weeks of harrowing uncertainty about the fate of their son or husband, who might have been reported in the newspaper casualty lists as "dangerously wounded" or "missing." In many cases that uncertainty lasted forever. Neither army provided soldiers with identity tags. More than half of the soldiers who died in the war were buried in graves—sometimes mass graves—without identification.

Walking through the Civil War section of a National or Confederate cemetery today and reading all of the stones marked "Unknown" gives one only a faint idea of the pain suffered by families who never saw the body of their soldier son or husband, never had an opportunity to say good-bye, never could visit his grave. "Death without dignity, without decency, without identity imperiled the meaning of the life that preceded it," writes Faust. "Americans had not just lost the dead; they had lost their own lives as they had understood them before the war."[40]

Efforts to counter this dismal fate made some progress during the war, especially in the North. The U.S. Sanitary Commission, the Christian Commission, and other private organizations worked with the army to identify deceased soldiers, notify their families, and in some cases to arrange for their shipment home, where families could have at least the comfort of burial in local cemeteries and markers to honor their sacrifice. The practice of embalming, rare in the United States before the Civil War, expanded greatly during the war and laid the foundations for a funeral "industry" after it. Embalming and coffins for shipment of bodies were expensive, however, and those whose remains received this treatment were mostly officers. But not entirely; of the 5,100 Union soldiers killed or mortally wounded at Gettysburg, an estimated 1,500 were interred or reinterred in their hometown cemeteries. Gettysburg, of course, was closer to Northern communities than any other major battlefield.

The rest of the Union dead at Gettysburg were buried in the soldiers' cemetery there, which provided a model for the government's principal effort to honor the memories of those who gave their lives for the republic and to provide at least some closure and comfort for their families. Although the Northern states whose men had fought at Gettysburg took the initiative in establishing that cemetery, the national government assumed responsibility for its maintenance and became the owner of the eventual total of seventy-four national military cemeteries (including Gettysburg) that were the final resting place for 303,536 Union war dead (and thousands of veterans of later wars as well).

As early as 1862 the U.S. Congress enacted legislation authorizing the president to purchase land "to be used as a national cemetery for the soldiers who shall die in the service of the country." Three such cemeteries in addition to Gettysburg were established during the war. But the greatest effort to find, identify, and reinter Union soldiers took place during the half-dozen years after the war, with generous appropriations authorized by the National Cemeteries Act of 1867. This undertaking was virtually unprecedented; except for "Republican Athens," noted a Northern journalist in 1866, "no people or nation had ever designated a burial place for the common soldier."[41]

This postwar program did something to atone for the government's haphazard record-keeping and treatment of the dead during the war's early years. Even though nearly half of those 303,536 Union soldiers in national cemeteries remained unknown, the re-interment program identified tens of thousands and gave comfort, Faust writes, to many families even of the unknown who could believe that their loved ones had been buried with dignity and marked with a stone—key elements in the ideal of a Good Death. "Such a consecration of a nation's power

and resources to a *sentiment*," wrote the army officer principally responsible for the reinterment project, "the world has never witnessed." Faust
agrees. "The reburial program represented an extraordinary departure
for the federal government," she maintains, "an indication of the very
different sort of nation that had emerged as a result of civil war." It
"would have been unimaginable before the war created its legions of
dead, a constituency of the slain and their mourners, who would change
the very definition of the nation and its obligations."[42]

What of the Confederate war dead and their constituency of
mourners? The United States obviously could not honor those soldiers
who fought against their country. During the war many Confederate
dead were buried in local cemeteries near where they fell—Oakwood
and Hollywood Cemeteries in Richmond, Blanford Cemetery in
Petersburg, and others around the South. But scores of thousands remained in unmarked graves from Pennsylvania to Louisiana. Southern
women formed Confederate Ladies Memorial Associations after the
war to locate battlefield and hospital burial sites and reinter the remains
of Southern soldiers in marked graves at Confederate cemeteries,
whose memorials and monuments matched those in national military
cemeteries.

These Civil War cemeteries, writes Faust, "were unlike any graveyards that Americans had ever seen." They "were not clusters of family
tombstones in churchyards, nor garden cemeteries symbolizing the reunion of man with nature." Rather they "contained ordered row after
row of humble identical markers, hundreds of thousands of men, known
and unknown, who represented not so much the sorrow or particu-
larity of a lost loved one as the enormous and all but unfathomable cost
of the war."[43]

Many of the Union war dead not buried in national cemeteries and
Southern soldiers not interred in designated Confederate burial grounds
were placed in civilian cemeteries or family graveyards, often with
elaborate tombstones that honored their sacrifices. Schantz's *Awaiting
the Heavenly Country* analyzes the funerary art that was an important

part of the American culture of death. One of the most popular Currier and Ives lithographs in that era was *The Soldier's Grave*, which showed a female mourner weeping next to a large gravestone commemorating "a brave and gallant soldier and a true patriot." These lithographs "created imaginary soldier's graves for those tens of thousands of Union troops who died many miles from their homes," Schantz writes. "In creating funerals for the mind and for the spirit," the lithographs "sustained Americans as they confronted loss of life on a mass scale."[44]

For both Schantz and Faust, this loss of life and the cultural institutions Americans constructed to cope with it are the most enduring legacy of the Civil War. The "horribly luminous" reality of 620,000 war dead, writes Schantz, "worked profound transformations on American society." For Faust, "death created the modern American union." The dying and killing "transformed society, culture, and politics in what became a broader republic of shared suffering." The "meaning of the war had come to inhere in its cost.... The Civil War Dead became both powerful and immortal, no longer individual men but instead a force that would shape American public life for at least a century to come."[45]

My discomfort with this conclusion does not stem solely from its apparent morbidity. Surely the legacy of the Civil War went beyond its cost in human lives. Both authors acknowledge that the war preserved the United States as one nation and, in Faust's words, "launched it on a trajectory of economic expansion and world influence." It also "ended slavery and helped to define the meanings of freedom, citizenship, and equality." But somehow these achievements seem to pale before the real "texture of the experience, its warp and woof...the presence of death."[46]

In my view, however, the meaning of the war inhered at least as much in its results as in its cost. Faust makes a strong case that the creation of national cemeteries with their constituency of mourners and the slain changed "the very definition of the nation and its obligations."[47] But I think that the Thirteenth, Fourteenth, and Fifteenth Amendments, which defined freedom, citizenship, and equal rights, were even more nationalizing and transformative. Despite the war's "harvest of death," three times more soldiers survived than died. Their veterans' reunions well into the twentieth century commemorated the sacrifices of comrades who had given their lives in the war, to be sure, but they also celebrated the achievements of the living. In neither respect, it seems clear, can this war that "wrought so profoundly upon the entire national character," as Mark Twain expressed it, be best understood in terms of its "remarkable restraint."

CHAPTER 5

American Navies and British Neutrality During the Civil War

Most civil wars in nation states through history have attracted foreign intervention of some kind, often military or diplomatic support for the faction rebelling against the established government. A very real possibility for such intervention existed during the American Civil War. Emperor Louis Napoleon of France looked with favor on the Confederacy, and the French economy was hurt by the sharp decline in the availability of Southern cotton. Several times during the war Napoleon pressed the British government to join France in an effort to mediate peace negotiations between the warring parties in America on the basis of Confederate independence. The British economy was hurt even more than France's by the loss of cotton from the South. Large numbers of Englishmen also sympathized with the Confederacy. But while Britain came dangerously close to intervention on two occasions, the ministry of Viscount Henry Palmerston backed off. Napoleon did not want to act without British cooperation. So in the end the Union and the Confederacy fought it out between themselves without official intervention by any foreign power. Still, it was a very near thing.

Several factors shaped British policy toward the American Civil War, including pressures both for and against intervention: the "cotton famine," as it was known especially in 1862, which caused massive unemployment and suffering among Lancashire textile workers; divisions between pro-Union and pro-Confederate elements of British public opinion; the importance to the British economy of foreign trade with the United States, as well as a desire for cotton from the Confederate states; the Palmerston ministry's fears that a rupture with the United States would jeopardize Britain's hold on its Canadian colonies; the slavery issue, especially after Abraham Lincoln's Emancipation Proclamation made it a war of freedom against slavery that strongly swayed British opinion toward the Union side; and international crises in Europe that diverted French as well as British attention from the war in America by 1863 and after.

But the single most important factor that directly or indirectly shaped Anglo-American and Anglo-Confederate relations, especially from 1861 to 1863, was the actions of Union and Confederate navies. Three such actions or proceedings played a crucial role in the international dimensions of the American Civil War and the potential for Anglo-American conflict: the "*Trent* Affair" in November and December 1861; the legal as well as economic aspects of the Union naval blockade of Confederate ports; and efforts by the Confederate navy to have warships built in private British shipyards.

First, the *Trent* affair. On November 8, 1861, the U.S. warship *San Jacinto*, patrolling the Old Bahama Channel off the northern coast of Cuba, fired a shot across the bow of the British packet steamer *Trent* and forced her to heave to in international waters. At the order of the *San Jacinto*'s captain, Charles Wilkes, the executive officer led armed sailors aboard the *Trent* and seized James Mason and John Slidell, who had escaped from Charleston aboard a blockade-runner and were on their way to Europe as Confederate envoys to Britain and France.

Wilkes was something of a loose cannon in the American navy. He had a bullying personality that demanded quick obedience from subordinates but often defied the orders of superiors. As a lieutenant twenty years earlier he had commanded an exploring expedition in the South Pacific that had produced much valuable information, including confirmation of Antarctica's continental status. But his violent disciplinary measures had earned the hatred of sailors and officers alike. He faced a court-martial upon his return to the United States in 1842 but escaped conviction.

For the next two decades Wilkes remained unpopular in the navy, and his career languished. But the need for experienced naval officers when the Civil War broke out caused Secretary of the Navy Gideon Welles to give him command of the *San Jacinto*. He was in the Caribbean hunting for the Confederate commerce raider CSS *Sumter*, which had captured and destroyed several American merchant vessels, when he learned from the American consul in Havana that Mason and Slidell were about to embark on the *Trent*. Here, thought Wilkes, was an even greater prize than the *Sumter*. He lay in wait for the *Trent* in the Old Bahama Channel. On November 8 the *Trent* steamed into sight, and Wilkes pounced.

Although the *Trent* was a ship of a neutral nation on its way from one neutral port to another, Wilkes informed Gideon Welles that he had consulted the books on international and maritime law on board the *San Jacinto* and learned that he had the right to capture enemy dispatches on a neutral ship. As diplomats, he wrote, Mason and Slidell were "the embodiment of dispatches." Whether this novel interpretation of international law would have stood up in a prize court is impossible to know, because Wilkes did not send the *Trent* to a port with a prize court. He was already shorthanded, Wilkes explained to Welles, and to have put a prize crew on board the *Trent* would have made him more so. The *Trent* was also carrying many passengers to England who would have been seriously inconvenienced by diversion to Key West or another American port. So he seized the Confederate diplomats and let the *Trent* go. Ironically, much of the angry British reaction would have been defused if he had sent her to a prize court.[1]

The Northern press lionized Wilkes as a hero. He was feted in Boston and lauded in Congress. In words he probably regretted later, Welles congratulated Wilkes "on the great public service you have rendered.... Your conduct in seizing these public enemies was marked by intelligence, ability, decision, and firmness." Even President Lincoln seemed to share the public mood of euphoria.[2]

But the president and other cabinet members soon had second thoughts. Even before the furious reaction from across the Atlantic reached American shores, Lincoln remarked to Attorney General Edward Bates: "I am not much of a prize lawyer, but it seems to me that if Wilkes saw fit to make that capture on the high seas he had no right to turn his quarter-deck into a prize court."[3] Charles Sumner, chairman of the Senate Foreign Relations Committee, reminded Lincoln that the United States had declared war on Britain in 1812 for behavior similar to Wilkes's seizure of Mason and Slidell. The American minister to Britain, Charles Francis Adams, made the same point to Secretary of State William H. Seward.

The jingo press in England clamored for revenge for this insult to the Union Jack. The Royal Navy strengthened its fleet in the western Atlantic and convoyed army reinforcements to Canada. The risk of war caused the American stock market to take a nosedive. Government bonds found no buyers. Southern newspapers speculated about the happy prospect of an Anglo-American war that would assure Confederate independence. The British cabinet drafted an ultimatum demanding an apology and the release of Mason and Slidell. Queen Victoria's consort, Prince Albert, ill and soon to die, suggested language that softened the ultimatum, which Foreign Secretary Lord John Russell accepted. Russell even suggested to Lord Lyons, the British minister to the United States, that if the Americans released the two Confederates the British could be "rather easy about the apology."[4]

By mid-December the Lincoln administration recognized that it must give in. Attorney General Bates, who had initially supported Wilkes, acknowledged that "to go to war with England now is to abandon all hope of suppressing the rebellion." While Lincoln realized that he must not have "two wars on his hands at a time," he also wanted to avoid the humiliation and political danger of appearing to give in to John Bull. Seward took a hint from Prince Albert's revision of the ultimatum. At cabinet meetings on Christmas and the following day, Seward presented a memorandum stating that Wilkes had acted without instructions (which was true) and had erred by failing to bring the *Trent* into port for adjudication by a prize court. As a face-saving gesture, Seward added that the United States was gratified by Britain's recognition of the neutral rights for which America had always contended.[5]

The cabinet endorsed this document, and the Confederate envoys made their ways to London and Paris, where they spent three futile years trying to win the foreign recognition and intervention that might have occurred if they had remained imprisoned at Fort Warren in Boston Harbor. The Lincoln administration suffered less political damage than the president had feared, for most of the Northern public had come to the same "one war at a time" conclusion that Lincoln had. And the reaction in Britain was surprisingly pro-American. Charles Francis Adams reported from the American legation in January 1862 that "the current which ran against us with such extreme violence six weeks ago now seems to be going with equal fury in our direction."[6] That favorable current had crucial significance for the U.S. Navy, for the question of the blockade's legitimacy under international law was coming to a head.

One of Lincoln's first actions as commander in chief after the Confederate attack on Fort Sumter was to declare a blockade of the Confederate coast, which eventually extended 3,500 miles from Virginia to Texas, including 189 harbors and coves where cargo could be landed. To block all of these holes was an impossible task. Only a dozen of these harbors had railroad connections to the interior, but imposing an effective blockade on just these ports would require large numbers of ships to cover the multiple channels and rivers and inland waterways radiating from or connecting several of them. Although the Navy Department purchased, chartered, and began to build vessels at a feverish pace in 1861 to create a large blockade fleet, the cordon was as leaky as a sieve at first. Most blockade-runners leaving or entering Confederate ports got through, as indeed they did throughout the war. But as time went on, the blockade became ever tighter, and those runners that did get through were built for speed and low visibility with limited carrying capacity, which much diminished Confederate seaborne trade at a time when the Southern ability to wage war required the importation of large amounts of war materiel and the export of cotton to pay for it. The blockade became an increasingly effective Union weapon by 1862, helping to cause shortages of almost everything in the South and a dizzying inflationary spiral that eventually ruined the Confederate economy.

The blockade had important diplomatic implications. In 1856 the leading maritime powers of Europe had adopted the Declaration of Paris, defining the international law of warfare at sea. A key part of this declaration stated: "Blockades, in order to be binding [on neutral powers] must be effective; that is to say, maintained by a force sufficient really to prevent access to the coast of the enemy."[7] The United States had not signed the declaration because it also outlawed privateering, which had been a potent American naval weapon in the Revolution and the War of 1812. Now that the United States was the victim of Confederate privateers in the early months of the Civil War, Secretary of State Seward was eager to sign. But the complications of doing so in the middle of a civil war postponed the question until some future time. Nevertheless, the provisions of the Declaration of Paris remained in force for European powers. Confederate envoys (including Mason and Slidell when they finally reached Europe) presented long lists of ships they claimed had evaded the blockade to prove that it was a mere "paper blockade" and therefore illegal under international law. Jefferson Davis condemned the North's so-called blockade as a "monstrous pretension."[8]

Their contention that many vessels breached the blockade was quite true. But they neglected to note that most of them were small coasting vessels traveling often on the inland waterways from one Southern port to another, not oceangoing ships or blockade-runners going to or from foreign ports. Nor did the Confederates help their cause by imposing an informal embargo on cotton exports in 1861 as a way to put pressure on Britain and France to intervene in the war to get cotton. By the time Confederate leaders realized that this embargo was counterproductive, the blockade had begun to tighten, and efforts to get cotton through it had become difficult.

Some did get through, however, and in November 1861 Foreign Secretary Lord Russell asked Lord Lyons for his opinion of Confederate claims about a paper blockade. Lyons confessed that he was "a good deal puzzled" about how to respond to Russell. He wrote that the blockade "is certainly by no means strict or vigorous along the immense extent of coast to which it is supposed to apply. On the other hand it is very far from being a mere Paper Blockade. A great many vessels are captured; it is a most serious interruption of trade; and if it were as ineffective as Mr. Jefferson Davis says in his message, he would not be so very anxious to get rid of it." When John Slidell presented French officials with yet another list of ships that had run the blockade, they asked him "how it was that so little cotton had reached neutral ports." Slidell answered that most of the successful runners had small cargo capacity, and "the risk of capture was sufficiently great to deter those who had not an adventurous spirit from attempting it."[9]

Fatal admission! The true measure of the blockade's effectiveness was not how many ships got through or even how many were captured, but how many never tried. Lord Russell said as much in a statement on February 2, 1862, when in effect he announced to Parliament a corollary to the Declaration of Paris: "Assuming...that a number of ships is stationed and remains at the entrance to a port, sufficiently really to prevent access to it *or to create an evident danger of entering or leaving it*...the fact that various ships may have successfully escaped through it...will not of itself prevent the blockade from being an effective one by international law."[10]

The Russell Corollary drove a stake through the heart of Confederate efforts to convince European governments of the blockade's illegitimacy.

But to the extent that the blockade was a practical as well as legal success, it ironically heightened the potential danger to the Union cause. Confederate diplomacy in 1862 switched its focus from discrediting the blockade to seeking diplomatic recognition of Confederate nationhood. The Southern nation was a going concern that had successfully defended its independence for a year. Recognition of this reality by foreign powers, argued Confederate leaders, could be the first step toward commercial treaties that might reopen trade and overcome the blockade-imposed cotton famine that was taking a rising toll on the British and French economies.

A good many Europeans shared this conviction. They viewed diplomatic recognition as part of a package that would include peace negotiations between the warring parties brokered by the British and French governments. Confederate military success in 1861 sustained a widespread belief in Europe that the Union cause was hopeless. Northern armies could never reestablish control over 750,000 square miles of territory defended by a determined and courageous people. Northern leaders greatly feared the possibility of European recognition of the Confederacy if Union armies did not do something to convince foreign nations of their ability to crush the rebellion. As Lord Robert Cecil told a Northern acquaintance in 1861: "Well, there is one way to convert us all—Win the battles, and we shall come round at once."[11]

In February 1862 Union forces did begin winning battles—Forts Henry and Donelson in Tennessee, Roanoke Island and a series of other victories in North Carolina, Pea Ridge in Arkansas, Shiloh in Tennessee, the capture of Nashville, New Orleans, Memphis, and Norfolk, and a massive invasion of Virginia that brought the Army of the Potomac to Richmond's doorstep by May. The Union navy played a key role in most of these victories, especially the capture of New Orleans. Although Confederate envoys continued to press for recognition, they now found a cold reception. In June 1862 British prime minister Palmerston observed in a letter that "this seems an odd moment to Chuse for acknowledging the separate Independence of the South when all the Seaboard, and the principal internal Rivers are in the hands of the North.... We ought to know that their Separate Independence is a Truth and a Fact before we declare it to be so."[12]

But even as Palmerston wrote these words, the pendulum of victory swung over to the Confederacy again. General Robert E. Lee's Army of Northern Virginia drove General George B. McClellan's Army of the Potomac back from Richmond in the Seven Days Battles and then inflicted a humiliating defeat on another Union army only twenty-five miles from Washington at the Second Battle of Bull Run. Confederate armies in Tennessee launched counteroffensives and invaded Kentucky in September while Lee invaded Maryland.

This startling reversal of momentum revived the possibility of European intervention, especially as the blockade-imposed cotton famine was devastating the British and French textile industries. Louis Napoleon pressed the British government to join France in an offer to mediate peace negotiations on the basis of Confederate independence. Palmerston and Foreign Secretary Russell now seemed almost ready for such an overture. Palmerston observed that at Second Bull Run the Federals "got a very complete smashing, and it seems not altogether unlikely that still greater disasters await them, and that even Washington or Baltimore might fall into the hands of the Confederates." If something like that happened, he asked Russell, "would it not be time for us to consider whether...England and France might not address the contending parties and recommend an arrangement on the basis of separation?" Russell needed little persuasion. He concurred, and added that if the Lincoln administration rejected an offer of mediation, "we ought ourselves to recognise the Southern States as an independent State."[13]

Palmerston and Russell planned to hold a cabinet meeting in October 1862 when they would vote on a proposal to the Union and Confederate governments of "an Armistice and Cessation of Blockades with a view to Negotiation on the Basis of Separation" to be followed by diplomatic recognition of the Confederacy. But they also agreed to take no action until the outcomes of the Confederate invasions of Maryland and Kentucky were more clear. "If the Federals sustain a great defeat...[their] Cause will be manifestly hopeless and the iron should be struck while it is hot," declared Palmerston. "If, on the other hand, they should have the best of it, we may wait a while and see what may follow."[14]

What followed was the battles of Antietam in Maryland and Perryville in Kentucky, which turned back the dual invasions and forced the Confederates to retreat. These were not tactically decisive Union victories, but they did have important strategic consequences, especially on the diplomatic front. Charles Francis Adams reported from London that most Englishmen had expected the Confederates to capture Washington, and "the surprise" at their retreat instead "has been quite in proportion....As a consequence, less and less seems to be thought of mediation and intervention."[15]

Palmerston did indeed back away from the idea of intervention. The only favorable condition for mediation would have been "the great success of the South against the North," he commented to Russell in October. "That state of things seemed ten days ago to be approaching," but at Antietam "its advance has been lately checked....I am therefore inclined to change the opinion I wrote you when the Confederates seemed to be carrying all before them, and I am [convinced]... that we must continue merely to be lookers-on till the war shall have taken a more decided turn."[16]

It never did take a decided enough turn toward the Confederates as far as Britain was concerned, especially because of another consequence of the Battle of Antietam: it gave Lincoln the Union victory he had been waiting for to issue the preliminary Emancipation Proclamation on September 22, followed by the final Proclamation on New Year's Day 1863. Young Henry Adams, who served as private secretary for his father at the legation in London, wrote on January 23 that "the Emancipation Proclamation has done more for us here than all our former victories and all our diplomacy. It is creating an almost convulsive reaction in our favor all over this country." Richard Cobden, a pro-Union member of the British Parliament, declared that the Proclamation "has had a powerful effect on our newspapers and politicians. It has closed the mouths of those who have been advocating the side of the South. Recognition of the South, by England, whilst it bases itself on Negro slavery, is an impossibility."[17]

Cobden's assertion was undoubtedly correct. But that did not end the danger of a rupture in Anglo-American relations that might redound to the benefit of the Confederacy. In the early months of the war, Confederate naval secretary Stephen Mallory had sent agents to Europe to purchase and contract for the building of warships to prey on American commerce and to attack Union blockade ships. The most successful of these agents was James D. Bulloch, a Georgia native and former officer in the U.S. Navy, who in 1861 contracted for two fast and powerful commerce raiders that became the CSS *Florida* and CSS *Alabama* when they were launched in 1862.

The building of these ships in Liverpool was an egregious violation of British neutrality. Britain's Foreign Enlistment Act prohibited the construction and arming of warships for a belligerent power. But Bulloch was a master of misdirection. The Confederate government itself was not named as a party to the contracts he negotiated. The ship that became the *Florida* was supposedly being built for a merchant in Palermo, Sicily. The American consul in Liverpool, Thomas H. Dudley, uncovered a great deal of evidence that the ship was in fact destined for the Confederacy. But the British government did not stop her from going to sea in March 1862 as an ostensible merchant vessel without any guns or other warlike equipment. In August she took on her armament, ammunition, and supplies that had been separately shipped to an uninhabited cay in the Bahamas. Soon afterward she sailed forth on a career that destroyed thirty-eight American merchant ships.

Even more deadly was the *Alabama*, which Bulloch managed to get out of Britain in July 1862 owing to the laxness of British enforcement of the Foreign Enlistment Act. In a contest of lawyers, spies, and double agents that would furnish material for an espionage thriller, Dudley amassed evidence of the ship's illegal purpose, and Bulloch struggled to slip through the legal net surrounding him. Once again bureaucratic negligence, legal pettifoggery, and the Confederate sympathies of the British customs collector in Liverpool gave Bulloch time to ready the ship for sea. When an agent informed him of the government's belated intention to seize the ship, Bulloch took her out for a "trial cruise" from which she never returned. She rendezvoused at the Azores with a tender carrying guns and ammunition sent separately from Britain. Under her redoubtable Confederate commander, Raphael Semmes, the *Alabama* roamed the seas for the next two years capturing and destroying sixty-four American merchant vessels and one naval ship before being sunk by the USS *Kearsarge* in a dramatic action near Cherbourg, France, in June 1864.

Encouraged by British negligence, which he interpreted as sympathy for the Confederacy, Bulloch aimed even higher. In 1862 he contracted with the same Liverpool firm that had built the *Alabama*, the Laird Brothers, for the construction of two powerful ironclad rams intended to raise havoc with the Union blockading fleets. Designed with two gun turrets and a lethal underwater ram, the warlike purpose of these formidable "Laird rams" was difficult to disguise. As they were nearing completion in 1863, another Confederate agent, Matthew Fontaine Maury, purchased a British steamer suitable for conversion into a commerce raider to be named the CSS *Georgia*. In March 1863 she was ready to sail from the obscure port of White Haven, and Maury sent coded messages to various Confederate officers in Britain to rendezvous there. The British Foreign Office woke up and tried to stop the ship's departure, but the telegram to White Haven sat in an outbox in London on March 31 until the port's telegraph office closed for the day. After midnight the *Georgia* sailed, took on her armament off Ushant, and began her career as a raider.[18]

The embarrassment caused by the *Georgia*'s escape made the Foreign Office determined to prevent any more such occurrences. Also in March

1863 a parliamentary committee issued a report condemning the British government for its failures to prevent the escape of the *Florida* and *Alabama*. And Charles Francis Adams continued to flood the Foreign Office with evidence of the Laird rams' Confederate provenance. Adams also pressed Foreign Secretary Russell to seize the *Alexandra*, a small steamer just completed in Liverpool as a commerce raider.

In April 1863 the government did seize the *Alexandra*. But the Court of Exchequer ruled the seizure illegal on the grounds that there was no proof of Confederate ownership or of the arming or fitting out of the vessel in England. That was technically true—it had been built for Fraser, Trenholm, and Company, a British firm that just happened to be the Confederacy's financial agent in London. The government appealed the Exchequer's decision and continued to detain the *Alexandra*. The officer slated to command the ship—one of several Southern naval officers in Britain awaiting assignment—complained that "it is clear that the English Government never intends to permit anything in the way of a man-of-war to leave its shores. I know Mr. Adams is accurately informed of the whereabouts and employment of every one of us, and that Yankee spies are aided by English Government detectives.... With the other vessels the same plan will be instituted as with the Alexandra. They will be exchequered, and thus put into a court where the Government has superior opportunities for instituting delays."[19]

Despite the obstacles that this precedent posed to getting the Laird rams into Confederate possession, Bulloch did not give up. He arranged for the dummy purchase of them by the French firm of Bravay and Company, ostensibly acting as agents for "his Serene Highness the Pasha of Egypt." This subterfuge fooled no one, but clear proof of Confederate ownership was elusive despite the mounting circumstantial evidence piled up by Thomas Dudley. Charles Francis Adams sent a series of increasingly ominous warnings to Foreign Secretary Russell against allowing the rams to escape, culminating in a dispatch on September 5, 1863, concluding that "it would be superfluous in me to point out to your Lordship that this is war."[20]

Despite the stark nature of Adams's words, his phraseology was actually ambiguous. Did he mean that the United States would respond to the escape of the rams with a declaration of war against Britain? Or that it would be seen as an act of war against the United States? Or was it a warning that it would make England complicit in the Confederate war against the United States? Whatever meaning Adams intended to convey, the matter was already moot when he wrote these words. Russell had given orders two days earlier for the detention of the ships, and they were subsequently purchased by the Royal Navy.

A disappointed and angry Bulloch moved his efforts to the friendlier environment of France, where he had reason to believe that Louis Napoleon's government would look the other way as he contracted with French shipbuilding companies for the construction of two ironclad warships and four corvettes as commerce raiders. After a promising beginning, however, Bulloch was dumbfounded in 1864 by the French government's decision to seize these vessels rather than risk rupture with the United States. Bulloch lamented this "most remarkable and astounding circumstance that has yet occurred in reference to our operations in Europe," which had caused him "greater pain and regret than I ever considered it possible to feel." John Slidell, who was still the Confederate envoy in Paris, confessed that this failure was "a most lame and impotent conclusion to all our efforts to create a Navy."[21]

In the end the American Civil War proved an exception to the rule that civil wars tend to attract foreign intervention. Neither the United States nor foreign powers, especially Britain, considered it in their self-interest to provoke or undertake such intervention and acted rationally to prevent it. The Lincoln administration determined in 1861 that it could only carry on "one war at a time" and let Mason and Slidell go. The British government decided in 1862 to recognize the legality of the Union blockade, in considerable part because Britain relied heavily on naval blockades in its own wars and did not want to create a precedent that might undermine the legitimacy of such a weapon in a future war. Later in 1862, the Palmerston ministry resolved that Confederate strategic defeats in the battles of Antietam and Per-ryville raised sufficient doubts about the ability of the Southern nation to sustain itself as to make it in British self-interest not to risk a break with the United States by recognizing the Confederacy. And for the same reason, Britain and France decided to clamp down on Confeder-ate efforts to build warships in the shipyards of those nations. These decisions prevented the American Civil War from becoming an inter-national war.

CHAPTER 6

The Rewards of Risk-Taking:
Two Civil War Admirals

In a letter to his wife in September 1864, Captain Charles Steedman of the U.S. Navy praised Rear Admiral David Glasgow Farragut for his decisive victory over Confederate forts and warships in the Battle of Mobile Bay the previous month. "That little man," wrote Steedman of the wiry Farragut, who was actually just under medium height, "has done more to put down the rebellion than any general except Grant and Sherman."[1]

Steedman's comment was not simply another example of naval boastfulness in the age-old rivalry between the army and the navy. After many years of studying the American Civil War, I am convinced that Steedman was right. Farragut's victory at Mobile Bay and his even more spectacular achievement in the capture of New Orleans back in April 1862, plus the part played by his fleet in the Mississippi River campaigns of 1862 and 1863, did indeed entitle him to virtually equal status with Grant and Sherman in winning the war.

But Steedman was making a larger point, with which I also agree: The Union navy deserves more credit for Northern victory than it has traditionally received. Ulysses S. Grant made a similar point in his famous *Memoirs* when he praised the role of the navy's Mississippi River Squadron in Grant's most significant success, the capture of Vicksburg in July 1863. "Without the navy's assistance," wrote Grant, "the campaign could not have been made."[2]

Farragut emerged as the Union navy's foremost hero in the Civil War, and he was appointed as the nation's first rear admiral in July 1862. But for the first year of the war, the most prominent and successful naval officer was Samuel Francis Du Pont, whose fleet won the most important Union victory in 1861 and who was subsequently named the third-ranking rear admiral in American history. Like General George B. McClellan, Du Pont was the great hope of the North in 1861; like Grant, Farragut labored in relative obscurity during most of the war's first year until they burst forth with major victories in early 1862, and went on thoroughly to eclipse McClellan and Du Pont in later stages of the war. And the similarities between McClellan and Du Pont on the one hand, and Grant and Farragut on the other, include character traits and qualities of leadership that explain how one pair has faded into obscurity and the other pair emerged into greatness.

Descended from one of the foremost families in America, Du Pont in 1861 was a veteran of forty-five years in the U.S. Navy. Although he was from the slave state of Delaware and several of his friends supported or at least sympathized with the Confederacy, Du Pont left no doubt about where he stood. "What has made me most sick at heart is to see the resignations from the Navy" of officers from Southern states, he said in 1861, as he stood tall and imposing with ramrod-straight posture and luxuriant muttonchop whiskers. "I stick by the flag and the national government," he declared, "whether my state do or not."[3]

About Farragut's allegiance, however, there were initially some doubts. He had served fifty of his fifty-nine years in the navy when the state he called home, Virginia, seceded in 1861. Farragut had been born in Tennessee and had married a Virginian. After his first wife died, he had married another Virginia woman. He had a brother in New Orleans and a sister in Mississippi. "God forbid I should ever have to raise my hand against the South," he said to friends in Virginia as the sectional conflict heated up. But when Abraham Lincoln called out the militia after the Confederates attacked Fort Sumter, Farragut expressed approval of his action. His Virginia friends told him that anyone holding this opinion could not live in Norfolk, then his home. "Well, then," Farragut replied, "I can live somewhere else." He decided to move to New York. "This act of mine may cause years of separation from your family," he told his wife, "so you must decide quickly whether you will go north or remain here." She went with him. As they prepared to leave, the thin-lipped Farragut offered a few parting words to his Norfolk neighbors: "You fellows will catch the devil before you get through with this business." And as matters turned out, they caught a good many devils from Farragut himself.[4]

Congressional legislation gave Secretary of the Navy Gideon Welles authority to ignore the traditional rule of seniority in making promotions during the Civil War. Welles was quick to weed out dead wood in the senior ranks of captains in order to promote younger and more promising officers over their heads. He did precisely that with Du Pont and Farragut. He jumped Du Pont over eighteen of his seniors and named him commander of the South Atlantic Blockading Squadron in September 1861. Du Pont had already achieved prominence as chairman of the Blockade Board that summer, which produced comprehensive strategic plans for organizing the blockade and capturing ports and cities along the Confederate coast. Du Pont himself would command the first of these efforts, a major campaign to capture Port Royal Sound in South Carolina.

To command the West Gulf Blockading Squadron, whose main objective in 1862 would be the capture of New Orleans, Welles named Farragut—who was thirty-seventh in seniority on the captain's list. Farragut was respected by many of his fellow officers but virtually unknown to the public at that time. As Welles wrote in his famous diary, "Neither the President nor any member of the Cabinet knew him, or knew of him. Members of Congress inquired who he was, and some of them remonstrated, and questioned whether I was making a mistake for he was a Southern man and had a Southern wife."[5] But Welles knew about Farragut's expressions of Unionism when he moved from

Norfolk to New York and was willing to gamble on his loyalty as well as his ability. Rarely in the history of naval warfare has a gamble paid off so handsomely.

Meanwhile Du Pont was putting together the largest fleet in American history to that time: seventeen warships with 157 guns, twenty-five colliers and supply ships, and thirty-three troop transports carrying thirteen thousand soldiers and six hundred marines to go ashore when the navy attacked the forts at the entrance to Port Royal Sound. This armada was more impressive in numbers than in the seagoing qualities of some of its vessels. In the rapid buildup of 1861, the navy had bought and chartered dozens of merchant ships and even several New York ferryboats and tugs never intended for open-water navigation. Some of these, in addition to regular navy warships, were part of Du Pont's fleet.

This fleet departed from Hampton Roads on October 29, 1861. As they emerged onto a smooth sea the first day, a lieutenant who commanded a gun crew on Du Pont's flagship, the forty-four-gun steam frigate USS *Wabash*, wrote that he looked out and saw "on either side of us, in line abreast, stretched for six miles the advanced guard of gunboats" followed by the transports. "Never did such a heterogeneous squadron venture upon the waters, nondescripts ad infinitum; vessels without shape before known to the maritime world. Had some homeward bound vessel helplessly got within our lines, surely would the bewildered skipper have imagined that 'Great Birnam Wood to high Dunsinane' had come against him."[6]

This literary image gave way to chaos and panic on November 1 as the fleet ran into what another officer on the *Wabash* described as "one of the severest gales I have ever experienced" off the North Carolina coast.[7] A steamer carrying three hundred marines went down; the sailing frigate USS *Sabine* rescued all but seven of them. Some ships had to turn back, including small steamers for towing surfboats to land troops. Much of the army's ammunition was lost. On the morning of November 2 only eight other ships were in sight from the *Wabash*. By the time the flagship reached the bar off Port Royal on November 4, however, most of the fleet was reunited. More vessels continued to arrive as the warships got over the bar on November 5 and prepared to attack the two Confederate earthwork forts mounting forty-three guns and situated three miles apart on either side of the wide channel.

This attack would have to be an all-navy show, for the loss of ammunition and surfboats made spectators of the army troops. Du Pont adopted a tactical plan made possible by steam power, which had revolutionized naval warfare during the past two decades. The ships would steam in an oval pattern between the two forts, pounding each in turn while presenting a moving target to the enemy. This movement up-ended the old adage from the days of sailing ships that one gun on shore in a fort was worth four on shipboard. At 9:26 A.M. on November 7, fourteen warships led by the *Wabash* moved up midchannel between Fort Beauregard to the north and the stronger Fort Walker to the south on Hilton Head Island, firing broadsides at both simultaneously. Du Pont placed five of his gunboats in a flanking position to protect the main fleet from the harassing fire of a small Confederate flotilla of converted tugs carrying one or two guns each. This so-called mosquito fleet soon fled up the Beaufort River out of range of the heavier Yankee guns. Du Pont turned back and brought the fleet close under the guns of Fort Walker, then turned again for a second pass up midchannel. On the second pass he was joined by the USS *Pocahontas*, which had just arrived after battling the storm that had separated the fleet. This ship was commanded by a South Carolina native, Percival Drayton, who had remained loyal to the United States while his brother Thomas had gone with the Confederacy and was a general now in command of Fort Walker, which came under fire from his brother's ship.

Most of the damage to the fort, however, was accomplished by the big 9-inch guns of the *Wabash*, which Du Pont brought to within five hundred yards of the fort on the second pass. A gun captain on the Wabash described the firing from the fort of "shell guns, Columbiads and rifled they cut us up in spars, rigging and hull pretty severely" but our guns "finally drove them out. They fled in all directions leaving some of the guns loaded, their arms, tents, etc." behind. The *Wabash* landed its marines and fifty sailors to take possession of Fort Walker. Across the entrance to the bay, Confederates also evacuated Fort Beauregard before the ships could make another turn to drive them out. Du Pont was elated by his victory. Several days later he wrote to a friend. "I never get *transporté*, as the French term it, but I will repeat, to the day of my death, that the second assault of this ship upon the forts, for rapidity, continuity, and precision of fire, has never been surpassed in naval warfare."[8]

Army troops landed and took possession of the forts, the town of Beaufort, and eventually most of the rich long-staple cotton plantations of the South Carolina and Georgia Sea Islands. White planters and their families fled to the mainland; almost ten thousand slaves stayed behind, making this campaign the largest emancipation of slaves in the war so far. Panic spread through the Carolina low country; Du Pont built up a large naval base at Port Royal and occupied other ports as far south as Fernandina and Jacksonville, Florida. Army artillery forced the surrender of Fort Pulaski at the mouth of the Savannah River in April 1862, pretty much sealing off Savannah from blockade-runners. Du Pont built up his blockade fleet in numbers and efficiency during 1862 and began planning for an attack on the cradle of secession, Charleston itself.

In the meantime, Farragut took command of the West Gulf Squadron and began building up his fleet for an effort to capture the biggest prize of all, the South's largest port and city, New Orleans. By April 1862 Farragut had gotten his fleet of twenty-two steam sloops and gunboats across the bar at the Southwest Pass of the Mississippi River where it empties into the Gulf of Mexico. They were supported by twenty schooners that had been modified to carry a 13-inch mortar to bombard the Confederate defenses at two forts flanking the Mississippi seventy miles below New Orleans, Forts Jackson and St. Philip. Together the forts mounted 126 big seacoast guns to try to blow out of the water any fleet trying to ascend the river. In addition, the Confederates had put together a squadron of eight gunboats converted from river steamboats, one small ironclad, and another large ironclad, the CSS *Louisiana*, which had its guns mounted but not yet its engines, so it was anchored near the forts as a kind of floating battery. Farragut's fleet was supported by an army of fifteen thousand Union soldiers commanded by General Benjamin Butler—who was not much of an asset for the Union effort. The public expected the navy to do the heavy work, just as it had done at Port Royal. Iowa senator James Grimes, a member of the Senate Committee on Naval Affairs, told Assistant Secretary of the Navy Gustavus Fox that "the country looks to the Navy. Don't wait for the Army; take New Orleans & hold it until the Army comes up."[9] And that is exactly how it happened.

The mortar schooners commanded by Farragut's foster brother, David Dixon Porter, were towed into position on April 18 to begin bombarding the forts. Over the next six days and nights they lobbed thousands of 216-pound shells into the forts, doing a lot of damage but not knocking out many of the guns. Farragut grew impatient and decided to run his fleet past the forts in the predawn darkness on April 24. This was not a popular decision among his ship captains, who had "little or no sanguine feeling of success," according to one of them. On April 22 Farragut called for a meeting of his captains to plan the attack. In military annals it was proverbial that councils of war never fight. But this one proved an exception. After Farragut outlined his plans for running past the forts in the darkness, he invited the responses of his captains. As one of the participants wrote: "The prevailing opinion seemed to be adverse to making the attempt to pass the forts at that time; that it was premature; that the forts had not yet been sufficiently reduced by the fire of the mortar vessels, and that the risk of the loss of too many vessels was too great to be run." But Farragut said that the mortars would soon exhaust their ammunition; it was now or never; and he concluded the meeting with the words: "I believe in celerity."[10]

"I believe in celerity" became Farragut's hallmark. At 2:00 A.M. on April 24 his seventeen ships carrying 154 guns that were to make the attempt weighed anchor and began moving upriver, with Farragut's flagship *Hartford* in the middle of three divisions of the fleet; the smaller gunboats were in the first and third divisions. The mortar fleet and the five steamers that towed them opened a furious fusillade to keep down the fire of the forts, while the ships of the three divisions also opened fire as they approached the forts; these forts began firing on the ships as they approached, and as the first ones got through, the Confederate gunboats above the fort also engaged. In this melee, scores of shells were in the air and exploding at the same time, in what was surely the most spectacular fireworks display in American history to that time. The Confederates had also prepared fire rafts—large rafts piled with kindling and logs soaked with oil, which they lit and floated down toward the Union ships.

As the *Hartford* approached the forts, Farragut climbed up the port mizzen ratline to get above the roiling smoke from the guns and fire rafts for a better view of the action. Holding on to the shrouds, he "stood there as cool as if leaning against a mantel in his own home," according to a sailor on the *Hartford*. Farragut's signal officer pleaded with him to come down. "We can't afford to lose you, Flag Officer," he shouted. "They'll get you up there, sure." Farragut finally came down, and as he reached the deck a shell exploded where he had been standing on the ratline.[11]

By this time the river was full of fire rafts. Veering to evade one of them, the *Hartford* ran aground under the guns of Fort St. Philip. A Confederate tug pushed the raft against her port quarter. Flames climbed up the side of the hull and shot halfway up the mast. "I thought it was all up with us," wrote Farragut later. But after a few seconds of confusion, the crew went to fire stations and began playing hoses on the burning ship. The hoses finally doused the fire, the engineers applied all power to back the *Hartford* off the mud, and she proceeded upriver.

Fourteen of the seventeen Union ships made it past the forts. Three were turned back by the forts as it began to grow light that morning, and one of the fourteen that got through was sunk by Confederate gunboats. But seven of those eight gunboats, plus the small ironclad CSS *Manassas*, were sunk by the Union fleet, and the other one was captured. At the cost of only 37 killed and 147 wounded, the Union fleet had won a remarkable victory.

But that victory was incomplete until New Orleans was in their possession. At midmorning on April 24, Farragut's surviving thirteen ships rendezvoused seven miles above the forts. They were all more or less damaged but still operational. Farragut decided to continue upriver and attack the city. The Confederate troops that had been stationed in New Orleans had been called upriver to Tennessee to meet the Union threat there after Grant had captured Fort Donelson, leaving behind only local militia, which fled at the approach of the fleet. The city was virtually defenseless except for two earthworks with fourteen guns flanking the river at Chalmette three miles downstream from New Orleans, where Andrew Jackson had stopped the British in 1815. But nothing was going to stop Farragut. Five of his ships, including the flagship *Hartford*, came on, firing first with their bow guns and then veering left or right to fire crushing broadsides into the works. In twenty minutes the Confederate guns were silenced. "Those who could run," Farragut reported to Secretary of the Navy Welles, "were running in every direction."[12]

Cut off and isolated downriver, with Butler's troops finally approaching the forts, the garrison at Fort Jackson mutinied, and both forts surrendered to the navy on April 28. The Confederates blew up their two big unfinished ironclads, CSS *Louisiana* and CSS *Mississippi*. The Union fleet proceeded to New Orleans, where they found all of the ships at the waterfront and thousands of bales of cotton on the wharfs on fire. Mobs rioted in the streets and threatened the Yankees with bloody vengeance. The future author seventeen-year-old George Washington Cable witnessed the fury of the mob. "The crowds on the levee howled and screamed with rage," he recalled. "The swarming decks answered never a word; but one old tar on the Hartford, standing with lanyard in hand beside a great pivot-gun, so plain to view that you could see him smile, silently patted its big black breech and blandly grinned." With naval guns trained on its streets, New Orleans sullenly surrendered, and Butler's troops finally arrived to preserve some kind of order. If the passage of the forts by the Union fleet was not quite "the night the war was lost," as the title of a modern book about this campaign would have it, the capture of New Orleans was unquestionably one of the most important Union victories of the war, with major consequences both at home and abroad.[13]

Farragut continued up the Mississippi River with part of his fleet to Vicksburg, where he met the gunboats of the Mississippi flotilla that had fought their way down the river in the spring of 1862, capturing Memphis in June. They bombarded Vicksburg, and Farragut twice ran his ships past the Confederate batteries there, once upriver and once down, but the combined fleets failed to force Vicksburg's surrender in 1862. The following March, as part of the eventually successful Union campaign to capture Vicksburg and Port Hudson, Farragut tried to pass the Confederate fortifications at Port Hudson, going upriver with seven ships, but only his flagship *Hartford* and a smaller gunboat consort got through. Two of *Hartford*'s sister ships were turned back with shots through their boiler and steam drum, and one other ship was sunk. When Farragut sat down next day to write his report to Welles, he began with the words "It becomes my duty to report disaster to my fleet."[14]

Welles, however, did not think it was a disaster at all, but a valiant action in which the *Hartford* and its gunboat consort gained a position to contest control of the 250 miles of river between Vicksburg and Port Hudson with the Confederates, and to blockade the mouth of the Red River, where supplies poured down to garrisons at Vicksburg and Port Hudson. Assistant Secretary Fox no doubt gladdened Farragut's heart with the assurance that "the President thinks the importance of keeping a force of strength in this part of the river is so great that he fully approves of your proceeding." And Farragut himself, looking back four months later, told his wife that "my last dash past Port Hudson was the best thing I ever did, except taking New Orleans. It assisted materially in the fall of Vicksburg and Port Hudson."[15]

While all of this was going on in the Mississippi Valley, matters at Charleston were coming to a head. The capture of this symbolic heart of the Confederacy had been a goal of Union strategy since Du Pont's success at Port Royal. But a fundamental difference existed between the Navy Department and Admiral Du Pont on how to carry out that strategy. Through the spring and summer of 1862 Du Pont and Assistant Navy Secretary Gustavus Fox carried on a correspondence about this matter in which they seemed to be talking past each other. Fox wanted it to be entirely a navy operation, on the model of Du Pont's capture of Port Royal and Farragut's capture of New Orleans. "Our summer's work must be Charleston by the navy," Fox wrote to Du Pont. "If we give you the *Galena* and *Monitor*"—the first two seagoing Union ironclads—"don't you think we can make it *purely navy?* Any other plan we shall play second fiddle" to the army, which "never does us justice, even when we win it," as at New Orleans. "The *Monitor* can go all over Charleston harbor and return with impunity. I feel that my duties are twofold; first, to beat our southern friends, second, to beat the Army."[16]

Du Pont was exasperated by this kind of talk. He believed that Charleston could only be captured by army troops moving against the forts and other defenses step by step, supported by the navy. "Do not go it half cocked about Charleston," he fold Fox. "Think coolly and dispassionately on the main object," which was to take Charleston, not to glorify the navy. "There is no running the gantlet" of forts at Charleston as there was at the forts below New Orleans, he reminded Fox. "The whole harbor is ringed with batteries; it is like a 'cul de sac' or bag." In a striking simile that he would repeat several times, Du Pont described the Charleston defenses as "like a porcupine's hide with quills turned outside in and sewed up at one end."[17]

In October 1862 Du Pont went north for a visit home and for consultations in Washington, where he and Fox discussed their differences face to face. "The number of forts and guns" in the Charleston defenses was "simply fabulous," Du Pont told Fox, to say nothing of obstructions strung across the channel between Forts Sumter and Moultrie, consisting of pilings, of logs strung together with ropes and chains, and of torpedoes—naval mines. But he could not get through to Fox, Du Pont complained to a friend. His "Navy feelings are so strong and his prejudices or dislike of Army selfishness so great that he listened unwillingly" to the idea of combined movements.[18]

Du Pont was nettled by Fox's frequent references to New Orleans: If Farragut could do it with wooden ships, why can't you do it with ironclads? A second generation of Monitor-class ironclads were becoming available, and nearly all of them went to Du Pont during the winter of 1862–63, with the idea that he could steam right past the heavy guns in Fort Sumter, Fort Moultrie, Fort Johnson, and several other batteries and compel the surrender of Charleston with naval guns trained on its streets, as Farragut had done at New Orleans. Fox waxed poetic in his vision of Du Pont's nine ironclads—which now included the twenty-gun *New Ironsides* of traditional frigate design as well as the new Monitor-class ships—"carrying in your flag supreme and superb, defiant and disdainful, silent amid the 200 guns, until you arrive at the center of this wicked rebellion" to "demand the surrender of the forts, or swift destruction. The President and Mr. Welles are very much struck with this program.... The sublimity of such a silent attack is beyond words to describe, and I beg of you not to let the Army spoil it."[19]

When Du Pont read these words, he wondered what Fox was smoking when he wrote them. Nevertheless, he replied to Fox that "we'll do it if it can be done—I would like to make you happy." But running silently past the forts was a nonstarter. "I think we shall have to pound and pound beyond any precedent in history" to subdue the forts so that army troops could advance step by step toward the city. The "idea that ironclads can go pirouetting around the harbor and that the forts can be 'run'—a la Mississippi" just would not work, he insisted.[20]

The closer the date for his attack approached, the more pessimistic Du Pont grew. "The probabilities are all against us," he told a friend. "Thirty-two guns to overcome or silence two or three hundred, which, however, would not disturb me much if it were not for the idea of the obstructions. To remove these under fire is simply absurd."[21] Du Pont's gloominess infected several of his ironclad captains, who also began to write home that *"we are not very sanguine* of the attack being successful" against enemy defenses "in every conceivable shape, such as torpedoes, obstructions of piles, and innumerable ropes in the channel to foul the propellers."[22] Two days before the scheduled beginning of his attack—which finally took place April 7, 1863—Du Pont forlornly referred to "these operations for the capture of Charleston, or what is more probable the *failure* of its capture."[23]

In Washington, Welles and Lincoln were increasingly disturbed by the defeatist tone of Du Pont's dispatches. They reminded Lincoln unpleasantly of McClellan. Welles was also a shrewd if sometimes harsh judge of character. He wrote in his diary: "I deplore the signs of misgiving and doubt that have recently come over" Du Pont. "Will and determination are necessary to success," but instead of emulating the "firm and impetuous Farragut," Du Pont "is getting as prudent as McClellan—is very careful—all dash, energy and force are softened under great responsibility. He has a reputation to preserve instead of one to make."[24]

The attack on April 7 by Du Pont's nine ironclads turned out just as he had feared—a self-fulfilled prophecy. The *New Ironsides* could not be controlled in the swift currents and had to anchor to avoid going aground, and got off only one ineffective broadside during the whole attack. Unknown to Du Pont, it anchored right over a 2,000-pound torpedo, which the Confederates on shore repeatedly tried to explode electrically, without success. (They later discovered that a wagon had run over the wires on Morris Island and cut them.)

That was the only thing that went right for Du Pont this day. The Monitor-class ironclads' rate of fire against the forts was too slow to do them much damage, and the forts in return, using prepositioned range markers, riddled the Union ships with accurate fire. The ships got off only 151 shots during the battle, while seventy-six guns in the forts fired 2,209 shots, of which a remarkable 520 struck the ironclads, partly disabling several and damaging the USS *Keokuk* so badly that she sank the next morning.

Du Pont broke off the action after two hours. He intended to renew it the next day, but at a conference that evening his ship captains told him that their vessels were so severely damaged that it would be suicidal to try it again. So Du Pont "determined not to renew the attack," as he reported to Welles, "for, in my judgment, it would have converted a failure into a disaster."[25]

In response to criticism that the attack failed because his heart was not in it, Du Pont wrote to a member of the Senate Naval Affairs Committee that "no officer living could have gone into the experiment with more earnest zeal than I did." This was disingenuous, to say the least. Soon after the battle, Du Pont had written to his wife: "We have failed, as I felt sure we would.... To me...there was no disappointment, for I expected nothing."[26]

Over the next few weeks, Du Pont became obsessed with defending himself against newspaper criticism, especially an article in a Baltimore newspaper that concluded: "Oh, that we had a Farragut here to take command at once, and do what has been so weakly attempted by Admiral Du Pont." Just as McClellan routinely blamed others for his failures, Du Pont openly criticized the defects of the ironclads, which, as he said, "are miserable failures where forts are concerned."[27]

Secretary Welles grew increasingly irritated with Du Pont for spending so much time and energy trying to justify himself instead of planning a new campaign against the enemy. In Du Pont's obsession with the supposed insult to his honor and self-esteem, Welles wrote in his diary, "he is evidently thinking much more of Du Pont than of the service or the country." Welles concluded that Du Pont "is against doing anything, he is demoralizing others. If anything is to be done, we must have a new commander." In June 1863 Welles accepted Du Pont's resignation and replaced him with Admiral John Dahlgren—whose efforts over the next several months to capture Charleston with combined army-navy operations also failed. Du Pont went home a bitter and in some ways broken man; he never again held an important command and died in 1865. He was, in the words of his most recent biographer, "Lincoln's tragic admiral."[28] His tragic flaw, like that of McClellan, was being unwilling to take large risks and then refusing to take responsibility for the failures that stemmed from this unwillingness.

The opposite was true of Farragut—he was willing to risk his fleet and his reputation on the effort to achieve victory, and he proved it again in August 1864 at the Battle of Mobile Bay. Ever since his capture of New Orleans two years earlier, Farragut had wanted to attack the forts guarding the entrance to Mobile Bay and shut down that port to blockade-running. But other priorities had intervened, and it was not until the summer of 1864 that the Navy Department turned him loose on Mobile Bay.

Farragut made the most of his opportunity. He now had four ironclads plus his fleet of wooden warships to take on the three forts plus a small Confederate fleet led by the formidable ironclad CSS *Tennessee*, and some 180 torpedoes that the Confederates had stretched across the entrance to the bay between the two main forts, leaving only a small opening. On August 5 the fleet weighed anchor and headed toward this opening, with the ironclads on the right closest to powerful Fort Morgan with its eighty-six big seacoast guns. The leading ironclad, USS *Tecumseh*, struck a torpedo and went down in less than a minute, taking ninety men with her. The captain of the USS *Brooklyn*, after watching this, hesitated at the line of torpedoes, and the whole fleet came to a halt under the punishing fire of Fort Morgan. Next in line behind the *Brooklyn* was Farragut's flagship, the *Hartford*. Without hesitating, Farragut ordered the *Hartford* to pass the *Brooklyn*, and in that moment one of the great legends in the history of the U.S. Navy was born. "Damn the torpedoes! Full speed ahead!" Farragut supposedly shouted.

Whether or not Farragut actually said these words, he certainly did order the *Hartford* to go ahead. Captain Percival Drayton, the fleet captain commanding the *Hartford*, described these events. When the *Tecumseh* went down, he wrote, "our line was getting crowded and very soon we should all have been huddled together, a splendid mark for the enemy's guns. The Admiral immediately gave the word to go ahead with the Hartford and pass the Brooklyn. We sheered to port and passed directly over the line of torpedoes planted by the enemy, and we could hear the snapping of the submerged devilish contrivances as our hull drove through the water—but it was neck or nothing, and that risk must be taken. All the other vessels followed in our wake and providentially all escaped."[29] The rapid and shifting currents in the channel off Fort Morgan had evidently broken loose some of the torpedoes and caused others to leak, dampening their powder—but of course Farragut could not have known that, especially after seeing what happened to the *Tecumseh*.

As the *Hartford* forged ahead dueling with the guns of Fort Morgan, Farragut climbed the rigging for a better view above the smoke and was lashed to the shrouds by the boatswain. A rifleman on the Confederate ironclad *Tennessee* fired several shots at him. If he had managed to hit him, Farragut might have become a martyred hero like Horatio Nelson at Trafalgar instead of merely the living hero of Mobile Bay. Once into the bay, the Union fleet engaged in a bloody firefight with the Confederate ships, especially the *Tennessee*, before eventually sinking or capturing two of the smaller ships and damaging the *Tennessee* so badly that she surrendered. Over the next two and one-half weeks the Union ships, with the help of army troops, forced the surrender of all the forts and gained control of the bay.[30] It was the first unequivocal strategic Union victory in 1864, and set the stage for several more victories in the following months that assured Lincoln's reelection and the final triumph at Appomattox.

In July 1866 Farragut became the first full admiral in American history, one day after Ulysses S. Grant became the first full general. In their epitaphs, it could have been written that they were willing to take great risks and accept the responsibility if they failed, and reaped the rewards of success they achieved by their willingness to take those risks.

CHAPTER 7

How Did Freedom Come?

Which was the most important result of the Civil War: preservation of the Union or abolition of slavery? These two results became inextricably linked as the war went on, and by 1864 it became impossible to separate them: slavery could not have been abolished without Union victory, and preservation of the United States as one nation became dependent on the destruction of slavery. Yet in the minds of most Americans today, the abolition of slavery stands out as the most dramatic result of the war, while preservation of the Union is something that we seem to take for granted. But in 1861 it could not be taken for granted. "Union" held profound meaning for many Americans, including even some Southerners (like Jefferson Davis) who embraced secession with heavy hearts and a conviction that it was the Northern people who had betrayed the great promise of 1776.

We rarely speak of the Union today except when referring to a labor organization. But to mid-nineteenth-century Americans "Union" carried powerful meanings, analogous with "nation" and "country." It "represented the cherished legacy of the founding generation," writes Gary Gallagher in *The Union War*, "a democratic republic with a constitution that guaranteed political liberty and afforded individuals a chance to better themselves economically." In this view of the Union, "slaveholding aristocrats who established the Confederacy ... posed a direct threat not only to the long-term success of the American republic but also to the broader version of democracy."[1]

The determination to uphold this vision sustained the Northern people and especially their president through four years of bloody war. Gallagher recaptures the meaning of Union to the generation that fought for it. He rescues the "Cause" for which they fought from modern historians who maintain that the abolition of slavery was the only achievement of the Civil War that justified all that death and destruction. In the process, however, he overstates the case against emancipation as an avowed purpose of the war for the Union. The very first sentence of *The Union War* states his thesis: "The loyal American citizenry fought a war for Union that also killed slavery."[2] "Also" is the key word here; it implies that the death of slavery was a mere by-product of the war. "Intention did not drive the process" by which the presence of Union soldiers in the South liberated slaves, Gallagher maintains. "Troops commanded by officers who cared nothing about black people proved as destructive to slavery as those led by ardent advocates of emancipation. No matter how prejudiced their own attitudes, Union soldiers functioned as cogs in a grand military mechanism that inexorably ground down slavery."[3]

Intentionality may have had more to do with the abolition of slavery than Gallagher is willing to grant. The invasion of slave states by the British army in the American Revolution liberated a good many slaves, but it did not end slavery because the British government had no intention of doing so. But from the beginning of the Civil War there were abolitionists and Republicans who believed that this war against a slaveholders' rebellion must end slavery, and their numbers grew as the war escalated. Congressional legislation confiscating the slave property of "rebels," the Emancipation Proclamation, and the Thirteenth Amendment to the Constitution expressed a growing determination that slavery and the Union were incompatible. Despite enormous pressure to drop abolition as one of his conditions for peace when the war was going badly for the North in the summer of 1864, Lincoln refused to do so. By that time more than one hundred thousand black soldiers were fighting for the Union. "If they stake their lives for us they must be prompted by the strongest motive—even the promise of freedom," said Lincoln. "And the promise being made, must be kept....Why should they give their lives for us, with full notice of our purpose to betray them? ... I should be damned in time and eternity for so doing. The world shall know that I will keep my faith to friends and enemies, come what will."[4]

Gallagher acknowledges that by 1864 the Lincoln administration "added emancipation to Union as a non-negotiable condition of any peace following United States victory."[5] The seeds of that nonnegotiable condition were sown in the first months of the war, according to Adam Goodheart's rich multi-tiered narrative of the North and its people as war descended on the land. At Fort Monroe, a Union garrison in Virginia at Hampton Roads, where the James River flows into Chesapeake Bay, three slaves sought asylum on May 24, 1861. They had escaped from a Confederate camp across the Roads where they had been building fortifications for the Southern army. Major General Benjamin Butler met with them and heard their story. On Butler's staff was Theodore Winthrop, who had told his family as he departed from Massachusetts for the front: "I go to put an end to slavery." When a Confederate officer, Major John Cary, came under a flag of truce to ask General Butler to return the three slaves, the following exchange took place:

CARY: What do you mean to do with those negroes?

BUTLER: I intend to hold them.

CARY: Do you mean, then, to set aside your constitutional obligation to return them?

BUTLER: I mean to take Virginia at her word, as declared in the ordinance of secession passed yesterday. I am under no constitutional obligations to a foreign country, which Virginia claims to be.

CARY: But you say we cannot secede, and so you cannot consistently detain the negroes.

BUTLER: But you say you have seceded, so you cannot
consistently claim them. I shall hold these negroes as
contraband of war, since they are engaged in the construction
of your battery and are claimed as your property.[6]

Contraband of war! This novel description of escaped slaves was like a
shot heard 'round the world. "An epigram abolished slavery in the
United States," wrote Theodore Winthrop shortly before he was killed
in action on June 10, 1861. Butler's epigram turned out to be the thin
edge of a wedge driven into the heart of slavery. From that moment,
slaves who came within Union lines—and there were soon thousands
of them—were known as contrabands. Some abolitionists complained
that this word dehumanized Negroes by equating them with property.
But "contraband" soon meant "freedman." The term became accept-
able and universal, even among freed slaves themselves. "Never was a
word so speedily adopted by so many people in so short a time," mar-
veled a Union officer.[7]

The Lincoln administration approved Butler's policy. The president was hearing from many of his constituents and from Republican
leaders that slavery must not survive this war for the Union. Senator
James Doolittle of Wisconsin told Lincoln that the war "is to result in
the entire abolition of Slavery." The president's private secretary, John
Hay, who opened Lincoln's mail, told him on May 7, 1861, that "his
daily correspondence was thickly interspersed with such suggestions."[8] The cause of Union and freedom would not be completely
fused for another three years, but as Goodheart neatly puts it, when
those three slaves showed up at Fort Monroe in May 1861 "they joined
the Union"—and the fusion began.[9]

Of course, Butler would not have had the opportunity to declare
these slaves contraband of war if they had not taken the initiative to
escape to Fort Monroe. Such proactive deeds by many others who followed raise the question of who was really responsible for the coming
of freedom. Perhaps the real story is not what happened in the White

House or the halls of Congress, but at thousands of places from Maryland to Texas when slaves ran away from their masters and entered the lines of Union armies, or when those armies occupied Southern cities and plantation districts. In his fascinating book *A Slave No More: Two Men Who Escaped to Freedom, Including Their Own Narratives of Emancipation*, David Blight enters a debate among historians about who deserves primary credit for freeing the slaves and ending slavery: Abraham Lincoln and his white Republican allies in Congress, or the slaves themselves.

The traditional answer to the question "Who freed the slaves?" was Abraham Lincoln. But many historians have placed greater emphasis on the initiative of the slaves themselves. They saw the Civil War as a potential war for abolition well before Lincoln did. By coming into Union military lines in the South, they forced the issue of emancipation on the administration. "While Lincoln continued to hesitate about the legal, constitutional, moral, and military aspects of the matter," wrote the historian and theologian Vincent Harding in 1981, "the relentless movement of the self-liberated fugitives into Union lines" soon "approached and surpassed every level of force previously known." Making themselves "an unavoidable military and political issue...this overwhelming human movement...of self-freed men and women...took their freedom into their own hands." The Emancipation Proclamation, when it finally came, merely "confirmed and gave ambiguous legal standing to the freedom which black people had already claimed through their own surging, living, proclamations."[10]

During the 1980s this self-emancipation thesis became dominant. It won the imprimatur of the foremost scholarly enterprise on the history of emancipation, the Freedmen and Southern Society project at the University of Maryland. By acting "resolutely to place their freedom—and that of their posterity—on the wartime agenda," wrote the editors of this project, the slaves were "the prime movers in securing their own liberty."[11] One of the historians associated with the Freedmen and Southern Society project, Barbara J. Fields, gave wide currency to this theme in her eloquent statements on camera in the Ken Burns PBS documentary *The Civil War* (viewed by more than forty million people) and in the book that accompanied the series. "Freedom did not come to the slaves from words on paper, either the words of Congress or those of the President," said Fields in 1990, but from "the initiative of the slaves" who "taught the nation that it must place the abolition of slavery at the head of its agenda."[12] A decade later Lerone Bennett Jr. declared that Lincoln's Emancipation Proclamation was a hoax. He "did not intend for it to free a single Negro....Lincoln didn't make emancipation; emancipation, which he never understood or supported, made Lincoln."[13]

Proponents of the traditional interpretation that Lincoln had something to do with freeing the slaves, and that the Emancipation Proclamation was an important step in that process, are quite ready to acknowledge that the actions of slaves who came into Union lines forced the Lincoln administration to decide what to do about them. Some Union generals wanted to return them to their owners. But both Congress and the administration rejected that alternative. Well before the end of the war's second year, the United States not only welcomed escaped slaves and enforced their freedom but also began arming freedmen to fight for freedom and nation as Union soldiers.

The Emancipation Proclamation officially made Union soldiers into an army of liberation. Northern troops carried copies of the Proclamation and distributed thousands of them as they penetrated into the heartland of the Confederacy. By the war's last year, more than 10 percent of these soldiers of freedom were black, most of them former slaves. That army was chiefly responsible for the freedom of slaves who came within its purview. By the end of the war, David Blight estimates, "some 600,000 to 700,000 out of the nearly four million African American slaves had reached some form of emancipation" by this process.[14] But most of them had done so by the Union army coming to them rather than by escaping to the Union army. The remaining 3.3 million slaves achieved freedom by the Thirteenth Amendment, whose adoption was possible only through Union military victory. And no one deserved more credit for that victory than Abraham Lincoln, commander in chief of an army of liberation.[15]

David Blight's *A Slave No More* publishes for the first time two autobiographies of former slaves that offer case studies of the process of emancipation during the Civil War. "Slave narratives" had long been a well-established literary genre. Before 1865 approximately sixty-five autobiographies of slaves who escaped or otherwise achieved freedom were published. Most of them were circulated (and some were ghost-written) by abolitionists as part of their antislavery crusade. After the Civil War some fifty or more former slaves wrote autobiographies, of which Booker T. Washington's *Up from Slavery* is by far the most widely read. The purpose of these postwar narratives, writes Blight, "was no longer to catalog the horrors of slavery, but to use memoir as a marker of racial uplift and respectability in the age of Jim Crow."[16]

The two narratives published in *A Slave No More* do not quite fit into either category. They do touch on some of the corrosive effects of slavery, and they also reveal, at least implicitly, the authors' striving for respectability. But in two important respects they are almost unique: They focus primarily on the authors' actions and experiences during the Civil War, and they were not written for publication, so they are unmediated by white editors or by the conventions of writing for a public audience. They were apparently written for the authors' children, to tell the next generation what their fathers had gone through to bring them into a world where they were free to achieve at least a modicum of mobility within a segregated society.

John Washington (1838–1918) and Wallace Turnage (1846–1916) were born slaves, respectively in Fredericksburg, Virginia, and on a farm near Snow Hill, North Carolina. Both had white fathers—which at the outset offers an insight into one of slavery's dirtiest secrets, the sexual exploitation of slave women by white men. Washington's mother taught him to read, while it is not clear how Turnage gained that precious knowledge. Both were exceptional in the degree of literacy they possessed when they emerged from slavery. They also shared the shock of separation from their mothers at a young age, another of the baneful features of enslavement. When Washington was twelve years old, his mother was hired out to a master in Staunton, Virginia, one hundred miles from Fredericksburg. Taking her other four children with her, she left John behind to work as a servant and errand boy for their owner. "Bitter pangs filled my heart" at this separation, wrote Washington more than twenty years later. "Then and there my hatred was kindled secretly against my oppressors, and I promised myself if I ever got an opportunity I would run away from these devilish slave holders."[17] Turnage endured even more bitter anguish when at the age of fourteen he was sold apart from his mother and taken seven hundred miles to a plantation in Alabama, where a burning desire to escape fueled every moment of his existence.

From this point on, the experiences of the two young slaves diverged. Living in the cosmopolitan town of Fredericksburg, Washington interacted with free blacks and fell in love with a light-skinned free woman whom he married in January 1862. His job as a steward at a hotel, whose proprietor rented him from his owner, and his literacy and access to books and newspapers kept him informed on national politics and the course of the war, which brought the Union army to Falmouth across the Rappahannock River from Fredericksburg in the spring of 1862.

Washington's desire for real freedom had only grown stronger during the years of quasi-freedom he had known as a hired slave doing the job of a free man. On April 18, 1862, he shouted across the river to Union troops that he wanted to come over. They sent a boat and rowed him to freedom. For several months he served as a cook and steward at a Union general's headquarters, until he could bring his wife and even his mother and siblings to Washington, where they joined a large and growing free black community liberated by the war.

Turnage's passage to freedom was much more tortuous than Washington's. The overseer on the cotton plantation in Alabama where he ended up liked to use the whip. Three times from 1860 to 1862 the teenage slave ran away in response to a whipping or to avoid one. Each time Turnage was caught and brought back—to face a whipping for running away. As Blight points out, "Wallace Turnage fought a war within a war well before he ever saw a Yankee soldier."[18]

By the time of Turnage's fourth attempt to escape in the fall of 1862, he was aware of the war and of the presence of Union troops in northern Mississippi 120 miles from his plantation. This time he almost made it, experiencing hardships, sleepless nights, and near-starvation along the way, which he described with untutored eloquence in his narrative. But Confederate cavalry caught him and returned him to his master, who decided that he no longer wanted this chronic runaway and sold him down the Tombigbee River to Mobile.

Having failed to reach the Yankees in 1862, Turnage ran away from his new owner when the Yankees came close to him in August 1864. Farragut's fleet and army troops captured the forts guarding the entrance to Mobile Bay. In his fifth escape attempt, Turnage journeyed thirty miles through swamps and across treacherous rivers dodging Confederate pickets and fending off poisonous snakes to reach Union lines. Within sight of his goal at Fort Powell on Dauphin Island he found a leaky dinghy and rowed out into the bay. A sudden storm almost capsized him before eight Union soldiers who had seen him coming rowed out in a skiff to rescue him.

Turnage remembered with vivid clarity his first day of freedom with the Yankees at Fort Powell. "The next morning I was up early," he wrote many years later, "and took a look at the rebels country with a thankful heart to think I had made my escape with safety after such a long struggle; and had obtained the freedom which I desired so long." Turnage offered a fervent expression of what freedom meant to him. "I now dreaded the gun, and handcuffs and pistols no more," he wrote. "Nor the blewing of horns and the running of hounds; nor the threats of death from the rebel's authority. I could now speak my opinion to men of all grades and colors, and no one question my right to speak."[19]

The welcome that Turnage and Washington received from Union soldiers challenges—or at least qualifies—the accounts by many historians that emphasize the racism and antiblack hostility of most soldiers. Both men have nothing but good words to say about their experiences after they reached Union lines. If they had been writing for a public (and predominantly white) readership, of course, we would be properly skeptical of such statements. But they were writing for themselves and their families, and we may infer that they were writing what they actually felt. There were many racist Union soldiers, to be sure. And the light color of both Washington and Turnage probably worked in their favor. Washington was so light that the Union soldiers he first encountered thought he was a white man and were astonished to learn that he had been a slave. His reception, and Turnage's, might have been less friendly if they had been really black.

Like Washington, Turnage became a cook for a Union officer (from Maryland) and served with him for the rest of the war. After their discharge they returned together to Baltimore, where Turnage lived for several years and eventually made contact with his mother and siblings. He married and moved to New York City, and several years later to Jersey City, where he lived the rest of his life and raised seven children, four of whom died young. Active in the Baptist church and a fraternal lodge, Turnage struggled to make a living for his family in various occupations: waiter, janitor, and watchman. Two of his children who grew to adulthood passed for white and disappeared into mainstream white society.

Also active in his Baptist church, John Washington lived most of his long life in the city of Washington, where he worked as a sign painter, waiter, and barkeeper. His four sons were educated in the capital's segregated public schools and found their ways into respectable middle-class and lower-middle-class occupations. Blight speculates that both men wrote their narratives of the journey from slavery to freedom to provide themselves and their families with a sense of identity and pride in an era of increasing segregation and racism. "In their own personal ways, Washington and Turnage are saying: Here is who I am; here is how I achieved freedom; and here is what it means to me."[20]

By editing and elaborating upon these striking autobiographies, David Blight has done an inestimable service to historians. He has also presented a way to resolve disagreements about the question of "who freed the slaves, Lincoln or blacks themselves?" The "Turnage and Washington stories answer conclusively that it was *both*," writes Blight. "Without the Union armies and navies, neither man would have achieved freedom when he did. But they never would have gained their freedom without their own courageous initiative, either."[21]

One might quibble about the "never" in that last sentence. Like the 3.3 million slaves who remained in bondage through the war, Washington and Turnage would have been freed by the Thirteenth Amendment in 1865 even if they had not demonstrated courageous initiative or come into contact with the Union army. But like many other bondsmen, Washington and Turnage did exhibit "the initiative of the slaves," in the words of Barbara Fields quoted earlier, "who taught the nation that it must place the abolition of slavery at the head of its agenda."

CHAPTER 8

Lincoln, Slavery, and Freedom

The Thirteenth, Fourteenth, and Fifteenth Amendments to the U.S. Constitution abolished slavery and barred states from abridging the equal civil and political rights of American citizens, including former slaves. Abraham Lincoln's native state of Kentucky was the only state that refused to ratify all three amendments. The region of southern Indiana, where Lincoln had lived from the age of seven to twenty-one (1816–30), was among the most proslavery and antiblack areas in the free states during those years. Its representative in Congress also voted against the Thirteenth Amendment. So did the congressman from central Illinois, where Lincoln had lived for three decades. Lincoln himself had represented this district in the state legislature for eight years and in the U.S. Congress for one term in the 1830s and 1840s. And in 1842 he married a woman from a prominent Kentucky slaveholding family.

One might therefore expect that the cultural influences surrounding Lincoln during the first half century of his life would shape his convictions about slavery and race in the same mold that characterized most politicians of his time and place. Instead, he was one of only two representatives in the Illinois legislature who presented a public "protest" against a resolution passed in 1837 by their colleagues that condemned abolitionist doctrines of freedom and civil equality and affirmed the right of property in slaves as "sacred to the slave-holding states."

Lincoln's protest acknowledged that the Constitution did indeed sanction slavery in those states but declared that nevertheless "the institution of slavery is founded on both injustice and bad policy."[1]

In 1854 Lincoln made an even stronger protest, this time in the form of eloquent speeches against the Kansas-Nebraska Act. Illinois senator Stephen A. Douglas, Lincoln's longtime political rival, had rammed this law through a divided Congress. It repealed the earlier ban on the expansion of slavery into territories carved out of the Louisiana Purchase north of latitude 36° 30'. Douglas's actions opened these territories to slavery and sparked the formation of the new "anti-Nebraska" Republican Party, which would nominate Lincoln for president six years later. Douglas had said that if the white people who moved to Kansas wanted slavery there, they should be allowed to have it. "This *declared* indifference, but as I must think, covert real zeal for the spread of slavery, I can not but hate," said Lincoln in 1854, "because of the monstrous injustice of slavery itself" and also "because it deprives our republican example of its just influence in the world—enables the enemies of free institutions, with plausibility, to taunt us as hypocrites."[2]

When he ran for the Senate in the famous contest against Douglas in 1858, Lincoln declared: "I have always hated slavery I think as much as any Abolitionist." Six years later he said, with feeling: "If slavery is not wrong, nothing is wrong. I can not remember when I did not so think, and feel."[3] As Eric Foner makes clear in *The Fiery Trial: Abraham Lincoln and American Slavery*, however, Lincoln was antislavery but not an abolitionist. That is, he considered slavery a violation of the natural rights to life, liberty, and the pursuit of happiness enunciated in America's founding charter (written by an antislavery slaveowner). Like Thomas Jefferson, Lincoln expected slavery eventually to die out in America. Preventing its spread into the territories was the first step, said Lincoln in 1858, toward putting it "in course of ultimate extinction."[4] But unlike the abolitionists, Lincoln and most Republicans in the 1850s did not call for the immediate abolition of slavery and the granting of equal citizenship to freed slaves.

Having grown up in Kentucky and the border regions of Indiana and Illinois, Lincoln also felt a degree of empathy with the South that was not shared by abolitionists of Yankee heritage. Although he hated slavery, he did not hate slaveowners. "I think I have no prejudice against the Southern people," he said at Peoria, Illinois, in 1854. "When Southern people tell us they are no more responsible for the origin of slavery, than we; I acknowledge the fact." Lincoln also said he could "understand and appreciate" how "very difficult" it would be "to get rid of" slavery "in any satisfactory way.... If all earthly power were given me, I should not know what to do" about the institution where it then existed. "My first impulse would be to free all the slaves, and send them to Liberia. But a moment's reflection would convince me" that even if such a project was feasible in the long run, "its sudden execution" was impossible. "What then? Free them all, and keep them among us as underlings? Is it quite certain that this betters their condition?"

What about the abolitionist proposal to "free them and make them politically and socially our equals?" Lincoln confessed that "my own feelings will not admit of this; and if mine would, we well know that those of the great mass of white people will not. Whether this feeling accords with justice and sound judgment, is not the sole question.... A universal feeling, whether well or ill-founded, can not be safely disregarded." The abolitionist program of immediate freedom was therefore unrealistic. "It does seem to me that systems of gradual emancipation might be adopted; but for their tardiness in this, I will not undertake to judge our brethren of the south." Lincoln could not "blame them for not doing what I should not know how to do myself."[5]

Proslavery Southern whites did not reciprocate Lincoln's expressions of empathy. To many of them, especially the radical disunionists known as fire-eaters, the divergence between "antislavery" and "abolitionist" was a distinction without a difference. In their view, anyone who considered slavery a monstrous injustice and spoke of placing it in the course of ultimate extinction was as dangerous as those who demanded its immediate extinction. When the "Black Republican"

Lincoln was elected president in 1860, they led their states out of the Union to prevent the feared extinction of their "peculiar institution." This preemptive action put in train a course of events that by 1864 brought about precisely what they feared.

By that time the nation was facing, as imminent realities, the same alternatives Lincoln had outlined as abstract possibilities in his famous Peoria speech ten years earlier: 1) free all the slaves and send them to Liberia (or elsewhere); 2) free them and keep them as "underlings" in the United States; or 3) free them and make them the political and social equals of white people (civil equality, in modern terms). In 1864 Lincoln had a much more definite idea of "what to do" and a great deal more "earthly power" to do it than in 1854. His "brethren of the south" were now "rebels" whose war against the United States had given him that power as commander in chief of an army of a million men, one hundred thousand of them the former slaves of those rebels.

Lincoln had tried a version of the first alternative (free slaves and send them abroad), but few wanted to go, and now that they were fighting so "gallantly in our ranks" their commander in chief no longer wanted them to go. By 1864 Lincoln therefore rejected that alternative and was looking beyond the second one of freeing them only to "keep them among us as underlings." In 1862 the president had proposed gradual emancipation during which most black people would indeed have remained as underlings for an indefinite period. But he was now moving toward a belief in immediate abolition and equal rights for all citizens. According to Foner, Lincoln "began during the last two years of the war to imagine an interracial future for the United States."[6]

When he was sworn in for his second term on March 4, 1865, writes Foner, "for the first time in American history companies of black soldiers marched in the inaugural parade. According to one estimate, half the audience that heard Lincoln's address was black, as were many of the visitors who paid their respects at the White House reception that day." For "Lincoln opened the White House to black guests as no president had before."[7]

The central theme of *The Fiery Trial* is Lincoln's "capacity for growth" in his "views and policies regarding slavery and race." Foner does not doubt the sincerity of his statement in 1858 that he had "always hated slavery." By the time of Lincoln's death, however, "he occupied a very different position with regard to slavery and the place of blacks in American society than earlier in his life."[8] In 1837 Lincoln described slavery as an injustice; by 1854 it was a monstrous injustice; in 1862 he told a delegation of five black men he had invited to the White House that "your race are suffering in my judgment the greatest wrong inflicted on any people." This was good abolitionist rhetoric. But Lincoln's purpose at this meeting in 1862 was to publicize his program for government assistance to blacks who volunteered to emigrate. Like his political heroes Thomas Jefferson and Henry Clay, Lincoln could not yet in 1862 imagine a future of interracial equity in the United States. "Even when you cease to be slaves," he told the five delegates, "you are yet far removed from being placed on an equality with the white race." Moreover, "there is an unwillingness on the part of our people, harsh as it may be, for you free colored people to remain with us....I do not propose to discuss this, but to present it as a fact with which we have to deal. I cannot alter it if I would....It is better for us both, therefore, to be separated."[9]

Despite overtones of empathy with the plight of blacks in a racist society, the condescension shown by these presidential remarks provoked widespread condemnation by abolitionists both black and white. "Pray tell us, is our right to a home in this country less than your own?" wrote one black man to the president. "Are you an American? So are we." Few blacks offered to emigrate, and a pilot project supported by the Lincoln administration to colonize several hundred black volunteers on a Haitian island was a failure. A good many Republicans agreed with one of their number who branded Lincoln's "scheme" of colonization as "simply absurd" and "disgraceful to the administration."[10]

Lincoln also came to see the "scheme" of colonization as unjust and impractical, though perhaps not disgraceful to his administration.

As Foner points out, after the president issued the Emancipation Proc-lamation and committed the government to the recruitment of black soldiers, Lincoln "abandoned the idea of colonization." He could scarcely ask black men to fight for their country and then tell them that they should leave it. "Black soldiers played a crucial role not only in winning the Civil War but also in defining its consequences," writes Foner, by putting "the question of postwar rights squarely on the national agenda." Because of Lincoln's admiration for the courage of black soldiers and their contribution to Union victories, his "racial views seemed to change" and his "sense of blacks' relationship to the nation also began to change." Their military service "implied a very different vision of their future place in American society than plans for settling them overseas."[11]

Foner is right on the mark here. Indeed, perhaps he could have emphasized even more the timing as well as the importance of Lincoln's praise for black soldiers. In August 1863 the president wrote one of his forceful public letters that served a purpose similar to a modern presi-dent's prime-time televised speech or news conference. This letter appeared in print just one year after Lincoln's colonization speech to blacks in the White House, and a month after white antidraft rioters in New York City lynched black men at almost the same moment black soldiers were dying in the attack on Fort Wagner in South Carolina (dra-matized in the movie *Glory*). Figuratively looking those draft rioters in the eye, Lincoln declared: "You say you will not fight to free negroes. Some of them seem willing to fight for you." When the war was won, Lincoln continued, "there will be some black men who can remember that, with silent tongue, and clenched teeth, and steady eye, and well-poised bayonet, they have helped mankind on to this great consumma-tion; while, I fear, there will be some white ones, unable to forget that, with malignant heart, and deceitful speech, they have strove to hinder it."[12]

A year later that "great consummation" seemed more distant than ever, as military stalemates on all fronts after enormous casualties that summer caused Northern morale to plummet to its lowest point yet.

Lincoln came under intense pressure to retreat from the abolition of slavery as one of his publicly stated prior conditions for negotiations to end the war. He refused. To back away from the promise of freedom would be an egregious breach of faith, declared Lincoln. "Could such treachery by any possibility, escape the curses of Heaven?" More than a hundred thousand black soldiers were then fighting for the Union. Lincoln expressed contempt for those who "have proposed to me to return to slavery [these] black warriors.I should be damned in time & in eternity for so doing. The world shall know that I will keep my faith to friends & enemies, come what will....Why should they give their lives for us, with full notice of our purpose to betray them?"[13]

What Lincoln and everyone else believed would come of this principled stand was his defeat for reelection in 1864. Two years after he had told African Americans that they should leave the country for the good of both races, he now staked his career and reputation on defending the freedom they had earned by fighting for their country. Northern battlefield victories in the fall of 1864 turned around both the military and political situations by 180 degrees. Instead of being "badly beaten" at the polls in November, as he had expected in August, Lincoln was decisively reelected. He then invoked his mandate and threw all of the resources of his administration into a successful fight to get the Thirteenth Amendment through Congress.

Two days after Confederate general Robert E. Lee surrendered his army at Appomattox, Lincoln gave a speech to an interracial crowd on the White House lawn. In this address he looked toward the future problem of reconstructing the war-torn South. At a time when black men could not vote even in most Northern states, the president expressed his preference for enfranchising literate blacks and all black Union military veterans in the new South. "This was a remarkable statement," Foner rightly asserts. "No American president had publicly endorsed even limited black suffrage."[14]

Lincoln's secretary of the interior considered this endorsement a critical step toward full and equal citizenship for all blacks. So did

John Wilkes Booth, who was in the crowd that heard Lincoln's words on April 11. "That means nigger citizenship," uttered Booth. "Now, by God, I'll put him through. That is the last speech he will ever make."[15]

Three days later Booth fulfilled his dark oath. Lincoln did not get the chance to continue the trajectory that had propelled him from the gradualist and colonizationist limitations of his antislavery convictions in earlier years toward the immediatist and egalitarian policies he was approaching by 1865. "Lincoln had changed enormously during the Civil War," Foner concludes. Most strikingly, "he had developed a deep sense of compassion for the slaves he had helped to liberate, and a concern for their fate."[16]

The nation's foremost black leader, Frederick Douglass, recognized this compassion in a memorial address he delivered in 1865. Lincoln was "emphatically, the black man's president," said Douglass, "the first to show any respect for their rights as men." A decade later, however, in a speech at the dedication of an emancipation monument in Washington, Douglass described Lincoln as "preeminently the white man's President." To his largely white audience on this occasion, Douglass declared that "you are the children of Abraham Lincoln. We are at best only his step-children." Later in the same speech, Douglass brought together his Hegelian thesis and antithesis in a final synthesis. Whatever Lincoln's flaws may have been in the eyes of racial egalitarians, "in his heart of hearts he loathed and hated slavery." His firm wartime leadership saved the nation and freed it "from the great crime of slavery.... The hour and the man of our redemption had met in the person of Abraham Lincoln."[17]

As James Oakes notes in his astute and polished study *The Radical and the Republican: Frederick Douglass, Abraham Lincoln, and the Triumph of Antislavery Politics*, Douglass's speech in 1876 "mimicked his own shifting perspective" on Lincoln over the previous two decades.[18] Born a slave on Maryland's Eastern Shore, Douglass escaped to the North and freedom in 1838 and soon emerged as one of the nation's leading abolitionists. During the Civil War he spoke out eloquently and repeatedly to urge expansion of this war for union into a war for black freedom. Because Lincoln seemed to move too slowly and reluctantly in that direction, Douglass berated him as a proslavery wolf in antislavery sheep's clothing. "Abraham Lincoln is no more fit for the place he holds than was James Buchanan," declared an angry Douglass in July 1862, "and the latter was no more the miserable tool of traitors than the former is allowing himself to be." Lincoln had "steadily refused to proclaim, as he had the constitutional and moral right to proclaim, complete emancipation to all the slaves of rebels.... The country is destined to become sick of...Lincoln, and the sooner the better."[19]

In Douglass's Hegelian dialectic attitude toward Lincoln, this was the time of his most outspoken opposition. He could not know that at the very moment he was condemning the president as no better than the proslavery Buchanan, Lincoln had decided to issue an emancipation proclamation that would accomplish most of what Douglass demanded. When Lincoln did precisely that, two months later, Douglass was ecstatic. "We shout for joy that we live to record this righteous decree," he announced.[20]

But in Douglass's view, Lincoln backslid after issuing the Proclamation. Just as the president had seemed too slow in 1862 to embrace emancipation, he now seemed similarly tardy in 1864 to embrace equal rights for freed slaves. For a time Douglass even supported efforts to replace Lincoln with a more radical Republican candidate for president in the election of 1864. In the end, however, when the only alternative to Lincoln was the Democratic nominee, George B. McClellan, whose election might jeopardize the antislavery gains of the previous two years, Douglass came out for Lincoln. "When there was any shadow of a hope that a man of more anti-slavery conviction and policy could be elected," he wrote, "I was not for Mr. Lincoln." But with the prospect of "the (miscalled) Democratic party...clearly before us, all hesitation ought to cease, and every man who wishes well to the slave and to the country should at once rally with all the warmth and earnestness of his nature to the support of Abraham Lincoln."[21]

James Oakes believes that Lincoln possessed as much "anti-slavery conviction" as Douglass himself. The difference between the two men was one of position and tactics, not conviction. Douglass was a radical reformer whose mission was to proclaim principles and to demand that the people and their leaders live up to those principles. Lincoln was a politician, a practitioner of the art of the possible, a pragmatist who subscribed to the same principles but recognized that they could only be achieved in gradual step-by-step fashion through compromise and negotiation, in pace with progressive changes in public opinion and political realities. Oakes portrays a symbiosis between the radical Douglass and the Republican Lincoln: "It is important to democracy that reformers like Frederick Douglass could say what needed to be said, but it is indispensable to democracy that politicians like Abraham Lincoln could do only what the law and the people allowed them to do."[22]

Looking back in 1876, Douglass acknowledged that while from the standpoint of the abolitionists "Lincoln seemed tardy, cold, dull, and indifferent," he was considerably to the left of the political center on the slavery issue. "Measure him by the sentiment of his country," a "sentiment he was bound as a statesman to consult," and Lincoln "was swift, zealous, radical, and determined."[23] Oakes carries this point a step further. Lincoln the politician was a master of misdirection, of appearing to appease conservatives while manipulating them toward acceptance of radical policies. Douglass and many other contemporaries failed to appreciate or even to understand Lincoln's political legerdemain. Many historians have similarly failed. But Oakes both understands and appreciates it, and he analyzes with more clarity and precision than anyone else what he describes as the "typically backhanded way" in which Lincoln handled slavery, a tactic that "obscured the radicalism of his move."[24]

Some examples. In August 1861 General John C. Frémont, commander of Union forces in the border slave state of Missouri, issued an edict freeing the slaves of all Confederate activists in the state. Radicals like Douglass rejoiced, but conservatives and border-state Unionists threatened to turn against the Union war effort if Frémont's decree was sustained. Lincoln ordered Frémont to modify his edict to conform to legislation enacted a few weeks earlier that "confiscated" (but did not specifically free) only those slaves who had actually worked on Confederate fortifications or on any other military projects. Radicals denounced Lincoln's action, especially the distinction between confiscation and emancipation. But Lincoln's main concern was to retain the loyalty of the border slave states. "Without them," as Oakes recognizes, "the North would probably have lost the war and the slaves would have lost their only real chance for freedom." Three months later, in his annual message to Congress (which we today call the State of the Union Address), Lincoln "let slip, as if in passing, one of the most important announcements of the war" when he casually referred to the slaves, now numbering in the thousands, who had been confiscated by coming into Union lines as having been "thus liberated." From then on, confiscation meant freedom; Lincoln accomplished this momentous step so subtly that nobody complained or even seemed to notice.[25]

By May 1862 the Union government had gained military and political control of the border states. Lincoln urged them to consider voluntary and compensated emancipation of their slaves (they ultimately rejected his appeal). In that month another of Lincoln's generals, David Hunter, issued an order abolishing slavery not only along the South Atlantic coast where Union forces had secured a foothold but also in the entire states of South Carolina, Georgia, and Florida—90 percent of which were under Confederate control.

Lincoln knew nothing of this order until he read it in the newspapers. He promptly rescinded it, stating privately that "no commanding general shall do such a thing, upon *my* responsibility, without consulting me." Publicly, however, he phrased it differently in his revocation of Hunter's order: "Whether it be competent for me, as Commander-in-Chief... to declare the slaves of any state or states, free" and whether at any time "it shall have become a necessity indispensable to the maintenance of the government, to exercise such power, are questions which, under my responsibility, I reserve to myself" and not to commanders in the field.[26] One does not have to read between the lines to discern the hint of possible future action—it is in the lines themselves. As Oakes comments, any diligent reader of Lincoln's words "might have found it odd that a proclamation ostensibly designed to overturn General Hunter's emancipation order" contained a paragraph "declaring the President's authority to free the slaves in the rebel states whenever 'military necessity' required it."[27]

The military-necessity argument took on added urgency in the summer of 1862 as Confederate counteroffensives in Virginia and Tennessee reversed earlier Union gains. Slaves constituted the majority of the Confederacy's labor force. They sustained the South's war economy and the logistics of Confederate armies. A strike against slavery would be a blow against the Confederacy's ability to wage war. Such a strike would have to be justified politically in the North not on abolitionist but on military grounds. The cause of the Union united the North; in 1862 the issue of emancipation still deeply divided it.

In August 1862 the influential *New York Tribune* published a signed editorial by Horace Greeley urging Lincoln to proclaim emancipation. The president had already decided to issue an emancipation proclamation but was waiting for a propitious moment to announce it. Greeley's editorial gave him an opportunity to respond with what Oakes describes as "a masterpiece of indirect revelation." "My paramount object" in this war "*is* to save the Union," wrote Lincoln in a public letter to Greeley, "and is not either to save or destroy slavery." If "I could save the Union without freeing *any* slave I would do it, and if I could save it by freeing *all* the slaves I would do it; and if I could save it by freeing some and leaving others alone I would also do that." Here was something for both radicals and conservatives—another hint that emancipation might be coming, but an assertion that if so, it would happen only because it was necessary to save the Union. Lincoln had again cloaked a radical measure in conservative garb. Many people then and since missed the point, including Douglass, who saw it only "as evidence that Lincoln cared a great deal about the restoration of the Union and very little about the abolition of slavery."[28]

Lincoln's racial attitudes were also a target of Douglass's criticism until 1864. On this subject, Oakes offers some original and incisive insights. The main charge of racism against Lincoln focuses on his statements during the debates with Stephen A. Douglas in 1858. Lincoln rejected Douglas's accusation that he favored racial equality—a volatile issue in Illinois that threatened Lincoln's political career if the charge stuck. Goaded by Douglas's repeated playing of the race card, Lincoln declared in one of the debates that "I am not, nor have ever been in favor of bringing about in any way the social and political equality of the races." It would be easy, comments Oakes, "to string such quotations together and show up Lincoln as a run-of-the-mill white supremacist." But in private, Lincoln was much less racist than most other whites of his time. He was "disgusted by the race-baiting of the Douglas Democrats," and he "made the humanity of blacks central to his antislavery argument."[29] In a speech at Chicago in 1858, Lincoln pleaded: "Let us discard all this quibbling about…this race and that race and the other race being inferior, and therefore they must be placed in an inferior position," and instead "once more stand up declaring that all men are created equal."[30]

Lincoln's statements expressing opposition to social and political equality, Oakes maintains, were in fact part of his antislavery strategy. Extreme racism was at the core of the proslavery argument: If the slaves were freed, they would aspire to equality with whites; therefore slavery was the only bulwark of white supremacy and racial purity. Lincoln "wanted questions about race moved off the table," writes Oakes, and "the strategy he chose was to *agree* with the Democrats" in opposition to social equality. Lincoln understood that most Americans—including most Northerners—believed in white supremacy, "and in a democratic society such deeply held prejudices cannot be easily disregarded." Thus the most effective way to convert whites to an antislavery position, Lincoln believed, was to separate the issue of bondage from that of race.[31]

The same strategy of taking race off the table elicited Lincoln's proposals for colonization of freed slaves in 1862. Frederick Douglass was outraged by the president's statement to the delegation of black men who came to the White House in August—that because whites did not like the presence of black people among them, "it is better for us both, therefore, to be separated." Douglass publicly rebuked Lincoln for his "pride of race and blood, his contempt for Negroes and his canting hypocrisy."[32] But again Douglass missed the point, according to Oakes. Lincoln was painfully aware that his forthcoming emancipation proclamation would provoke a racist backlash. By signaling the possibility of colonizing some freed slaves elsewhere, Lincoln hoped to defuse part of that backlash. Some Republicans understood the strategy. "I believe practically [colonization] is a damn humbug," said one, "but it will take with the people." Lincoln's remarks to the black delegation were a staged performance. The president had invited a stenographer from the *New York Tribune* to report his words. Lincoln "was once again using racism strategically" to "make emancipation more palatable to white racists," writes Oakes, who admires Lincoln's skill but acknowledges that this time he may have overdone the tactic. "It was a low point in his presidency."[33]

After issuing the Emancipation Proclamation on January 1, 1863, Lincoln stopped using racism as a strategic diversion. By March 1863 he strongly endorsed the recruitment of black soldiers to fight for the Union, and in response to prodding by Douglass and other abolitionists he supported the successful passage of legislation to equalize the pay of black and white soldiers. Lincoln's refusal to back away from his insistence on the abolition of slavery as a precondition for peace negotiations in 1864 convinced Douglass that the president was the black man's genuine friend. Lincoln twice invited Douglass to the White House for private consultations on racial policies and also invited him to tea at the Lincolns' summer cottage. Douglass discovered at these meetings "a deeper moral conviction against slavery than I had ever seen before in anything spoken or written by him." Douglass also found that Lincoln in person had none of that "pride of race" he had earlier accused him of possessing. "In his company I was never in any way reminded of my humble origin, or my unpopular color," wrote Douglass. The president received him "just as you have seen one gentleman receive another." Lincoln was "one of the very few Americans, who could entertain a negro and converse with him without in anywise reminding him of the unpopularity of his color."[34]

Douglass outlived Lincoln by thirty years. In the latter half of that period the nation receded from its Reconstruction promise of racial justice, and Southern blacks were forced into second-class citizenship. As this trajectory spiraled downward, the Civil War president looked better and better in retrospect. If Lincoln were alive today, Douglass said in 1893, "did his firm hand now hold the helm of state...did his wisdom now shape and control the destiny of this otherwise great republic," the national government would not be making the "weak and helpless" claim that "there is no power under the United States Constitution to protect the lives and liberties" of Southern blacks "from barbarous, inhuman and lawless violence."[35] Seventy years later, Martin Luther King Jr. stood in front of the Lincoln Memorial in Washington and described his dream that one day the nation would live up to the ideals of Douglass and Lincoln.

CHAPTER 9

A. Lincoln, Commander in Chief

When the American Civil War began with the Confederate attack on Fort Sumter, U.S. president Abraham Lincoln was far less prepared for the task of commander in chief than his Southern adversary. Jefferson Davis had graduated from West Point, served in the regular army for seven years, commanded a regiment that fought intrepidly at Buena Vista in the Mexican War, and compiled a record as an outstanding secretary of war in the Franklin Pierce administration from 1853 to 1857. Lincoln's only military experience had come twenty-nine years earlier, when he was captain of a militia unit that saw no action in the Black Hawk War. During Lincoln's one term in Congress, he made a speech in 1848 mocking his military career. "Did you know I am a military hero?" he said. "I fought, bled, and came away" after "charges upon the wild onions" and "a good many bloody struggles with the Musquetoes."[1]

When he called state militias into federal service on April 15, 1861, to put down "combinations too powerful to be suppressed by the ordinary course of judicial proceedings," Lincoln therefore faced a steep learning curve as commander in chief. He went at the task diligently. His experience as a largely self-taught lawyer with a keen analytical mind who had mastered Euclidean geometry for mental exercise enabled him to learn on the job. He read and absorbed works on military history and strategy; he observed the successes and failures of his own and the enemy's military commanders and drew apt conclusions; he made mistakes and learned from them; he applied his large quotient of common sense to slice through the obfuscations and excuses of military subordinates. By 1862 his grasp of strategy and operations was firm enough almost to justify the overstated but not entirely wrong conclusion of the historian T. Harry Williams in 1952: "Lincoln stands out as a great war president, probably the greatest in our history, and a great natural strategist, a better one than any of his generals."[2] This assertion was incorrect in one respect: Lincoln was not a "natural strategist"; he had to work hard to achieve a grasp of strategy.

Williams belonged to a generation of historians who recognized that Lincoln's role as commander in chief was central to his place in history. The sixteenth president has been (so far) the only one whose presidency was wholly bounded by war. On the day Lincoln took office, the first document placed on his desk was a letter from Major Robert Anderson at Fort Sumter, informing him that the garrison there must be withdrawn or resupplied at the risk of war. Lincoln chose to take that risk. Four years later he was assassinated five days after General Robert E. Lee surrendered at Appomattox but while several other Confederate armies were still in the field.

During those four years Lincoln spent more time in the War Department telegraph office than anywhere else except the White House or his summer residence at the Soldiers' Home. Military matters required more of his time and energy than anything else. He rarely left Washington except to visit the Army of the Potomac at the front, as he did eleven times for a total of forty-two days with the army. As T. Harry Williams and other historians who were writing during the era from the 1920s to the 1950s understood, not only Lincoln's success or failure as president but also the very survival of the *United* States depended on how he performed his duties as a military leader.[3]

Since the 1960s, however, military history has fallen out of fashion among professional academic historians. Social history in its various forms that focus on themes of race, class, ethnicity, and gender has replaced political, diplomatic, and especially military history as a leading historiographical category. This change affected scholarship about Lincoln. One of the best reference works on Lincoln, Mark E. Neely's *The Abraham Lincoln Encyclopedia* (1982), devoted less than 5 percent of its space to military matters. Of the seventeen collected essays on Lincoln published in 1987 by the late Don E. Fehrenbacher, one of the foremost Lincoln scholars of his time, not one dealt with the president as a military leader. On the 175th anniversary of Lincoln's birth in 1984, Gettysburg College hosted a conference on recent Lincoln scholarship. There were three sessions on psychobiography, two on the assassination, two on Lincoln's image in photographs and popular prints, one each on his economic ideas, religion, humor, Indian policy, and slavery. But there were no sessions on Lincoln as commander in chief—a remarkable irony, given the site of the conference. In 1994 the historian Merrill Peterson published his splendid study *Lincoln in American Memory*, highlighting 130 years of the sixteenth president's image in American historiography and popular culture. There are chapters on Lincoln and the South, religion, politics, Reconstruction, civil rights, and several other themes, but no chapters on Lincoln and the army.[4]

Perhaps it is time to recognize the truth expressed by Lincoln himself in his second inaugural address when the Civil War had been raging for almost four years: On "the progress of our arms…all else chiefly depends."[5] "All else" included many of the questions and developments that social historians consider important: the fate of slavery; the definition of freedom; the destruction of the Old South's socioeconomic system and the triumph of entrepreneurial free-labor capitalism as the national norm; a new definition of American nationalism; the origins of a new system of race relations; the very survival of the United States in a manner that laid the foundations for the nation's emergence as a world power.

The issue of slavery and its abolition offers a striking illustration of this point. Much recent writing about the wartime emancipation of hundreds of thousands of slaves has viewed this process mainly through the lens of social history, "history from the bottom up." Of their own volition many slaves escaped from their masters and won freedom by coming into Union lines. But this process could not have occurred if there had been no Union lines to which they could escape. And in most cases it was the military lines that came to the slaves, not vice versa, as Northern armies penetrated deeper into the South. It was the commander in chief of these armies who oversaw these events and who made the crucial decisions to convert a *strategy* of liberating slaves to weaken the Confederacy into a *policy* of abolishing slavery as a war aim second in importance only to preserving the Union. Freedom quite literally came from the barrel of a gun. The story of how this happened cannot be fully understood without at least some attention to military history.

As commander in chief in time of war a president performs or oversees five functions in diminishing order of direct activity: policy, national strategy, military strategy, operations, and tactics. Neither Lincoln nor anyone else defined these functions in a systematic way during the Civil War. If they had, their definitions might have looked something like this: *Policy* refers to war aims, the political goals of the nation in time of war. *National strategy* refers to mobilization of the political, economic, diplomatic, and psychological as well as military resources of the nation to achieve these war aims. *Military strategy* refers to plans for the employment of armed forces to win military victories that will further the political goals. *Operations* refers to the actual organization, logistics, and movements of armies in particular campaigns to carry out the purposes of military strategy. *Tactics* refers to the formations and fighting of an army in actual battle.

As president of the nation and leader of his party as well as commander in chief, Lincoln was principally responsible for shaping and defining national policy. From first to last, that policy was preservation of the United States as one nation, indivisible, and as a republic based on majority rule. In May 1861 he explained that "the central idea pervading this struggle is the necessity that is upon us, of proving that popular government is not an absurdity. We must settle this question now, whether in a free government the minority have the right to break up the government whenever they choose."[6] Secession "is the essence of anarchy," said Lincoln on another occasion, for if one state may secede at will, so may any other until there is no government and no nation. In the Gettysburg Address, Lincoln offered his most eloquent statement of policy: The war was a test of whether the nation conceived in 1776 "might live" or would "perish from the earth." This issue of national sovereignty over a union of all the states was nonnegotiable. No compromise between a sovereign *United* States and a separately sovereign *Confederate* States was possible. This issue "is distinct, simple, and inflexible," said Lincoln in 1864. "It is an issue which can only be tried by war, and decided by victory."[7]

The next level of Lincoln's duty as commander in chief was to mobilize the means to achieve that policy by winning the war. The president, of course, shared with Congress and key cabinet members the tasks of raising, organizing, and sustaining an army and navy, preventing foreign intervention in the conflict, and maintaining public support for the war. But no matter how much this national strategy required maximum effort at all levels of government and society, the ultimate responsibility was the president's in his dual roles as head of government and commander in chief. And this responsibility was as much a political as a military one, especially in a civil war whose origins lay in a political conflict and was precipitated by political decisions. Although Lincoln never read Carl von Clausewitz's famous treatise *On War* (*Vom Kriege*), his actions were a consummate expression of Clausewitz's central argument: "The political objective is the goal, war is the means of reaching it, and means can never be considered in isolation from their purpose. Therefore, it is clear that war should never be thought of as something autonomous but always as an instrument of policy."[8]

Some professional military men tended to think of war as "something autonomous" and deplored the intrusion of political considerations into military matters. Take the notable example of "political generals." Lincoln appointed numerous prominent politicians with little or no military training or experience to the rank of brigadier or major general. Some of them received these appointments so early in the war that they subsequently outranked professional, West Point–educated officers. Lincoln also commissioned important ethnic leaders as generals with little regard to their military merits. Some of these political and ethnic generals proved to be incompetent on the battlefield. "It seems but little better than murder to give important commands to such men as [Nathaniel] Banks, [Benjamin] Butler, [John] McClernand, and Lew Wallace," sighed the thoroughgoing professional Henry W. Halleck in 1864, "but it seems impossible to prevent it."[9]

Historians who likewise deplore the abundance of political generals sometimes cite an anecdote to mock the process. One day in 1862, so the story goes, Lincoln and Secretary of War Edwin M. Stanton were going over a list of colonels for promotion to brigadier general. Coming to the name of Alexander Schimmelfennig, the president said that "there has got to be something done unquestionably in the interest of the Dutch, and to that end I want Schimmelfennig appointed." Stanton protested that there were better qualified German Americans. "No matter about that," said Lincoln, "his name will make up for any difference there may be."[10]

General Schimmelfennig is remembered today mainly for hiding three days in a woodshed next to a pigpen to escape capture at Gettysburg. Other political generals are also remembered more for their military defeats or supposed blunders than for any positive achievements: Nathaniel Banks for the Red River campaign and other defeats; John C. Frémont for the mess he made of affairs in Missouri and western Virginia; Daniel Sickles for endangering the Army of the Potomac and losing his leg by moving out to the Peach Orchard at Gettysburg; Benjamin Butler for alleged corruption in New Orleans and for botching the first attack on Fort Fisher; and so on.

Often forgotten are the excellent military records of some political generals like John A. Logan and Francis P. Blair Jr. (among others). And some West Pointers, notably Ulysses S. Grant and William T. Sherman, might have languished in obscurity if it had not been for the initial sponsorship of Grant by Congressman Elihu Washburne and of Sherman by his brother John, a U.S. senator.

Even if all political generals, or generals in whose appointments politics played a part, turned out to have mediocre military records, however, the process would have had a positive impact on *national* strategy. The main purpose of commissioning prominent political and ethnic leaders was to mobilize their constituencies for the war effort. The U.S. Army on the eve of the war consisted of approximately 16,400 men. By April 1862, when the war was a year old, the volunteer Union army consisted of 637,000 men. This mass mobilization of volunteers could not have taken place without an enormous effort by local and state politicians as well as by prominent ethnic leaders. In New York City, for example, the Tammany Democrat Daniel Sickles raised a brigade and earned a commission as brigadier general, the Irish-born Thomas Meagher helped raise the famous Irish Brigade, and the German American leader Carl Schurz helped raise several German regiments and eventually became a major general. Northern state governors, nearly all Republicans, played an essential part in raising and organizing regiments and claimed brigadier generalships for their political allies in return. At the same time, Lincoln needed the allegiance of prominent Democrats like John McClernand and John Logan in southern Illinois, for example, where support for the war was questionable. These two men "have labored night and day to instruct their fellow citizens in the true nature of the contest," acknowledged the Republican *Chicago Tribune* in September 1861, "and to organize their aroused feelings into effective military strength. They have succeeded nobly."[11] Both eventually became major generals. And of course, prominent Republicans could not be ignored. Lincoln's party supplied most of the energy and manpower for the war effort. John C. Frémont, who had been the first Republican presidential candidate in 1856, and Nathaniel P. Banks, former Speaker of the House and governor of Massachusetts, were made major generals early in the war.

By the war's second year, the need for politically motivated commissions to cement allegiances and to reward support had declined. Performance in action became the principal determinant for promotion, though politics could never be completely absent from the process. With Lincoln's approval, the War Department issued General Order No. 111 in August 1862, stipulating that "hereafter no appointments of major generals or brigadier generals will be given except to officers of the regular army for meritorious and distinguished service during the war, or to volunteer officers who, by some successful achievement in the field shall have displayed the military abilities required for the duties of a general officer." This order was sometimes honored in the breach. Schimmelfennig, for example, was promoted to brigadier general in November 1862, while Carl Schurz and Julius Stahel were promoted to major general in January 1863—all in the name of rewarding "our sincere friends" in the German American community, as Lincoln put it.[12]

Nevertheless, General Order No. 111 did herald the advent of a more professional criterion for promotion in the Union army. The national strategy of mobilizing political support for the war through military patronage had served its purpose. "The political generals' reputation for battlefield defeats is certainly accurate for many in this group," writes a recent historian of the subject, "but this orthodox caricature neglects their vital contribution in rallying support for the war and convincing the people to join the mass citizen army as volunteers." Lincoln would have agreed.[13]

Some of the higher-ranking political generals helped shape military strategy and thus straddled the boundary between national and military strategy. Another important issue that began as a question of national strategy eventually crossed the boundary to become policy as well. That was the issue of slavery and emancipation. During the war's first year, one of Lincoln's top priorities was to keep border-state unionists and northern antiabolitionist Democrats in his war coalition. He feared, with good reason, that the balance in three border slave states might tip to the Confederacy if his administration took a premature step toward emancipation. When General Frémont issued a military order freeing the slaves of Confederate supporters in Missouri, Lincoln revoked it in order to quell an outcry from the border states and northern Democrats. To sustain Frémont's order, Lincoln believed, "would alarm our Southern Union friends, and turn them against us—perhaps ruin our rather fair prospect for Kentucky....I think that to lose Kentucky is nearly the same as to lose the whole game. Kentucky gone, we can not hold Missouri, nor as I think, Maryland. These all against us, and the job on our hands is too large for us. We would as well consent to separation at once, including the surrender of this capitol."[14]

During the next nine months, however, the thrust of national strategy shifted away from conciliating the border states and antiemancipation Democrats. The antislavery Republican constituency grew louder and more demanding. The argument that the Slave Power had brought on the war and that restoration of the Union with slavery still in it would only sow the seeds of another war became more insistent. The evidence that slave labor sustained the Confederate economy and the logistics of Confederate armies grew stronger. Counteroffensives by Southern armies in the summer of 1862 wiped out many of the Union gains of the winter and spring. Many Northerners, including Lincoln, became convinced that bolder steps were necessary. To win a war over an enemy fighting *for* and sustained *by* slavery, the North must strike *at* slavery.

In July 1862 Lincoln therefore decided on a major change in national strategy. Instead of deferring to the border states and Northern Democrats, he would activate the dynamism of the Northern antislavery majority that had elected him and mobilize the potential of black manpower by issuing a proclamation of freedom for slaves in rebellious states. "Decisive and extensive measures must be adopted," Lincoln told members of his cabinet, according to Secretary of the Navy Gideon Welles. Emancipation was "a military necessity, absolutely necessary to the preservation of the Union. We must free the slaves or be ourselves subdued. The slaves [are] undeniably an element of strength to those who have their service, and we must decide whether that element should be with us or against us.... We [want] the army to strike more vigorous blows. The administration must set the army an example and strike at the heart of the rebellion."[15]

After a two-month wait for a Union military victory to give an emancipation edict credibility as a positive war measure instead of as a desperate appeal for a slave uprising, Lincoln issued a preliminary proclamation five days after the Battle of Antietam. It warned that on January 1, 1863, the president would invoke his war powers as commander in chief to seize enemy property (slaves) by proclaiming emancipation in all states or parts of states in rebellion. January 1 came, the rebellion still raged, and Lincoln issued his historic proclamation.

Emancipation thus became a crucial part of the North's national strategy as an attempt to convert a Confederate resource to Union advantage. But this step opened up a potential inconsistency between national strategy and policy. The Emancipation Proclamation might free many slaves if Northern armies could conquer the states to which it applied. But what about slaves in the states to which it did not apply? What force would the Proclamation have once the war was over? Could the North fight a war using the strategy of emancipation to restore a Union in which slavery still existed and to uphold a Constitution that still sanctioned bondage? During the last two years of the war the abolition of slavery evolved from a *means* of winning the war to a *war aim*—from national strategy to national policy. Lincoln was reelected in 1864 on a platform calling for "unconditional surrender" of the Confederacy and a Thirteenth Amendment to abolish slavery everywhere and forever.[16]

Lincoln's shift from a national strategy of opposing the recruitment of black soldiers to one of vigorous support for that action lagged a few months behind his similar shift on emancipation. The idea of putting arms in the hands of black men provoked even greater hostility among Democrats and border-state Unionists than emancipation itself. In

August 1862 Lincoln told delegates from Indiana who offered to raise two black regiments that "the nation could not afford to lose Kentucky at this crisis" and that "to arm the negroes would turn 50,000 bayonets from the loyal border States against us that were for us."[17]

Three weeks later, however, the president quietly authorized the War Department to begin organizing black regiments on the South Carolina Sea Islands. The Emancipation Proclamation openly endorsed the recruitment of black soldiers and sailors. And by March 1863 Lincoln told his military governor of occupied Tennessee that "the colored population is the great *available* and yet *unavailed* of, force for restoring the Union. The bare sight of fifty thousand armed, and drilled black soldiers on the banks of the Mississippi, would end the rebellion at once. And who doubts that we can present that sight, if we but take hold in earnest."[18]

This prediction proved overoptimistic. But in August 1863, after black regiments had proved their worth at Fort Wagner and elsewhere, Lincoln told opponents of their employment that these soldiers had already made a contribution to the "great consummation" of Union victory. A year later, with more than a hundred thousand black men under arms, Lincoln considered their role to be essential. Without those soldiers, he said, "we can not longer maintain the contest...& we would be compelled to abandon the war in 3 weeks."[19]

Lincoln's dominant role in determining policy and national strategy is scarcely surprising. But he also took a more active, hands-on part in shaping military strategy than presidents have done in most other wars. This was not necessarily by choice. Lincoln's lack of military training inclined him at first to defer to General in Chief Winfield Scott. But Scott's age, poor health, and lack of energy placed a greater burden on the president than he had anticipated. Lincoln was also disillusioned by Scott's advice in March 1861 to yield both Forts Sumter and Pickens and by the seemingly passive strategy of the Anaconda Plan. Scott's successor, General George B. McClellan, proved to be an even greater disappointment to Lincoln. Henry W. Halleck did not measure up to expectations as Lincoln's third general in chief. Neither did field commanders Don Carlos Buell, John Pope, Ambrose Burnside, Joseph Hooker, and William S. Rosecrans. When Ulysses S. Grant became general in chief in March 1864, Lincoln told him (according to Grant's memoirs) that "he had never professed to be a military man or to know how campaigns should be conducted, and never wanted to interfere in them: but that procrastination on the part of commanders" had compelled him to take a more active part.[20] Grant's account does not ring entirely true. By that time Lincoln had a pretty definite idea how campaigns should be conducted. But it is certain that "procrastination," especially by McClellan and Buell, caused Lincoln to become in effect his own general in chief as well as commander in chief during key campaigns.

Perhaps he should have played an even more assertive role. In early December 1861, after McClellan had been commander of the Army of the Potomac for more than four months and had done little with it except to conduct drills and reviews, Lincoln drew on his reading and discussions of military strategy to propose a campaign against Confederate general Joseph E. Johnston's army, occupying the Manassas-Centreville sector twenty-five miles from Washington. Under Lincoln's plan, part of the Army of the Potomac would feign a frontal attack while the rest would use the Occoquan Valley to move up on the flank and rear of the enemy, cut its rail communications, and catch it in a pincers.[21]

It was a good plan; indeed, it was precisely what Johnston most feared. McClellan rejected it in favor of his proposal for a deeper flanking movement all the way south to Urbana on the Rappahannock River. Lincoln posed a series of questions to McClellan, asking him why his distant-flanking strategy was better than his, Lincoln's, short-flanking plan. Three sound premises underlay Lincoln's questions: First, the enemy army, not Richmond, should be the objective; second, Lincoln's plan would enable the Army of the Potomac to operate near its own base (Alexandria), while McClellan's plan, even if successful, would draw the enemy back toward its base (Richmond) and lengthen the Union supply line; and third, "does not your plan involve a greatly larger expenditure of *time*...than mine?"[22]

McClellan brushed off Lincoln's questions and proceeded with his own plan, bolstered by an 8–4 vote of his division commanders in favor of it, which caused Lincoln reluctantly to acquiesce. Johnston then threw a monkey wrench into McClellan's Urbana strategy by withdrawing from Manassas to the south bank of the Rappahannock—in large part to escape the kind of maneuver Lincoln had proposed. McClellan now shifted his campaign all the way to the Virginia Peninsula between the York and James Rivers. Instead of attacking the line near Yorktown, held by fewer than seventeen thousand Confederates in early April, with his own army, then numbering seventy thousand, McClellan settled down for a siege that gave Johnston time to bring his whole army down to the Peninsula. An exasperated Lincoln telegraphed McClellan on April 6: "I think you better break the enemies' line from York-town to Warwick River, at once. They will probably use *time*, as advantageously as you can." McClellan's only response was to comment petulantly in a letter to his wife that "I was much tempted to reply that he had better come & do it himself."[23]

Three days later Lincoln wrote McClellan a letter reiterating what was becoming a hallmark of his strategic thinking, the importance of time. "By delay the enemy will relatively gain upon you—that is, he will gain faster, by *fortifications* and *re-inforcements*, than you can by re-inforcements alone."[24] Lincoln's point was exactly right. McClellan's repeated delays yielded the initiative time and again to Johnston and later to Robert E. Lee, and ruined McClellan's Peninsula Campaign.

In his April 9 letter to the general, Lincoln enunciated another major theme of his military strategy: The war could be won only by fighting the enemy rather than by endless maneuvers and sieges to occupy *places*. "Once more," wrote Lincoln, "let me tell you, it is indispensable to you that you strike a blow. You will do me the justice to remember I always insisted, that going down the Bay in search of a field, instead of fighting at or near Manassas, was only shifting, and not surmounting, a difficulty—that we would find the same, or equal intrenchments, at either place. The country will not fail to note—is now noting—that the present hesitation to move upon an intrenched enemy, is but the story of Manassas repeated." Lincoln assured McClellan that "I have never written you, or spoken to you, in greater kindness of feeling than now, nor with a fuller purpose to sustain you.... *But you must act*."[25]

The general who acquired the nickname of Tardy George never learned that lesson. The same was true of several other generals who did not live up to Lincoln's expectations. They seemed to be paralyzed by responsibility for the lives of their men as well as the fate of their army and nation. This intimidating responsibility made them risk-averse. Afraid of a failure that might lose everything, they chose the safe course of doing as little as possible. This risk-averse behavior especially characterized commanders of the Army of the Potomac, who operated in the glare of media publicity with the government in Washington looking over their shoulders. In contrast, officers like Ulysses S. Grant, George H. Thomas, and Philip H. Sheridan got their start in the Western theater, hundreds of miles distant, where they worked their way up from command of a regiment or brigade step by step to larger responsibilities away from media attention. They were able to grow into these responsibilities and to learn the necessity of taking risks without the fear of failure that unnerved McClellan.

General William T. Sherman was something of an exception that proved the rule. Thrust into command of the entire Department of the Cumberland in October 1861, he broke down under the pressure and had to be relieved. He started over again as the officer in charge of a supply base at Cairo, Illinois, under Grant, and then found himself as a division commander at Shiloh, which became the solid bottom rung for his successful climb up the ladder of command. In 1864 Sherman persuaded Grant and an initially reluctant Lincoln to let him take the greatest risk of all, to cut loose from his base and march through the enemy heartland 285 miles from Atlanta to the sea. This spectacular feat evoked from Lincoln praise for the risk-taking characteristics he wanted in a general: "When you were about leaving Atlanta for the Atlantic coast, I was *anxious*, if not fearful; but feeling that you were the better judge, remembering that 'nothing risked, nothing gained' I did not interfere. Now, the undertaking being a success, the honor is all yours; for I believe none of us went farther than to acquiesce."[26]

In October 1862, after the Battle of Antietam, Lincoln had prodded McClellan to pursue and attack the retreating Confederates more aggressively by offering the same "nothing risked, nothing gained" advice. "I say 'try,' " the commander in chief told McClellan; "if we never try, we shall never succeed." But the general did not try. Lincoln finally gave up on him and removed McClellan from command. He could no longer "bore with an auger too dull to take hold," he told one of McClellan's supporters.[27]

Meanwhile Lincoln's frustration with the lack of activity in the Kentucky-Tennessee theater had elicited from him an expression of another important strategic concept. Generals Halleck and Buell commanded in the two Western theaters separated by the Cumberland River. Lincoln urged them to cooperate in a joint campaign against the Confederate army defending a line from eastern Kentucky to the Mississippi River. Both responded in early January 1862 that they were not yet ready. On the back of a copy of a letter from Halleck, explaining why he could not move against the Confederate defenses at Columbus, Kentucky, Lincoln wrote: "It is exceedingly discouraging. As everywhere else, nothing can be done."[28]

Lincoln was provoked by Halleck's pedantic explanation of why he and Buell could not cooperate. "To operate on exterior lines against an enemy occupying a central position will fail," wrote Halleck. "It is condemned by every military authority I have ever read." By this time Lincoln had read some of those authorities (including Halleck) and was prepared to challenge the general's reasoning. "I state my general idea of the war," he wrote to both Halleck and Buell, "that we have the *greater* numbers, and the enemy has the *greater* facility of concentrating forces upon points of collision; that we must fail, unless we can find some way to making *our* advantage an over-match for his; and that this can be only done by menacing him with superior forces at *different* points, at the *same* time; so that we can safely attack, one, or both, if he makes no change; and if he *weakens* one to strengthen the other, forbear to attack the strengthened one, but seize and hold the weakened one, gaining so much."[29]

Lincoln clearly expressed here what military theorists define as "concentration in time" to counter the Confederacy's advantage of interior lines that enabled Southern forces to concentrate in space. The geography of the war required the North to operate generally on exterior lines while the Confederacy could use interior lines to shift troops to the point of danger. By advancing on two or more fronts simultaneously, Union forces could neutralize this advantage, as Lincoln understood but Halleck and Buell seemed unable to grasp.

Not until Grant became general in chief in 1864 did Lincoln have a commander in place who carried out this strategy. In his final report on the 1864–65 campaigns that won the war, Grant noted that prior to these operations, Union armies in different theaters had "acted independently and without concert, like a balky team, no two ever pulling together." Employing concentration in time, Grant ordered five separate Union armies to operate from exterior lines against as many smaller Confederate armies to prevent any of them from reinforcing another. Lincoln was impressed. He told his private secretary John Hay that Grant's plans reminded him of his own "suggestion so constantly made and as constantly neglected, to Buell & Halleck et al to move at once upon the enemy's whole line so as to bring into action to our advantage our great superiority in numbers."[30]

Grant's strategy of attacking the enemy wherever he found them also carried out Lincoln's strategy of trying to cripple the enemy army as far from Richmond (or any other base) as possible rather than maneuver to occupy or capture *places*. From February to June 1862, Union

forces had enjoyed remarkable success in capturing Confederate territory and cities along the southern Atlantic coast and in Tennessee and
the lower Mississippi Valley, including the cities of Norfolk, Nashville,
New Orleans, and Memphis. But Confederate counteroffensives in the
summer recaptured much of this territory (though not these cities).
Clearly, the conquest and occupation of places would not win the war
so long as enemy armies remained capable of reconquering them.

Lincoln viewed these Confederate offensives more as an opportunity than a threat. When the Army of Northern Virginia began to move
north in the campaign that led to Gettysburg, General Hooker proposed to cut in behind them and attack Richmond. Lincoln rejected the
idea. *"Lee's* Army, and not *Richmond*, is your true objective point," he
wired Hooker on June 10, 1863. "If he comes toward the Upper Potomac, follow on his flank, and on the inside track, shortening your
[supply] lines, whilst he lengthens his. Fight him when opportunity
offers." A week later, as the enemy was entering Pennsylvania, Lincoln
told Hooker that this invasion "gives you back the chance that I thought
McClellan lost last fall" to cripple Lee's army far from its base.[31]

Hooker's complaints and bickering with Halleck finally caused
Lincoln to replace Hooker with George Gordon Meade, who punished but did not destroy Lee at Gettysburg. When the rising Potomac
trapped Lee in Maryland, Lincoln urged Meade to close in for the kill.
If Meade could "complete his work, so gloriously prosecuted thus far,"
said Lincoln, "by the literal or substantial destruction of Lee's army,
the rebellion will be over."[32]

Lincoln was distressed by Meade's congratulatory order to his
army after Gettysburg, which closed by saying that the country now
"looks to the army for greater efforts to drive from our soil every ves-
tige of the presence of the invader." "Great God!" cried Lincoln. "This
is a dreadful reminiscence of McClellan," who had proclaimed a great
victory when the enemy retreated across the river after Antietam. "Will
our Generals never get that idea out of their heads? The whole country
is *our* soil." That, after all, was the point of the war.[33]

When word came that Lee had escaped across the Potomac, Lincoln was both angry and depressed. He wrote to Meade: "My dear general, I do not believe you appreciate the magnitude of the misfortune involved in Lee's escape. He was within your easy grasp, and to have closed upon him would, in connection with our other late successes [mainly the capture of Vicksburg and Port Hudson with their thirty-six thousand defenders], have ended the war. As it is, the war will be prolonged indefinitely.... Your golden opportunity is gone, and I am distressed immeasurably because of it."[34]

Having gotten these feelings off his chest, Lincoln filed the letter away unsent. But he never changed his mind. And two months later, when the Army of the Potomac was maneuvering and skirmishing again over the devastated land between Washington and Richmond, the president declared that "to attempt to fight the enemy back to his intrenchments in Richmond...is an idea I have been trying to repudiate for quite a year....I have constantly desired the Army of the Potomac, to make Lee's army, and not Richmond, its objective point. If our army can not fall upon the enemy and hurt him where he is, it is plain to me it can gain nothing by attempting to follow him over a succession of intrenched lines into a fortified city."[35]

Five times in the war Lincoln tried to get his field commanders to trap enemy armies that were raiding or invading northward by cutting in south of them and blocking their routes of retreat: during Stonewall Jackson's drive north through the Shenandoah Valley in May 1862; Lee's invasion of Maryland in September 1862; Braxton Bragg's and Edmund Kirby Smith's invasion of Kentucky in the same month; Lee's invasion of Pennsylvania in the Gettysburg campaign; and Jubal Early's raid to the outskirts of Washington in July 1864. Each time his generals failed him, and in most cases they soon found themselves relieved of command: John C. Frémont and James Shields after failing to intercept Jackson; McClellan after letting Lee get away; Buell after Bragg and Kirby Smith got safely back to Tennessee; and David Hunter after Early's raid. Meade retained his command despite Lincoln's disappointment but played second fiddle to Grant in the war's last year.

In all of these cases the slowness of Union armies trying to intercept or pursue the enemy played a key part in their failures. Lincoln expressed repeated frustration with the inability of his armies to march as light and fast as Confederate armies. Much better supplied than the enemy, Union forces were actually slowed down by the abundance of their logistics. Most Union commanders never learned the lesson pronounced by Confederate General Richard Ewell that "the road to glory cannot be followed with much baggage."[36]

Lincoln's efforts to get his commanders to move faster with fewer supplies brought him into active participation at the operational level of his armies. In May 1862 he directed General Irvin McDowell to "put all possible energy and speed into the effort" to trap Jackson in the Shenandoah Valley. "It is, for you, a question of legs. Put in all the speed you can. I have told Frémont as much, and directed him to drive at them as fast as possible."[37] Jackson's troops marched twice as fast as those of Frémont and of McDowell's lead division under Shields, and the Confederates slipped through the trap with just hours to spare.

Lincoln was disgusted with the excuses offered by Frémont for not moving faster. The same pattern of excuses from Buell during his pursuit of Bragg after the Battle of Perryville and from McClellan after Antietam deepened his disgust. Lincoln told Buell that he could "not understand why we cannot march as the enemy marches, live as he lives, and fight as he fights, unless we admit the inferiority of our troops and our generals."[38] Lincoln probably did not fully appreciate the logistical difficulties of moving large bodies of troops, especially in enemy territory. On the other hand, the president did comprehend the reality expressed by the Army of the Potomac's quartermaster in response to McClellan's incessant requests for more supplies before he could advance after Antietam, that "an army will never move if it waits until all the different commanders report that they are ready and want no more supplies." Lincoln told another general in November

1862 that "this expanding, and piling up of *impedimenta*, has been, so far, almost our ruin, and will be our final ruin if it is not abandoned.... You would be better off...for not having a thousand wagons, doing nothing but hauling forage to feed the animals that draw them, and taking at least two thousand men to care for the wagons and animals, who might otherwise be two thousand good soldiers."[39]

With Grant and Sherman, Lincoln finally had generals in top commands who followed Ewell's dictum about the road to glory and who were willing to demand of their soldiers—and of themselves—the same exertions and sacrifices that Confederate commanders required of their men. After the Vicksburg campaign Lincoln said of General Grant, whose rapid mobility and absence of a cumbersome supply line were a key to its success, that "Grant is my man and I am his the rest of the war!" Perhaps one of the reasons for Lincoln's praise was a tongue-in-cheek report from Elihu Washburne, who traveled with Grant for part of the campaign. "I am afraid Grant will have to be reproved for want of style," Washburne wrote to Lincoln on May 1, 1863. "On this whole march for five days he has had neither a horse nor an orderly or servant, a blanket or overcoat or clean shirt, or even a sword....His entire baggage consists of a toothbrush."[40] To Lincoln, the contrast with the headquarters pomp or bloated logistics of a Frémont or McClellan could not have been greater.

Lincoln had opinions about battlefield tactics, but he rarely made suggestions to his field commanders for that level of operations. One exception, however, occurred in the second week of May 1862. Upset by McClellan's month-long siege of Yorktown without any apparent result, Lincoln, Secretary of War Stanton, and Secretary of the Treasury Salmon P. Chase sailed down to Hampton Roads on May 5 to discover that the Confederates had evacuated Yorktown before McClellan could open with his siege artillery.

Norfolk remained in enemy hands, however, and the feared CSS *Virginia* (former *Merrimack*) was still docked there. On May 7 Lincoln took direct operational control of a drive to capture Norfolk and to push a gunboat fleet up the James River. The president ordered General John Wool, commander at Fort Monroe, to land troops on the south bank of Hampton Roads. Lincoln even personally carried out a reconnaissance to select the best landing place. On May 9 the Confederates evacuated Norfolk before the Northern soldiers could get there. Two days later the *Virginia*'s crew blew her up to prevent her capture. An officer on the USS *Monitor* wrote that "it is extremely fortunate that the President came down as he did—he seems to have infused new life into everything." Nothing was happening, he said, until Lincoln began "stirring up dry bones." Chase rarely found opportunities to praise Lincoln, but on this occasion he wrote to his daughter: "So has ended a brilliant week's campaign of the President; for I think it quite certain that if he had not come down, Norfolk would still have been in possession of the enemy, and the 'Merrimac' as grim and defiant and as much a terror as ever.... The whole coast is now virtually ours."[41]

Chase exaggerated, for the Confederates would have had to abandon Norfolk anyway to avoid being cut off when Johnston's army retreated up the north side of the James River. But Chase's words can perhaps be applied to Lincoln's performance as commander in chief in the war as a whole. He enunciated a clear national policy, and through trial and error evolved national and military strategies to achieve it. The nation did not perish from the earth but experienced a new birth of freedom.

CHAPTER 10

The Commander Who Would Not Fight:
McClellan and Lincoln

On September 7, 1862, Major General George B. McClellan wrote to his wife exultantly that "my enemies are crushed, silent, and disarmed." What did he mean? Had he won a great battle against the Army of Northern Virginia that has somehow escaped the attention of historians? This was far from the only time that McClellan referred to titanic struggles with his enemies. "I am in a *battle* & must fight it out," he wrote on another occasion. My "bitter enemies...are making their last grand attack. I *must & will* defeat them."[1] Abraham Lincoln would have been startled by such bellicose language from McClellan, whom he once compared to "an auger too dull to take hold." McClellan, said the president, was a commander who "would not fight."[2]

Lincoln was right. McClellan's "bitter enemies" whom he had "crushed" in September 1862 were not Confederates but instead other generals in the Union army and high officials in the U.S. government— Generals John Pope and Irvin McDowell, who had been relieved of command and whose troops had been absorbed into McClellan's Army of the Potomac, and Secretary of War Edwin M. Stanton, who had wanted to cashier McClellan. If McClellan had exerted as much energy and determination in his battles against the enemy army as he did against these supposed enemies in his own army and government, the North might have won the war in 1862.

The strongest language McClellan used against Confederates was "those rascals," while he described his adversaries in the Union Congress, administration, and army as "heartless villains . . . wretches . . . incompetent knaves a most despicable set of men."[3] When Winfield Scott was still general in chief and McClellan's commanding officer in 1861, the thirty-four-year-old McClellan described him as "a dotard" and "a perfect imbecile." He privately ridiculed Lincoln in the fall of 1861 as "nothing more than a well meaning baboon . . . 'the *original gorilla.*'"[4] As for members of Lincoln's cabinet, Secretary of State William H. Seward was "a meddlesome, officious, incompetent little puppy," and Secretary of the Navy Gideon Welles was "weaker than a garrulous old woman."[5] McClellan reserved his greatest animosity for Stanton, who had been the general's confidant and supporter before he became secretary of war in January 1862 and lost faith in McClellan's competence and determination. McClellan made Stanton the scapegoat for the failure of his Peninsula Campaign in 1862. The secretary of war, he wrote his wife, was "the most depraved hypocrite & villain" he had ever known. If he "had lived in the time of the Saviour, Judas Iscariot would have remained a respected member of the fraternity of Apostles."[6]

McClellan certainly had powerful paranoid tendencies, but he did not make up this vision of "bitter enemies" out of whole cloth. His sharpest critics were Radical Republicans in Congress and the cabinet—especially the congressional Joint Committee on the Conduct of the War and Secretary of the Treasury Salmon P. Chase, as well as Stanton. All of them had once been McClellan backers but had become profoundly disillusioned. After the Army of the Potomac was driven back from Richmond in the Seven Days Battles, Senator Zachariah Chandler of Michigan, a leading member of the Joint Committee on the Conduct of the War, wrote privately that "McClellan is an imbecile if not a traitor. He has virtually lost the army of the Potomac" and "deserves to be shot."[7] After McClellan disobeyed orders to reinforce General Pope with the 6th and 2nd Corps at the Second Battle of Bull Run on August 29–30, 1862, Stanton wanted McClellan court-martialed, and Chase said he should be shot.[8]

How had matters come to such a pass by August 1862? To answer this question, we must go back to the last week of July 1861. Lincoln had called McClellan to Washington after the Union defeat at First Bull Run to become commander of the newly named Army of the Potomac. Fresh from commanding a small Union force whose victories in western Virginia helped put that Unionist region on the path to becoming the new state of West Virginia, McClellan received a hero's welcome in the capital. The press lionized him as a "young Napoleon"; the correspondent of the *Times* (London) described him as "the man on horseback" to save the country; the president of the U.S. Sanitary Commission said that "there is an indefinable air of success about him and something of the 'man of destiny.' "[9]

This adulation first surprised McClellan and then went to his head. The day after arriving in Washington, he wrote, "I find myself in a new & strange position here—Presdt, Cabinet, Genl Scott & all deferring to me—by some strange operation of magic I seem to have become *the* power of the land." Three days later he went to Capitol Hill and was "quite overwhelmed by the congratulations I received & the respect with which I was treated." Congress seemed willing to "give me my way in every thing." McClellan developed what can only be called a messiah complex during these first weeks in Washington. "God has placed a great work in my hands," he wrote. "I was called to it; my previous life seems to have been unwittingly directed to this great end."[10]

But God also seemed to place obstacles in McClellan's path. The first of them was General in Chief Winfield Scott. A hero of the War of 1812 and conqueror of Mexico in 1847, Scott was America's greatest soldier since George Washington. Old and infirm by 1861, however, he could work only a few hours each day, while the young Napoleon put in sixteen hours, organizing and training his new army. Tension and then conflict between the old and new military titans soon erupted. McClellan attended a cabinet meeting on his second day in Washington, to which Scott was not invited. McClellan bypassed Scott frequently and communicated directly with Lincoln and other cabinet members—including

Seward, even as the general was privately condemning the secretary of state as an incompetent and meddlesome puppy.

The action that most angered Scott was a memorandum from McClellan on August 8, 1861, sent to both Lincoln and Scott, that highlighted what turned out to be McClellan's main defect as a military commander—an alarmist tendency to inflate enemy strength and intentions. The Confederate army in his front, only twenty miles from Washington, McClellan insisted, had a hundred thousand men (their real numbers were about forty thousand), and reinforcements were passing through Knoxville to join them. Washington itself was in danger of attack by this huge force, McClellan told Scott (and Lincoln). "Our present army in this vicinity is entirely insufficient for the emergency," McClellan warned, so he advised Scott to order forward all troops scattered in other places within reach of Washington to meet this "imminent danger."[11]

Scott regarded this communication as an insult to his own authority and his management of the army. He also scoffed at McClellan's estimate of enemy numbers and his fears of an imminent attack. He called McClellan to his headquarters and apparently dressed him down. At the same time, Scott asked then–Secretary of War Simon Cameron to place him on the retired list—in effect submitting his resignation as general in chief.[12] Lincoln was upset by this contretemps between his two top commanders. He stepped into the quarrel between McClellan and the first of the young Napoleon's many "enemies"—a task that the beleaguered president would have to repeat many times in the next fifteen months. He persuaded Scott to stay on and persuaded McClellan to withdraw his offending letter. In what passed for an apology, McClellan promised to "abstain from any word or act that could give offense to General Scott or embarrass the President." He also offered his "most profound assurances of respect for General Scott and yourself."[13]

At this very time, however, McClellan was writing privately that the Confederate army in his front now numbered 150,000 men. "I am here in a terrible place," he fumed. "The enemy have 3 to 4 times my force.... Genl Scott is the most dangerous antagonist I have ... a perfect imbecile.... He will not comprehend the danger & is either a traitor or an incompetent.... The President is an idiot, the old General in his dotage—they cannot or will not see the true state of affairs."[14]

Although Lincoln had managed to defuse a blow-up between his two top generals, tensions continued to simmer for the next two months. McClellan persisted in leaving Scott out of the loop of his communications with the president and cabinet. During these months several Republican leaders in Congress, as well as broad segments of the Northern press, grew restless as McClellan continued to train his expanding army and to hold impressive reviews but did nothing to advance against the main Confederate army or to prevent the enemy from establishing batteries on the Potomac below Washington to blockade the river. McClellan declined to cooperate with the navy in an expedition to capture these batteries and end what had become by October 1861 a national humiliation. When Assistant Secretary of the Navy Gustavus V. Fox informed Lincoln of McClellan's failure to provide troops for this purpose, the president, according to Fox, "manifested more feeling and disappointment than I have seen him before exhibit."[15]

At about the same time, Senator Benjamin F. Wade, soon to become chairman of the Joint Committee on the Conduct of the War, wrote to his colleague Zachariah Chandler: "The present state of things must not be suffered to continue.... We have vast armies in the field maintained at prodigious and almost ruinous expense. Yet they are suffered to do nothing with the power in our hands to crush the rebellion.... We are in danger of having our army set into winter quarters with the capitol in a state of siege for another year."[16] McClellan met with the senators and managed to convince them that he wanted to advance but that Scott held him back. They went to Lincoln and pressed him to force Scott out. The president had Scott's earlier request for retirement on his desk; Scott renewed the request, citing continued deterioration of his health.[17]

McClellan was pulling every string he could to get himself appointed as Scott's successor. But the old general wanted that job to go to Henry

W. Halleck, author and translator of books on military strategy and history. Like McClellan, Halleck had resigned from the army in the 1850s to pursue a more rewarding civilian career. He returned to the army in August 1861 with a commission as major general. Scott hoped that Halleck could get to Washington from California in time for Lincoln to appoint him rather than McClellan as Scott's replacement. But it was not to be. On October 18, Lincoln persuaded the cabinet to accept Scott's request to retire. McClellan learned of this decision from one of his sources in the cabinet—probably Montgomery Blair, but perhaps Chase, a McClellan ally at this time. McClellan wrote to his wife on October 19: "It seems to be pretty well settled that I will be Comdr in Chf within a week. Genl Scott proposes to retire in favor of Halleck. The presdt and Cabinet have determined to accept his retirement, but not in favor of Halleck," who was at sea and would not arrive for another two or three weeks.[18]

On November 1 McClellan achieved his goal: Scott retired and McClellan became the youngest general in chief of U.S. armies in history—as well as field commander of the Army of the Potomac. Lincoln expressed some concern that "this vast increase in responsibilities...will entail a vast labor upon you." "I can do it all," McClellan replied.[19]

Having convinced Radical Republican senators—and perhaps Lincoln also—that it was only Scott's timidity that had kept him on a leash, McClellan now faced expectations that he would advance. But in conversations with the president he immediately began backtracking. In his mind the Confederate forces in northern Virginia now numbered 170,000 (three times their actual size). He reminded Lincoln of what had happened at Bull Run in July when the Union army fought a battle before it was trained and disciplined. The disastrous outcome of a reconnaisance in force toward Leesburg on October 21, when several Union regiments were ambushed at Ball's Bluff and Lincoln's friend Colonel Edward Baker was killed, lent legitimacy to McClellan's counsel of caution. "Don't let them hurry me," McClellan urged Lincoln.

"You shall have your own way in the matter," the president assured him. But he also warned the general that the pressure for the army to do *something* instead of dress parades and reviews was "a reality and should be taken into account. At the same time General you must not fight till you are ready."[20]

McClellan proved to have a tin ear about that ever-present "reality," which the president could not ignore. But the general heard loud and clear Lincoln's counsel not to fight until he was ready. The problem was that he was perpetually *almost* but never *quite* ready to move. The enemy always outnumbered him, and his own army was always lacking something. In response to Lincoln's request, the new general in chief prepared a memorandum stating that "winter is approaching so rapidly" that unless the Army of the Potomac could be increased from its current strength of 134,000 men to 208,000, the only alternative to taking the field "with forces greatly inferior" to the enemy was "to go into winter quarters."[21] Since Lincoln was well aware that the army could not be increased by that much before the end of the year, if ever, his shoulders must have slumped when he read these words. They slumped more as week after week of unusually mild and dry weather slipped by in November and December with no advance in Virginia and no military success anywhere except the capture of Port Royal Bay and the adjacent Sea Islands by the navy under Flag Officer Samuel Francis Du Pont.

Lincoln began dropping by McClellan's headquarters or his home near the White House almost daily to consult with him. McClellan grew to resent these visits as a waste of time or an unwanted form of pressure. More than once he hid himself away "to dodge all enemies in shape of 'browsing' presdt etc."[22] On November 13 Lincoln and Seward, along with the president's secretary John Hay, called unannounced on McClellan at home but learned that he was at a wedding. When the general returned an hour later, the porter told him that Lincoln was waiting to see him. McClellan said nothing and went upstairs to bed. The president and secretary of state waited another half hour before a servant deigned to tell them that the general was asleep.

Hay was furious at "this unparalleled insolence of epaulettes," but as they walked back to the White House Lincoln told him that it was "better at this time not to be making points of etiquette and personal dignity." Significantly, however, from then on Lincoln almost always summoned McClellan to his office when he wanted to talk with the general. After one such occasion four days later, McClellan wrote to his wife that at the White House "I found 'the *original gorilla*,' about as intelligent as ever. What a specimen to be at the head of our affairs!"[23]

About December 1, despairing of any initiative by McClellan, Lincoln drafted a proposal for part of the army to make a feint toward Centreville to hold the enemy in place while two other columns moved south along the Potomac—one by road and the other by water—to turn the Confederate flank and move up the Occoquan Valley to Brentsville southwest of Manassas. On paper, at least, this plan reflected what Lincoln had learned from his recent reading of works on military history and strategy—including one of Halleck's books. Lincoln's plan would avoid a frontal attack on Confederate defenses at Centreville and Manassas, which McClellan claimed were impregnable. The general rejected the plan, however, because he said that the enemy's greatly superior numbers would enable him to detach mobile reserves to counterattack and defeat the flanking force.[24]

Meanwhile the confrontation with Britain over the seizure of James Mason and John Slidell from the British ship *Trent* caused a diplomatic crisis and dried up the sale of bonds to finance the war. Just before Christmas, McClellan fell sick with typhoid fever. Northern morale and Lincoln's own mood plunged to a low point in the first days of the New Year. On January 10 the president dropped in at the office of Quartermaster General Montgomery C. Meigs. "General, what shall I do?" asked Lincoln. "The people are impatient; Chase has no money...the General of the Army has typhoid fever. The bottom is out of the tub. What shall I do?" Meigs advised him to assert his prerogative as commander in chief and set in motion a campaign without regard to McClellan, who might not be able to resume duty for weeks.[25]

This counsel echoed similar advice from Attorney General Edward Bates. Except for Lincoln's insistence the previous June that Scott order the army forward toward Manassas—against Scott's judgment—Lincoln had deferred to Scott and then to McClellan on military strategy. The unhappy outcome of the Manassas campaign had sobered the president. With no military training or experience, Lincoln recognized the need to rely on professionals. But the professionals had disappointed him—and now the chief disappointment was ill. Having begun a cram course of reading in military strategy, Lincoln was open to Bates's urging that, "being 'Commander in chief' by law, he *must* command" rather than continue "this injurious deference to his subordinates."[26]

So Lincoln walked out of Meigs's office on January 10 and summoned to his own office two of the Army of the Potomac's division commanders, Brigadier Generals Irvin McDowell and William B. Franklin. The army's senior division commander, McDowell was also the choice of the Joint Committee on the Conduct of the War to replace McClellan. Franklin was one of McClellan's personal friends and protégés. These two seemed an unpromising combination to carry out Lincoln's insistence on action. Nevertheless, the president figuratively knocked their heads together at the meeting on January 10. According to McDowell's notes, Lincoln said that "if General McClellan did not want to use the army, he would like to *borrow* it."[27] Lincoln ordered the two generals to come up with a plan and to meet the next day with him and Meigs (who would be responsible for logistics) plus several cabinet members.

They came up with two plans. McDowell formulated a short-range flanking movement via the Occoquan River similar to Lincoln's earlier proposal. Franklin sketched out a deep flanking movement all the way down the Chesapeake Bay to Fort Monroe to operate against Richmond via the peninsula between the York and James Rivers. McClellan had been mulling a similar operation for some time, and Franklin was privy to it—while McDowell and the president obviously were not. Most of those at the January 11 meeting favored McDowell's plan. McClellan got wind of this meeting, probably from Chase, and rose from his sickbed to meet with the same group on the thirteenth. He refused to reveal his plan to them, stating that he feared a leak. But when he assured Lincoln that he actually *had* a plan and a timetable to carry it out, the president once again deferred to him and adjourned the meeting.[28]

Five days later, Lincoln's confidant Senator Orville H. Browning of Illinois wrote in his diary that the president had "expressed great confidence" in McClellan. But when two more weeks went by and matters continued "All Quiet Along the Potomac," as a popular song had it, Lincoln's confidence waned. On January 31 he issued Special Order No. 1, specifying that the Army of the Potomac must move against the enemy at Centreville and Manassas by February 22.[29] As intended, this order forced McClellan for the first time to reveal his plans in detail. Instead of moving via the Occoquan against Manassas, he proposed to take the army a hundred miles farther by water down the Potomac and the Chesapeake Bay and up the Rappahannock River to Urbana, Virginia. From there he would have a secure supply base to launch a fifty-mile campaign to Richmond. This move, he said, would force the Confederates to evacuate Manassas and retreat south to defend Richmond, which McClellan predicted he might reach before the enemy could get there.[30]

Lincoln was concerned that the enemy instead might attack Washington before McClellan got anywhere near Richmond. But despite his reservations, the president again deferred to the general's supposedly superior professional qualifications and reluctantly approved McClellan's plan. Assembling the shipping and other logistical resources for McClellan's campaign would take several weeks. That was one of the reasons why Lincoln had questioned it. Meanwhile other Union forces won a string of victories in Tennessee, North Carolina, Florida, and Arkansas that made the Army of the Potomac's continuing inactivity seemingly more humiliating by comparison.

Ugly rumors began to circulate in Republican circles that McClellan, a Democrat, did not really want to crush the rebellion. The general had made little secret of his dislike of abolitionists and Radical Republicans.

His closest political associates—including his favorite division commanders, Fitz John Porter and William B. Franklin—were Democrats
who wanted to restore the Union on the basis of something like the Crittenden Compromise that would preserve slavery and the political power
of Southern Democrats. Some of the generals serving in the Confederate
army confronting McClellan "were once my most intimate friends," he
acknowledged (privately) in November 1861. He did not want to fight the
kind of war the Radicals were beginning to demand—a war to destroy
slavery and the planter class and to give the restored Union a new birth of
freedom. McClellan wrote in November 1861 to an influential Democratic
friend: "Help me dodge the nigger....*I* am fighting to preserve the integ-
rity of the Union....To gain that end we cannot afford to raise up the
negro question."[31]

Radical Republican senators Benjamin Wade and Zachariah
Chandler had played a significant role in boosting McClellan to the
position of general in chief the previous November. Four months had
passed, and in their view McClellan had betrayed them by doing
nothing. They were suspicious of his politics and perhaps half believed rumors of his disloyalty, but the main reason for their conversion from supporters of McClellan to his most vocal critics was the
general's military inactivity. On March 3, 1862, Lincoln met with members of the Joint Committee on the Conduct of the War. They gave the
president an earful of complaints about McClellan. Committee chairman
Ben Wade urged Lincoln to remove him from command. If he did so,
Lincoln asked, who should replace him? "Why, anybody!" Wade
reportedly responded. "Wade," Lincoln supposedly said, "anybody
will do for you, but not for me. I must have somebody."[32]

Despite Lincoln's deflection of Wade, the president was in fact
considering the removal of McClellan. Four weeks had gone by since
Lincoln had lukewarmly approved the general's Urbana plan. The army
was still in winter quarters. The day after his meeting with the committee, Lincoln told a Pennsylvania congressman that unless McClellan
moved soon he would be replaced.[33] Three days later Lincoln summoned

McClellan to the White House and told him with unprecedented bluntness that his tenure was short unless he got moving. The president also hinted—perhaps stated openly—that some influential men believed that the real purpose of his Urbana plan was to leave Washington uncovered so the enemy could capture it. McClellan was outraged, but Lincoln assured the general that he did not believe a word of the rumors.

With his tin ear for the political realities of both his and the president's positions, McClellan said that he would resolve any doubts about his Urbana plan by submitting it to a vote of his eleven division commanders and the army's chief engineer officer. They voted 8–4 in favor of the plan—not surprising, perhaps, since most of those eight owed their positions to McClellan's sponsorship. Three of the four division commanders with the greatest seniority voted against the plan.[34] Next day Lincoln issued an order organizing the Army of the Potomac into four corps and appointed the four senior generals—including the three who voted against the plan—as corps commanders. If McClellan failed to get the message, Lincoln added more clarity three days later by relieving McClellan from duty as general in chief because, as commander of an army about to take the field, he could no longer "do it all." For the time being, Lincoln and the new secretary of war, Stanton, would do the job of general in chief.[35]

On the very day that a majority of generals voted for the Urbana plan, Confederate general Joseph E. Johnston made it irrelevant by withdrawing from the Centreville-Manassas line to Culpeper south of the Rappahannock River, where he was in a position to block McClellan's intention to move toward Richmond. The Union commander immediately led the Army of the Potomac on what he called a "practice march" to the abandoned Confederate works. Northern journalists who accompanied the army discovered that the Confederate defenses were by no means as formidable as McClellan had claimed, and the camps had room for only about half as many men as McClellan had estimated. And several of the heavy artillery redoubts mounted logs painted black rather than large-caliber cannons. These "Quaker guns" caused McClellan much embarrassment. Already doubtful of his estimates of enemy numbers and strength, Lincoln and Stanton never again gave credence to the general's perpetual complaints of inferior numbers.

Johnston's retreat compelled McClellan to shift his proposed flanking movement all the way to Fort Monroe at the tip of the Virginia Peninsula. This time all four corps commanders voted for the plan, and Lincoln reluctantly approved—provided McClellan left behind sufficient force to protect Washington. The general promised to do so but failed to consult with Lincoln about what constituted a sufficient force. After he departed for the Peninsula, McClellan sent back a memorandum summarizing the units he had left to defend the capital. Lincoln and Stanton soon discovered that the number of these troops was considerably less than McClellan had stated, so the president held back McDowell's corps. Thus began a prolonged and increasingly bitter controversy in which McClellan blamed the government for failing to support his campaign against an enemy whose numbers he consistently inflated by a factor of two or three.

The details of the Peninsula Campaign are beyond the scope of this essay. McClellan yielded the initiative to the enemy, especially after Robert E. Lee became commander of the Army of Northern Virginia on June 1. McClellan's list of "enemies" in his own government and in the Northern press grew longer as he blamed others but never himself for the failure of the Peninsula Campaign. In the middle of the Seven Days Battles, on June 28, he sent a telegram to Stanton that concluded with these words: "I have lost this battle because my force was too small.... [The Government] has not sustained this army.... If I save this army now, I tell you plainly that I owe no thanks to you or to any other persons in Washington. You have done your best to sacrifice this army."[36]

Shocked by the two concluding sentences, the head of the War Department telegraph office recopied the dispatch without them before sending it on to Stanton, so he and Lincoln never saw the sentences. Nevertheless, they were well aware that Stanton had become McClellan's chief whipping boy and that some of that hostility spilled over to the president himself. After Lincoln had given his consent to the Peninsula plan in March, McClellan had written to a prominent Democrat: "The President is all right—he is my strongest friend." But now, three months later, he wrote to his wife that "Honest A[be] has again fallen into the hands of my enemies."[37]

After McClellan retreated to the James River in the Seven Days Battles, Lincoln called Henry W. Halleck from the West to become general in chief. McClellan added Halleck to his list of enemies when he advised Lincoln to withdraw the Army of the Potomac from the Peninsula to reinforce Major General John Pope's newly created Army of Virginia southwest of Washington. Pope also joined the list. McClellan predicted that Pope would be "badly thrashed" by Lee. "Very badly whipped he will be & ought to be—such a villain as he is ought to bring defeat upon any cause that employs him."[38] These startling sentiments help explain why McClellan resisted repeated orders from Halleck to rush the 6th and 2nd Corps of the Army of the Potomac to Pope's aid during the Second Battle of Bull Run. Lincoln was shocked by McClellan's actions. He "wanted Pope defeated," the president told his private secretary.[39]

But through thick and thin, soldiers in the Army of the Potomac remained fiercely loyal to McClellan. Even those in the Army of Virginia preferred him to Pope. When Major General Ambrose E. Burnside turned down Lincoln's offer of command of the Army of the Potomac, Lincoln felt he had no choice but to retain McClellan in command of that army and to merge the Army of Virginia into it. The president was painfully aware that both armies were "utterly demoralized." McClellan was the only man who could "reorganize the army and bring it out of chaos," Lincoln said. He "has the army with him . . . [and] we must use the tools we have. There is no man . . . who can . . . lick these troops of ours into shape as well as he. . . . If he can't fight himself, he excels in making others ready to fight."[40]

Events of the next two months confirmed Lincoln's judgment. As the Army of Northern Virginia invaded Maryland, McClellan did reorganize the two armies into one and lick them into shape. He also prepared them to fight, which they did at South Mountain and Antietam on September 14 and 17. When McClellan telegraphed an exaggerated report of his victory at South Mountain, Lincoln wired back congratulations and added: "Destroy the rebel army, if possible."[41] When the president learned that McClellan had held back his reserves at Antietam instead of exploiting potential break-throughs because he feared a counterattack by an enemy whose numbers he inflated by a factor of three, and that he had not renewed the attack on September 18 but instead let the enemy escape across the river, Lincoln again evinced disappointment.

The president visited the army during the first four days of October to pump some energy and aggressiveness into McClellan. When Lincoln returned to Washington, he had Halleck send an order to McClellan that any other general would have considered peremptory: "Cross the Potomac and give battle to the enemy....Your army must move now while the roads are good." McClellan stayed north of the Potomac for almost three more weeks. In a letter whose sentiments surely echoed Lincoln's, Halleck expressed enormous frustration: "I am sick, tired, and disgusted," he wrote. "There is an immobility here that exceeds all that any man can conceive of. It requires the lever of Archimedes to move this inert mass."[42]

Lincoln finally gave up on "tardy George." On November 7 he removed him from command and appointed a reluctant Ambrose Burnside to replace him. Lincoln explained his decision to John Hay: "I peremptorily ordered him to advance....He kept delaying on little pretexts of wanting this and that. I began to fear he was playing false—that he did not want to hurt the enemy. I saw how he could intercept the enemy on the way to Richmond. I determined to make that the test. If he let them get away I would remove him. He did so & I relieved him."[43]

Seventeen months and three commanders of the Army of the Potomac later, Lieutenant General Ulysses S. Grant, who had also learned that it seemed to require the lever of Archimedes to move that army, asked cavalry commander James H. Wilson: "What's wrong with this army?"[44] Wilson did not have any good answers. If Grant had asked Lincoln this question, the president might accurately have replied that McClellan had created the army in his own image, and even Grant would find it a hard job to overcome that legacy.[45]

CHAPTER 11

Lincoln's Legacy for Our Time

When Abraham Lincoln breathed his last at 7:22 A.M. on April 15, 1865, Secretary of War Edwin M. Stanton intoned: "Now he belongs to the ages." Stanton's remark was more prescient than he knew, for Lincoln's image and legacy became the possessions not only of future ages but also of people of other nations. On the centenary of Lincoln's birth in 1909, Leo Tolstoy described him as "a Christ in miniature, a saint of humanity." An Islamic leader projected a more militant image of Lincoln, declaring that America's sixteenth president "spoke with a voice of thunder...and his deeds were as strong as the rock." When Jacqueline Kennedy lived in the White House, she sought comfort in the Lincoln Room in times of trouble. "The kind of peace I felt in that room," she recalled, "was what you feel when going into a church. I used to feel his strength, I'd sort of be talking to him."[1]

Lincoln could not have anticipated the reverence that millions would feel for him in future ages. But he *was* intensely aware, as he told Congress in December 1861 when America was engulfed in a tragic civil war, that this struggle to preserve the Union "is not altogether for today—it is for a vast future also."[2] Lincoln had a profound sense of history. He did not acquire it from formal education. He did not study history in college or high school; indeed, he did not study it in school at all, for he had less than a year of formal schooling, which included no history courses. The only work of history that Lincoln seems to have read as a boy was "Parson" Weems's famous filiopietistic biography of George Washington, with its apocryphal story of the hatchet and cherry tree.

That book nonetheless made a lasting impression on Lincoln. Forty years after he first read it, President-elect Lincoln addressed the New Jersey legislature in Trenton, near the spot where Washington's ragged troops had won the victory the day after Christmas 1776 that saved the American Revolution from collapse. Lincoln told the legislators: "I remember all the accounts" in Weems's book "of the battle-fields and struggles for the liberty of the country, and none fixed themselves upon my imagination so deeply as the struggle here at Trenton.... The crossing of the river; the contest with the Hessians; the great hardships endured at that time, all fixed themselves on my memory more than any single revolutionary event....I recollect thinking then, boy even though I was, that there must have been something more than common that those men struggled for."[3]

These words were not merely an exercise in nostalgia. As always, Lincoln invoked the past for a purpose. On this occasion he shifted from the Revolution to the present and future. Prospects for the United States in that present and future were dark. The country of which Lincoln would become president eleven days later was no longer the United States but the *dis*-United States. Seven slave states, fearing for the future of their "peculiar institution" in a nation governed by the new antislavery Republican Party, had seceded from the Union in response to Lincoln's election. Several more states were threatening to withdraw. Even as Lincoln spoke in Trenton, delegates from those first seven states were meeting in Montgomery, Alabama, to form the independent nation of the Confederate States of America. Civil war, or a permanent division of the country with its dire precedent for further divisions, or both, loomed on the horizon. Thus, it is not surprising that when Lincoln shifted from his discussion of the Revolution to the present, he began: "I am exceedingly anxious" that what those men fought for, "that something even more than National Independence;

that something that held out a great promise to all the people of the world [for] all time to come; I am exceedingly anxious that this Union, the Constitution, and the liberties of the people shall be perpetuated in accordance with the original idea for which that struggle was made."[4]

The next day, Washington's Birthday, Lincoln spoke at Independence Hall in Philadelphia, where he spelled out more fully what he believed was at stake both in the Revolution and in the crisis of 1861. "I have often inquired of myself," said Lincoln, "what great principle or idea it was that kept this [Union] so long together. It was not the mere matter of the separation of the colonies from the motherland, but that sentiment in the Declaration [of Independence] which gave liberty, not alone to the people of this country, but hope to the world for all future time." At this point in Lincoln's remarks, the newspaper text indicated "Great applause" from the audience, which included the city council and leading citizens of Philadelphia. Lincoln told them: "I have never had a feeling politically that did not spring from the sentiments embodied in the Declaration of Independence" ("Great cheering," according to the press). The ringing phrases that "all men are created equal, that they are endowed by their Creator with certain unalienable Rights, that among these are Life, Liberty, and the pursuit of Happiness," said Lincoln in 1861, gave not only "promise" to Americans but also "hope to the world" that "in due time the weights should be lifted from the shoulders of all men, and that *all* should have an equal chance. (Cheers.)"[5]

The sincerity of some in the audience who cheered Lincoln's egalitarian sentiments might be questioned. But Lincoln was quite sincere in his endorsement of them. He was, of course, painfully aware that many Americans enjoyed neither liberty nor equality. Four million were slaves, making the United States—the self-professed beacon of liberty to oppressed masses everywhere—the largest slaveholding country in the world. Lincoln grasped this nettle. "I hate...the monstrous injustice of slavery," he had said in his famous Peoria speech of 1854. "I hate it because it deprives our republican example of its just influence in the world—enables of the enemies of free institutions, with plausibility, to taunt us as hypocrites."[6]

As for equality, said Lincoln on another occasion, the author of the Declaration of Independence and the Founding Fathers who signed it clearly "did not intend to declare all men equal *in all respects*." They did not even "mean to assert the obvious untruth" that all men in 1776 were equal in rights and opportunities. Rather, "they meant to set up a standard maxim for free society, which should be . . . constantly looked to, constantly labored for, and even though never perfectly attained, constantly approximated, and thereby constantly spreading and deepening its influence, and augmenting the happiness and value of life to all people of all colors everywhere."[7]

Like Thomas Jefferson, Lincoln asserted a universality and timelessness for the principles of liberty, equal rights, and equal opportunity on which the nation was founded. And Lincoln acknowledged his intellectual debt to Jefferson—not Jefferson the slaveholder, not Jefferson the author of the Kentucky Resolutions of 1799 asserting the superiority of state over federal sovereignty, not even Jefferson the president, but Jefferson the philosopher of liberty, author of the Northwest Ordinance that kept slavery out of future states comprising 160,000 square miles at a time when most existing states of the Union still had slavery, and the Jefferson who, though he owned slaves, said of the institution that "he trembled for his country when he remembered that God was just." This was the Jefferson, said Lincoln in 1859, who "in the concrete pressure of a struggle for national independence by a single people had the coolness, forecast, and capacity to introduce into a merely revolutionary document"—the Declaration of Independence—"an abstract truth, applicable to all men and all times."[8]

Universal and timeless this truth may be, but in Jefferson's time it remained mostly as Lincoln described it—abstract. Fate decreed that it fell to Lincoln, not Jefferson, to give substance and meaning to what Jefferson had called a self-evident truth. Ironically, it was the slaveholders who provided Lincoln with the opportunity to do so, for by taking their states out of the Union they set in train a progression of events that destroyed the very social and political order founded on slavery that they had seceded to preserve.

Secession transformed the main issue before the country from slavery to disunion. When Lincoln became president, the question he confronted was not what to do about slavery but what to do about secession. On this question, Lincoln did not hesitate. Branding secession as "the essence of anarchy," he insisted in 1861 that "the central idea pervading this struggle is the necessity that is upon us, of proving that popular government is not an absurdity. We must settle this question now, whether in a free government the minority have the right to break up the government whenever they choose. If we fail it will go far to prove the incapability of the people to govern themselves."[9]

Lincoln had come a long way in his understanding of history since his boyhood reading of Weems's biography of Washington. Like other thoughtful Americans, he was acutely aware of the unhappy fate of most republics in the past. The United States stood almost alone in the mid-nineteenth century as a democratic republic in a world bestrode by kings, queens, emperors, czars, petty dictators, and theories of aristocracy. Some Americans alive at midcentury had seen two French republics rise and fall. The hopes of 1848 for the triumph of popular government in Europe had been shattered by the counterrevolutions that brought a conservative reaction in the Old World. Would the American experiment in government of, by, and for the people also be swept into the dustbin of history?

Not if Lincoln could help it. "Our popular government has often been called an experiment," he told a special session of Congress that met on July 4, 1861. "Two points in it, our people have already settled— the successful *establishing*, and the successful *administering* of it. One still remains—its successful *maintenance* against a formidable internal attempt to overthrow it." If that attempt succeeded, said Lincoln, the forces of reaction in Europe would smile in smug satisfaction at this proof that the upstart republic launched in 1776 could not last.[10]

Many in the North shared Lincoln's conviction that democracy was on trial in this war. "We must fight," proclaimed an Indianapolis newspaper two weeks after Confederate guns opened fire on Fort Sumter. "We must fight because we *must*. The National Government has been assailed. The Nation has been defied. If either can be done with impunity neither Nation nor Government is worth a cent.... War is self preservation, if our form of Government is worth preserving. If monarchy would be better, it might be wise to quit fighting, admit that a Republic is too weak to take care of itself, and invite some deposed Duke or Prince of Europe to come over here and rule us. But otherwise, *we must fight.*"[11]

The outbreak of war brought hundreds of thousands of Northern men to recruiting offices. A good many of them expressed a similar sense of democratic mission as a motive for fighting. "I do feel that the liberty of the world is placed in our hands to defend," wrote a Massachusetts soldier to his wife in 1862, "and if we are overcome then farewell to freedom." In 1863, on the second anniversary of his enlistment, an Ohio private wrote in his diary that he had not expected the war to last so long, but no matter how much longer it took, it must be carried on "for the great principles of liberty and government at stake, for should we fail, the onward march of Liberty in the Old World will be retarded at least a century, and Monarchs, Kings, and Aristocrats will be more powerful against their subjects than ever."[12]

Some foreign-born soldiers appreciated the international impact of the war more intensely than native-born men who took their political rights for granted. A young British immigrant in Philadelphia wrote to his father back in England explaining why he had enlisted in the Union army. "If the Unionists let the South secede," he wrote, "the West might want to separate next Presidential Election.... [O]thers might want to follow and this country would be as bad as the German states." Another English-born soldier, a forty-year-old corporal in an Ohio regiment, wrote to his wife in 1864, explaining why he had decided to reenlist for a second three-year hitch. "If I do get hurt I want you to remember that it will be not only for my Country and my Children but for Liberty all over the World that I risked my life, for if Liberty should be crushed here, what hope would there be for the cause of Human Progress anywhere else?" An Irish-born carpenter, a private in the 28th Massachusetts Infantry of the famous Irish Brigade, rebuked both his wife in Boston and his father-in-law back in Ireland for questioning his judgment in risking his life for the Union. "This is the first test of a modern free government in the act of sustaining itself against internal enemys," he wrote almost in echo of Lincoln. "If it fails then the hopes of millions fall and the designs and wishes of all tyrants will succeed the old cry will be sent forth from the aristocrats of Europe that such is the common lot of all republics."[13] Both this Irish-born private and the English-born Ohio corporal were killed in action in 1864.

The American sense of mission invoked by Lincoln and by these soldiers—the idea that the American experiment in democracy was a beacon of liberty for oppressed people everywhere—is as old as the Mayflower Compact and as new as American victory in the Cold War. In our own time this sentiment sometimes comes across as self-righteous posturing that inspires more resentment than admiration abroad. The same was true in Lincoln's time, when the resentment was expressed mainly by upper-class conservatives, especially in Britain. But many spokesmen for the middle and working classes in Europe echoed the most chauvinistic Yankees. During the debate that produced the British Reform Act of 1832, the London Working Men's Association pronounced "the Republic of America" to be a "beacon of freedom for all mankind," while a British newspaper named the *Poor Man's Guardian* pointed to American institutions as "the best precedent and guide to the oppressed and enslaved people of England in their struggle for the RIGHT OF REPRESENTATION FOR EVERY MAN."[14]

In the preface to the twelfth edition of his *Democracy in America*, written during the heady days of the 1848 democratic uprisings in

Europe, Alexis de Tocqueville urged the leaders of France's newly created Second Republic to study American institutions as a guide to the "approaching irresistible and universal spread of democracy throughout the world." When instead of democracy France got the Second Empire under Napoleon III, the republican opposition to his regime looked to the United States for inspiration. "Many of the suggested reforms," wrote the historian of the French opposition, "would have remained utopic had it not been for the demonstrable existence of the United States and its republican institutions." The existence of the United States remained a thorn in the side of European reactionaries, according to a British radical newspaper, which stated in 1856 that "to the oppressors of Europe, especially those of England," the United States was "a constant terror, and an everlasting menace," because it stood as "a practical and triumphant refutation of the lying and servile sophists who maintain that without kings and aristocrats, civilized communities cannot exist."[15]

Once the war broke out, some European monarchists and conservatives did indeed make no secret of their hope that the Union would fall into the dustbin of history. The powerful *Times* of London considered the likely downfall of "the American colossus" a good "riddance of a nightmare.... Excepting a few gentlemen of republican tendencies, we all expect, we nearly all wish, success to the Confederate cause." The Earl of Shrewsbury expressed his cheerful belief "that the dissolution of the Union is inevitable, and that men before me will live to see an aristocracy established in America."[16] In Spain the royalist journal *Pensamiento Español* found it scarcely surprising that Americans were butchering each other, for the United States, it declared editorially, "was populated by the dregs of all the nations of the world.... Such is the real history of the one and only state in the world which has succeeded in constituting itself according to the flaming theories of democracy. The example is too horrible to stir any desire for emulation." The minister to the United States from Czar Alexander II echoed this opinion in 1863. "The republican form of government, so much talked about by the Europeans and so much praised by the Americans, is breaking down," he wrote. "What can be expected from a country where men of humble origin are elevated to the highest positions?" He meant Lincoln, of course. "This is democracy in practice, the democracy that European theorists rave about. If they could only see it at work they would cease their agitation and thank God for the government which they are enjoying."[17]

French republicans, some of them in exile, supported the North as "defenders of right and humanity." In England, John Stuart Mill expressed the conviction that the American Civil War was "destined to be a turning point, for good and evil, in the course of human affairs." Confederate success, said Mills, "would be a victory for the powers of evil which would give courage to the enemies of progress and damp the spirits of its friends all over the civilized world."[18]

Clearly, opinion in Europe supported Lincoln's contention that the very survival of democracy was at stake in the Civil War. But in the first year and a half of the war, the problem of slavery muddied the clarity of this issue. The Confederacy was a slave society, which should have strengthened the Union's image abroad as the champion of liberty and equal rights. As Lincoln put it in a private conversation in January 1862: "I cannot imagine that any European power would dare to recognize and aid the Southern Confederacy if it became clear that the Confederacy stands for slavery and the Union for freedom." The problem was, at that time the Union did not yet stand for the freedom of slaves. Constitutional constraints plus Lincoln's need to keep Northern Democrats and the border slave states in his war coalition inhibited efforts to make it a war against slavery. This restraint puzzled and alienated many potential European friends of the Union cause. An English observer asked in September 1861: Since "the North does not proclaim abolition and never pretended to fight for anti-slavery," how "can we be fairly called upon to sympathize so warmly with the Federal cause?"[19]

Lincoln recognized the validity of this question. In September 1862 he agreed with a delegation of antislavery clergymen that "emancipation would help us in Europe, and convince them that we are incited by something more than ambition." When he said this, Lincoln had made up his mind to issue an emancipation proclamation. The balance of political forces in the North and military forces on the battlefield had shifted just enough to give this decision the impetus of public support. Basing his action on the power of the commander in chief to seize enemy property being used to wage war against the United States— slaves were property and their labor was essential to the Confederate war economy—Lincoln issued a preliminary Emancipation Proclamation in September 1862 and the final one on January 1, 1863, justifying it as both a "military necessity" and an "act of justice."[20]

The Emancipation Proclamation not only laid the groundwork for the total abolition of slavery in the United States, which was accomplished by the Thirteenth Amendment to the Constitution in 1865. It also emancipated Lincoln from the contradiction of fighting a war for democratic liberty without fighting a war against slavery. Emancipation deepened Lincoln's sense of history. As he signed the Proclamation on that New Year's Day in 1863, he said to colleagues who gathered to witness this historic occasion: "I never, in my life, felt more certain that I was doing right than I do in signing this paper.... If my name ever goes into history it will be for this act, and my whole soul is in it."[21]

Lincoln here connected the act of emancipation with the future, as he had earlier connected the war for the Union with a past that had given Lincoln's generation the legacy of a united country. Just as the sacrifices of those who had fought for independence and nationhood in 1776 inspired Lincoln and the people he led, their sacrifices in the Civil War would leave a legacy of freedom and democracy to future generations. Lincoln sent his second annual message to Congress in December 1862, just before he issued the final Emancipation Proclamation. On this occasion he defined the war's meaning by linking past, present, and future in a passage of eloquence and power. "Fellow-citizens, we cannot escape history," he said. "We of this Congress and this administration, will be remembered in spite of ourselves.... The fiery trial through which we pass, will light us down, in honor or dishonor, to the latest generation.... We shall nobly save, or meanly lose, the last best, hope of earth.... The dogmas of the quiet past, are inadequate to the stormy present....In *giving* freedom to the *slave*, we *assure* freedom to the *free*....We must disenthrall ourselves, and then we shall save our country."[22]

Lincoln surpassed even the eloquence of this passage a year later in the prose poem of 272 words that we know as the Gettysburg Address. In this elegy for Union soldiers killed at the Battle of Gettysburg, Lincoln wove together past, present, and future with two other sets of three images each: continent, nation, battlefield; and birth, death, rebirth. The Gettysburg Address is so familiar that, like other things we can recite from memory, its meaning sometimes loses its import. At the risk of destroying the speech's poetic qualities, let us disaggregate these parallel images of past, present, future; continent, nation, battlefield; and birth, death, rebirth. To do this will underscore the meaning of the Civil War not only for Lincoln's time but also for generations into the future.

Four score and seven years in the *past*, said Lincoln, our fathers *brought forth* on this *continent* a *nation* conceived in liberty. *Today*, he continued, our generation faces a great test of whether a nation so conceived can survive. In dedicating the cemetery on this *battlefield*, the living must take inspiration to finish the task that those who lie buried here "so nobly advanced" by giving their "last full measure of devotion." Life and *death* in this passage have a paradoxical relationship: men died that the nation might live, yet the old Union also died, and with it would die the institution of slavery. After these deaths the nation must have a "*new birth* of freedom" so that government of, by, and for the people that our fathers conceived and brought forth in the *past* "shall not perish from the earth" but live into the *future*.

Although Lincoln gave this address at the dedication of a cemetery, its rhetoric was secular. As the war went on, however, Lincoln's efforts to come to grips with the mounting toll of death, destruction, and suffering became more infused with religious inquiry. Perhaps God was punishing Americans with "this mighty scourge of war" for some great sin. By the time of his inauguration for a second term, Lincoln believed that he had identified that sin. If God willed that the war continue "until all the wealth piled by the bond-man's two hundred and fifty years of unrequited toil shall be sunk, and until every drop of blood drawn with the lash, shall be paid by another drawn with the sword, as was said three thousand years ago, so still it must be said 'the judgments of the Lord, are true and righteous altogether.' "[23]

The war lasted only another few weeks after Lincoln's second inauguration. In the twenty-first century, however, we may well wonder if we are still paying for the blood drawn with the lash of slavery. But the impact abroad of Union victory was almost immediate. In Britain, a disgruntled Tory member of Parliament expressed disappointment that the Union had not broken in "two or perhaps more fragments," for he considered the United States "a menace to the whole civilized world." A Tory colleague described this menace as "the beginning of an Americanizing process in England. The new Democratic ideas are gradually to find embodiment." Indeed they were. In 1865 a liberal political economist at University College in London, Edward Beesly, who wanted the expansion of voting rights in Britain, pointed out the moral of Union victory across the Atlantic. "Our opponents told us that Republicanism was on trial" in the American Civil War, said Beesly. "They told us that it was forever discredited in England. Well, we accepted the challenge. We staked our hopes boldly on the result.... Under a strain such as no aristocracy, no monarchy, no empire could have supported, Republican institutions have stood firm. It is we, now, who call upon the privileged classes to mark the result.... A vast impetus has been given to Republican sentiments in England."[24]

Queen Victoria's throne was safe. But a two-year debate in Parliament, in which the American example figured prominently, led to enactment of the Reform Bill of 1867, which nearly doubled the eligible electorate and enfranchised a large part of the British working class for the first time. With this act, the world's most powerful nation took a long stride toward democracy. What might have happened to the Reform Bill if the North had lost the Civil War, thereby confounding liberals and confirming Tory opinions of democracy, is impossible to say.

The end of slavery in the re-United States sounded the death knell of the institution in Brazil and Cuba, the only other places in the Western Hemisphere where it still existed. Commending the Brazilian government's first steps toward the abolition of slavery in 1871, an abolitionist in that country was glad, as he put it, "to see Brazil receive so quickly the moral of the Civil War in the United States."[25]

Even without Northern victory in the war, slavery in the United States, Brazil, and Cuba would have been unlikely to survive into the next millennium. But it might have survived into the next century. And without the Fourteenth and Fifteenth Amendments to the U.S. Constitution, which, like the Thirteenth, were a direct consequence of the war and which granted equal civil and political rights to African Americans, the United States might have developed into even more of an apartheid society in the twentieth century than it did.

After decades in which those constitutional amendments slumbered in a near coma, they have finally become living realities in the United States of our own time. Several years ago the Huntington Library sponsored an essay contest about Lincoln for high school students in connection with a major Lincoln exhibit. One of the finalists was a seventeen-year-old girl from Texas, whose forebears had immigrated to the United States from India. She wrote that "if the United States was not in existence today, I would not have the opportunity to excel in life and education. The Union was preserved, not only for the people yesterday, but also for the lives of today."[26]

Lincoln would surely have applauded this statement. In 1861 he said that the struggle for the Union involved not only "the fate of these United States" but also that of "the whole family of man."[27] It was a struggle "not altogether for today" but "for a vast future also." We are living in that vast future. Lincoln's words resonate in the twenty-first century with as much relevance as they did more than seven score years ago.

CHAPTER 12

War and Peace in the Post–Civil War South

I n his formal acceptance of the Republican presidential nomination in 1868, General Ulysses S. Grant concluded with four words that struck a deep chord with voters: "Let us have peace."[1] For more than twenty years the country had been wracked by conflict over slavery and its aftermath. Historians have described the conflict in Vietnam as America's longest war. But, arguably, the nineteenth-century decades of sectional strife punctuated by a four-year conflict Americans call the Civil War truly represented the nation's longest war. It was certainly its most intense and violent war. In a country with less than one-sixth of the population it contained a century later, the number of American soldier deaths (including Confederates) in the Civil War was thirteen times greater than those in Vietnam. And to this total of 750,000 Civil War dead, one must add hundreds more in the Kansas wars of the 1850s that anticipated the war of 1861–65 and the thousands of deaths in the paramilitary clashes in the South during Reconstruction. The Civil War illustrated the famous aphorism of the Prussian military theorist Carl von Clausewitz that war is the continuation of politics by other means. In 1865 Americans would discover what might be described as a corollary to Clausewitz: Postwar reconstruction was a continuation of war by other (but distressingly similar) means.

Grant's plea for peace in 1868 resonated with such meaning because the country had not known real peace since the outbreak of war with Mexico in 1846. During congressional debates over the issue of slavery in the territories acquired from Mexico, fistfights broke out on the floor of the House, Senator Jefferson Davis of Mississippi challenged an Illinois congressman to a duel, Senator Henry Foote (also of Mississippi) drew a loaded revolver on the Senate floor, and Congressman Alexander Stephens of Georgia declared that to resist "the dictation of the Northern hordes of Goths and Vandals" the slave states must make "the necessary preparations of men and money, arms and ammunitions, etc., to meet the emergency."[2]

The initial crisis subsided with the Compromise of 1850 but flared up again after passage of the Kansas-Nebraska Act in 1854. At least two hundred men lost their lives in fighting between proslavery and antislavery forces in Kansas. Congressman Preston Brooks of South Carolina clubbed Senator Charles Sumner of Massachusetts almost to death with a heavy cane on the floor of the Senate in 1856. Two years later, a congressional debate over the question of admitting Kansas as a slave state under its fraudulent Lecompton Constitution provoked a shoving and pummeling fight between Northern and Southern congressmen in the House. "There were some fifty middle-aged and elderly gentlemen pitching into each other like so many Tipperary savages," wrote a journalist with some amusement, "most of them incapable, from want of wind and muscle, of doing each other any serious harm." But one representative commented that "if any weapons had been on hand it would probably have been a bloody one."[3]

After John Brown's raid on Harpers Ferry in 1859, which stirred fear, outrage, and retaliation in the South, men began coming armed to the floor of Congress. One of them observed, with some hyperbole, that "the only persons who do not have a revolver and knife are those who have two revolvers." A Southerner reported that a good many slave-state congressmen expected—even wanted—a shootout on the floor of the House; they were "willing to fight the question out, and settle it right there." The governor of South Carolina wrote to one of his state's representatives: "If . . . you upon consultation decide to make an issue of force in Washington, write or telegraph me, and I will have a regiment in or near Washington in the shortest possible time."[4]

The war of 1861–65 transferred these conflicts from the political arena to the battlefield. Appomattox and the subsequent surrenders of other Confederate armies ended that battlefield war. But they did not end the cultural and ideological struggle between slavery and freedom in which the military contest was embedded. The Civil War was actually two wars. One of them ended in 1865. Real peace was impossible until the other one ended as well. Some contemporaries recognized this truth. Two months after Appomattox, the Boston lawyer and author (*Two Years before the Mast*), Richard Henry Dana, the federal district attorney for Massachusetts, gave a widely publicized speech in which he declared that "a war is over when its purpose is secured. It is a fatal mistake to hold that this war is over, because the fighting has ceased. This war is not over," and until the North had secured "the fruits of victory" it must continue to hold the South in "the grasp of war."[5]

These phrases, "fruits of victory" and "grasp of war," became part of the public discourse during the year immediately after the end of fighting between the armies. What did they mean? At a minimum, they meant that the victorious North had the power and responsibility to impose terms on which the South would be reincorporated into the Union. Suffering from the shock of defeat, many ex-Confederates were despondent and listless, without the will to resist any terms of reconstruction the North saw fit to impose. "They expect nothing," wrote a Northern journalist, "were prepared for the worst; would have been thankful for anything.... They asked no terms, made no conditions." Even South Carolinians admitted that "the conqueror has the right to make the terms, and we must submit."[6]

The problem was that the conquerors could not agree on what those terms should be. The assassination of Lincoln had removed a firm hand from the helm. At first his successor, Andrew Johnson, seemed to favor draconian terms. Having fought the secessionists on the ground in Tennessee, the new president thundered that "treason is a crime.... Traitors must be punished and impoverished. Their great plantations must be seized and divided into farms, and sold to honest, industrious men."[7]

This rhetoric seemed to place Johnson at the same end of a spectrum of Northern opinion with Thaddeus Stevens and other Radical Republicans who wanted to overthrow the power of the old Southern ruling class, confiscate their land, and distribute it among freed slaves and Unionist whites. It also meant disfranchising leading ex-Confederates and enfranchising freed slaves. The planter class had brought on secession and war, they believed. The United States would never achieve genuine peace until the planters were shorn of their wealth and replaced by a democratized biracial yeoman class that would constitute the backbone of the New South.

At heart, however, Johnson was a Democrat and a white supremacist, whom the Republicans had placed on the ticket in 1864 to broaden their appeal to War Democrats and border-state Unionists. Johnson's nomination gave Republicans a short-term advantage in helping to win the election but at the cost of disastrous long-term consequences in winning the peace. Not long after declaring that traitors must be punished and impoverished, Johnson began a migration toward the conservative and even Democratic end of the spectrum. From there, he and like-minded Democrats saw Reconstruction as a minimalist process that would establish a mechanism by which former Confederate states could return to the Union with little or no change except for the abolition of slavery. For the proponents of such a policy, the fruits of victory included simply the restoration of the old Union and a grudging admission that slavery was gone with the wind. They could best achieve a real and permanent peace, they believed, by the maximum conciliation of former enemies consistent with the actual outcome of the war.

Between these alternatives of Reconstruction as revolution or as minimum change were the imprecise and shifting ideas held by the majority of the Republican Party. For them, the fruits of victory included an irrevocable repudiation of secession, ratification of the Thirteenth

Amendment, some kind of federal guarantee for the civil rights of former slaves if not their immediate enfranchisement as voters, security and power for Southern white Unionists, and at least temporary political disqualification of leading ex-Confederates. When Johnson moved toward the conservative end of the spectrum in 1865–66, the moderate Republicans moved in countervailing fashion closer to the radical position. This process produced a growing polarization between the president and Congress, which in turn led to Johnson's impeachment in 1868 and his escape from conviction by a single vote in the Senate.

In the spring and summer of 1865, Johnson issued proclamations of amnesty and reconstruction that offered pardons and restoration of property—except slaves—to most ex-Confederates who were willing to take an oath of allegiance to the United States. The president exempted several classes of high-ranking Confederate civil and military officers and wealthy Southerners. However, these exempted individuals could apply for individual pardons. Johnson thereupon pardoned them in large numbers—more than thirteen thousand. Once pardoned, they could proceed to join with amnestied whites and those who had never supported the Confederacy to adopt new state constitutions and elect new governors, legislatures, congressmen, and senators.

Freed slaves remained excluded from this process. In fact, several of the new state governments enacted "Black Codes" that codified explicit second-class citizenship for freedpeople. Johnson's restoration of property to amnestied and pardoned ex-Confederates also drove tens of thousands of freedmen off land they had farmed for themselves that year. Moreover, the president vetoed a Freedmen's Bureau bill that would have given the Bureau authority to place freedmen on abandoned land in the former Confederacy.

Under the new state governments, voters elected hundreds of ex-Confederate officials to state offices, along with no fewer than nine Confederate congressmen, seven Confederate state officials, four generals, four colonels, and Confederate vice president Alexander H. Stephens to the

U.S. Congress. To angry Republicans it appeared that the rebels, unable to capture Washington in war, were about to do so in peace. They were determined not to let this happen. In December 1865 the *Chicago Tribune* expressed a growing sentiment in the North. Its editorial focused in particular on the Mississippi Black Code but, by implication, addressed the growing defiance of Southern whites in general. "We tell the white men of Mississippi," thundered the *Tribune*, "that the men of the North will convert the state of Mississippi into a frog pond before they will allow such laws to disgrace one foot of the soil in which the bones of our soldiers sleep and over which the flag of freedom waves."[8]

For the next two years a bitter struggle in Washington made a mockery of the hopes for peace that had blossomed at Appomattox. With their three-quarters majority in Congress, Republicans refused to admit the representatives and senators elected by the Southern states. Congress passed a civil rights bill and a Freedmen's Bureau bill over Johnson's vetoes and adopted the Fourteenth Amendment to the Constitution, which Johnson counseled Southern state legislatures to reject.

In the midterm elections of 1866, Northern voters resoundingly repudiated a conservative coalition that Johnson's supporters had cobbled together. The Republicans maintained their three-quarters majority in both houses of Congress. They proceeded in 1867 to enact a series of laws over Johnson's vetoes that mandated new state constitutions in the South providing for universal manhood suffrage and for temporary disfranchisement and political disqualification of many ex-Confederates. New Republican-controlled state governments came into existence in 1868 and 1869, which created public school systems in the South and enacted other progressive social legislation. They also ratified the Fourteenth and Fifteenth Amendments that banned racial discrimination in civil and voting rights.

President Johnson tried to hinder every step of this process by executive obstruction, which is why the House impeached him and the Senate almost convicted him in 1868. The most pernicious effect of Johnson's obstructionism was to encourage growing white resistance in the South. By the fall of 1865 the immediate postwar passivity of Southern whites was metamorphosing into defiance. After all, the president of the United States appeared to be on their side. In September 1865 a leading Alabama politician scoffed at Republican insistence on guarantees of Southern white loyalty and good behavior. "It is you, proud and exultant Radical, who should give guarantees, guarantees that you will not again...deny any portion of the people their rights." Two months later Wade Hampton, one of the South's richest antebellum planters and a Confederate cavalry commander, commented that "it is our duty to support the President of the United States so long as he manifests a disposition to support all our rights as a sovereign State."[9]

This sounded like 1860 all over again. Many Southern whites agreed with South Carolina's Thomas Pickney Lowndes, who wrote several years later that "for us the war is not ended. We had met the enemy in the field and lost our fight, but now we were threatened with a servile war, a war in which the negro savage backed by the U.S. and the intelligent white scoundrel as his leader was our enemy."[10]

White Southerners acted on this premise. Violent acts spread throughout the South, ranging from midnight assassinations of black and white Republicans to full-scale riots in Memphis and New Orleans in 1866 that killed forty-six and thirty-seven blacks, respectively. A shadowy organization with the ominous sounding name of Ku Klux Klan carried out many of these actions. Similar secret societies arose in other states. Louisiana experienced the worst of the violence. Hundreds of victims of guerrilla attacks met their deaths in that state in the three years between Appomattox and Grant's nomination for president.[11]

Paramilitary groups composed mostly of Confederate veterans killed hundreds more in other states. Federal occupation troops were too few and spread too thinly to prevent most of the killings. Little wonder that people longed for surcease from constant strife and crisis. "Let us have peace," echoed many newspapers when they published Grant's acceptance letter. If anyone could win the peace, they hoped, it was the man who had won the war.

But there would be no peace. It was not for lack of trying. In several Southern states, Republican governors organized militia companies to suppress the violence. In Tennessee, Arkansas, and other places, they had some success. But positive results were exceptional. In many areas, county sheriffs organized posses, but they were often outgunned by counter-Reconstruction guerrillas. The sheriff of Fayette County, Alabama, put his finger on another problem. "When I gather my posse," he testified, "I could depend on them; but as soon as I get home, I meet my wife crying, saying that they have been there shooting into the house. When we scatter to our houses, we do not know at what time we are to be shot down; and living with our lives in our hands in this way, we have become disheartened."[12]

If the militia or sheriffs did manage to apprehend Klansmen, what then? Even in Republican counties it proved difficult to impanel a jury that would convict. Although militia or federal troops might be able to protect witnesses and jurors during trials, they could not prevent retaliation on a dark night months later. And sometimes the intimidation occurred during the trial itself. To cite just one example, the district attorney in northern Mississippi saw a case fall apart when five key witnesses were murdered. The example was not lost on witnesses elsewhere.

North Carolina's Governor William W. Holden came to grief because of his attempts to stamp out the Klan. County sheriffs and civil courts proved helpless to contain a rising tide of terror that swept over the state in early 1870. The legislature authorized Holden to proclaim a state of insurrection but refused him the power to declare martial law or to suspend the writ of habeas corpus. Knowing that nothing short of these measures would do the job, Holden in effect declared martial law by executive order. The militia arrested scores of Klansmen, while dozens of others turned state's evidence in hope of light or suspended sentences. In response to the mounting pressure, Holden dropped his plan to try offenders in military courts. As usual, the civil courts failed to convict any of those arrested. After the Democrats won control of the legislature (with the aid of Klan violence) in 1870, they impeached and convicted Holden in March 1871 for having illegally declared martial law. He was the first governor in American history to be removed from office by impeachment.[13]

As the death toll from Klan violence mounted during 1870, Southern Republicans desperately petitioned the Grant administration for help. Rigorous legislation to enforce the Fourteenth and Fifteenth Amendments became major items of congressional business. A stumbling block to such legislation was the federal system, under which the states had jurisdiction over the crimes of murder, assault, arson, and the like. In the view of moderate Republicans, the prosecution of such crimes by federal officials would stretch the Constitution to the breaking point. Nevertheless, the clauses of the Fourteenth and Fifteenth Amendments, giving Congress power to enforce their provisions by appropriate legislation, seemed to provide constitutional sanction for a departure from tradition.

Missouri's Senator Carl Schurz, a refugee from the revolutions of 1848 in Germany, a founder of the Republican Party, and a major general in the Union army during the Civil War, eloquently supported an enforcement law. In a Senate speech he scorned the incessant harping by Democrats on what they euphoniously called "self government and...State sovereignty....In the name of liberty [they] assert the right of one man, under State law, to deprive another man of his freedom. [But] the great constitutional revolution" accomplished by the war had brought in its wake "the vindication of individual rights by the National power. The revolution found the rights of the individual at the mercy of the States...and placed them under the shield of national protection." And how did the Democrats respond? asked Schurz rhetorically. "As they once asserted that true liberty implied the right of one man to hold another man as his slave, they will tell you now that they are no longer true freemen in their States because...they can no longer deprive other men of their rights."[14]

In May 1870 Congress passed an enforcement act that made interference with voting rights a federal offense and defined as a felony any attempt by one or more persons to deprive another person of his civil or political rights. Mindful of opposition charges of military dictatorship and "Caesarism," Grant initially did little to enforce this law. Klan violence continued to increase. Grant and his new attorney general, Amos Akerman, finally decided to take off the velvet glove that had cloaked the iron fist. Congress helped by passing an even stronger law at a special session in April 1871, popularly known as the Ku Klux Act. This law empowered the president to use the army to enforce the 1870 law, declare martial law, suspend the writ of habeas corpus in areas that he declared to be in a state of insurrection, and purge suspected Klansmen from juries by an oath backed with stiff penalties for perjury.

Under these laws the Grant administration cracked down on the Klan. Government detectives infiltrated the order and gathered evidence of its activities. In 1871 a congressional committee conducted an investigation of the Klan that produced twelve thick volumes of testimony documenting its outrages. The president sent cavalry to the South to supplement the federal infantry to cope with the fast-riding Klansmen.

Grant also suspended the writ of habeas corpus in nine counties of South Carolina. There and elsewhere, federal marshals aided by soldiers arrested thousands of Klansmen. Hundreds of others fled their homes to escape arrest. Federal grand juries handed down more than three thousand indictments. Several hundred defendants pleaded guilty in return for suspended sentences. The Justice Department (established in 1870) dropped charges against nearly two thousand others in order to clear clogged court dockets for trials of major offenders. Approximately six hundred of these were convicted and 250 acquitted. Of those convicted, most received fines or light jail sentences, but sixty-five were imprisoned for sentences of up to five (in a few cases, ten) years in the federal penitentiary at Albany, New York.[15]

The government's main purpose in this crackdown was to destroy the Klan and restore a semblance of law and order in the South rather than to secure mass convictions. Thus the courts granted clemency to many convicted defendants and Grant used his pardoning power liberally. By 1875 all the imprisoned men had served out their sentences or received pardons. The government's vigorous actions in 1871–72 did bring at least a temporary peace to large parts of the former Confederacy. As a consequence, blacks voted in solid numbers, and the 1872 election was the fairest and most democratic presidential election in the South until 1968.

This experience confirmed a reality that had existed since 1865: While counter-Reconstruction guerrillas assaulted unarmed white and black Republicans, teachers in freedpeople's schools, sheriffs' posses, and state militias, they carefully avoided conflict with federal troops. Yet the success of federal enforcement in 1871–72 contained seeds of future failure. Southern whites and Northern Democrats hurled charges of "bayonet rule" against the Grant administration. Southern Democrats learned that the Klan's tactics of terrorism—midnight assassinations and whippings by disguised vigilantes operating in secret organizations—were likely to bring down the heavy hand of federal retaliation. They did not forswear violence, but openly formed organizations that they described as "social clubs"—which just happened to be armed to the teeth. Professing to organize only for self-defense against black militias, "carpetbagger corruption," and other bugbears of Southern white propaganda, they named themselves White Leagues (Louisiana), White Liners or Rifle Clubs (Mississippi), or Red Shirts (South Carolina). They were, in fact, paramilitary organizations that functioned as armed auxiliaries of the Democratic Party in Southern states in their drive to "redeem" the South from "black and tan Negro-Carpetbag rule."

Most of the paramilitaries, like those who had constituted Klan personnel, were Confederate veterans. A careful study of the White League in New Orleans analyzes the membership of this order and finds that 88 percent of its officers "can be positively identified as Confederate veterans who served in Louisiana during the Civil War."[16] But they were not eager to reprise the war of 1861–65, so they too were careful to avoid conflict with the dwindling number of federal troops stationed in the South and to portray their increasingly murderous attacks on blacks and Republicans as purely defensive.

The most notorious confrontation occurred in 1873 at Colfax on the Red River in the plantation country of western Louisiana. Colfax was the parish seat of Grant Parish, whose population was almost equally divided between whites and blacks. Disputed elections had left rival claimants for control of both the parish and state governments. Simmering warfare between the White League and black militia came to a head in Colfax on Easter Sunday in 1873. Claiming that "Negro rule" in the parish had produced corruption, pillage, and rape, the White League vowed to reassert white rule. Occupation of the courthouse by armed blacks provoked whites into a frenzy. On April 13 nearly three hundred armed whites rode into Colfax pulling a cannon on a farm wagon. Using tactics learned as Confederate soldiers, they attacked the courthouse from three directions. After shooting down in cold blood several blacks trying to escape, they set the building on fire, burning several men alive and killing the rest as they came out to surrender. At least seventy-one blacks (by some accounts as many as three hundred) and three whites were killed—two of the latter by shots fired from their own side. Federal troops steaming upriver from New Orleans arrived in time only to count the dead.

A federal grand jury indicted seventy-two whites under the Enforcement Act of 1870 for violating black civil rights. Only nine came to trial, and three were convicted. These three went free in 1876 when the Supreme Court ruled (*U.S. v. Cruikshank*) that the enforcement act was unconstitutional because the Fourteenth Amendment prohibited only states, not individuals, from violating civil rights. "The power of Congress...to legislate for the enforcement of such a guarantee," declared the Court, "does not extend to the passage of laws for the suppression of ordinary crime within the states.... That duty was originally assumed by the States; and it still remains there."[17] The Court failed to specify what recourse victims might have if a state did not or could not suppress such crimes.

In Louisiana and Mississippi, White Leaguers and White Liners carried on their campaigns of intimidation and murder with little regard for courts, either federal or state. Federal troops were too few or too late to protect most targets of violence. Tensions rose in 1874 as elections approached. The White League in the Red River Parish southwest of Shreveport forced six white Republicans to resign their offices on pain of death—and then brutally murdered them after they had resigned.[18]

"For many former Confederates, this was a glorious time," writes Nicholas Lemann in his history of these events. "After years of defeat and loss of power and control, it looked as if they might be winning again." They "were taking their homeland back from what they saw as a formidable misalliance of the federal government and the Negro. The drama of it was so powerful that killing defenseless people registered in their minds as acts of bravery, and refusal to obey laws that protected other people's rights registered as acts of high principle."[19]

Two weeks after the Red River Parish murders, New Orleans on September 14 became the scene of a battle between the White League on one side and the police and state militia on the other. The commander of the state forces, which included both white and black units, was none other than former Confederate general James Longstreet, who had become a Republican after the war and was now fighting against men who had once served under him. Longstreet's little army killed twenty-one White Leaguers and wounded nineteen but suffered eleven killed and sixty wounded—including Longstreet—in the course of being routed by the White Leaguers.

The White League installed its own claimant to the governorship (from the disputed election of 1872), but President Grant then stepped in and put an end to the exercise. Three regiments of U.S. infantry and a battery of artillery arrived in New Orleans (then the capital), supported by a flotilla of gunboats anchored in the river with a full complement of marines. "New Orleans became host to the largest garrison of federal troops in the United States," writes the historian James Hogue, "and assumed the appearance of an occupied city, much as it had during the Civil War."[20] The soldiers ensured a fair election in the city. Grant also sent part of the 7th Cavalry (George Armstrong Custer's regiment) to patrol the turbulent Red River parishes.

In addition, Grant ordered to Louisiana his top field commander, General Philip H. Sheridan. This hotheaded fighter had pulled no punches in his Civil War career, nor did he now. "I think the terrorism now existing in Louisiana, Mississippi, and Arkansas could be entirely removed, and confidence and fair dealing be established, by the arrest and trial of ringleaders of the armed White Leagues," Sheridan wired the secretary of war in a dispatch that was widely published in the press. "If Congress would pass a bill declaring them banditti, they could be tried by a military commission." The "ringleaders of this banditti, who murdered men here on the 14th of September, and also more recently at Vicksburg, Miss., should, in justice to law and order...be punished." If "the President would issue a proclamation declaring them banditti, no further action need to be taken except that which would devolve on me."[21]

We shall never know if Sheridan's approach would have worked, for it was never tried. His banditti dispatch provoked a firestorm of condemnation in the North as well as in the South. Instead of bringing peace, Grant's Southern policy seemed to be causing ever more turmoil. Many Northerners adopted a "plague on both your houses" attitude toward the White Leagues and the "Negro-Carpetbag" state governments. Withdraw the federal troops, they argued, and let the Southern people work out their own problems, even if that meant a solid South for the white-supremacy Democratic Party and curtailment of black civil and political rights.

"People are becoming tired of...abstract questions, in which the overwhelming majority of them have no direct interest," declared the leading Republican newspaper in Washington in 1874. "The Negro question, with all its complications, and the reconstruction of the Southern States, with all its interminable embroilments, have lost

much of the power they once wielded." A Republican politician commented even more bluntly the following year that "the truth is that our
people are tired of this worn out cry of 'Southern outrages'!!! Hard
times and heavy taxes make them wish the 'nigger,' 'everlasting nigger,'
were in _____ or Africa."[22]

Benefiting from this sentiment as well as from an anti-Republican
backlash caused by the economic depression that followed the Panic
of 1873, Democrats gained control of the House of Representatives and
several Northern governorships for the first time in almost two decades. And the Supreme Court was already sending signals that it
might strip the 1870–71 enforcement laws of their teeth.

Despite the presence of federal troops in Louisiana, the election of
state legislators in 1874 produced a new round of disputed results.
Democrats appeared to have won a majority in the lower house. But the
Republican "returning board" threw out the results in several parishes
on the grounds of intimidation. The board certified the election of fifty-
three Republicans and fifty-three Democrats, with five cases undecided
and referred to the lower house itself. When this body convened on
January 4, 1875, Democrats carried out a well-planned maneuver to seat
the five Democratic claimants before the befuddled Republicans could
organize to prevent that action. In response, the Republican governor
asked federal troops to eject the five Democrats who had no election
certificates. Soldiers marched into the House and escorted the Democrats out.

This affair caused an uproar in Congress as well as in the country.
Even a good many Republicans condemned the unprecedented military
invasion of the legislature. Carl Schurz, who had spoken so powerfully for
federal enforcement of Reconstruction five years earlier, with troops if
necessary, had changed his tune by 1875. "Our system of republican government is in danger," he proclaimed in a Senate speech. "Every American who truly loves his liberty will recognize the cause of his own rights
and liberties in the cause of Constitutional government in Louisiana."
The "insidious advance of irresponsible power" had drawn sustenance

from the argument that it was "by federal bayonets only that the colored man may be safe." Schurz conceded that "brute force" might make "every colored man safe, not only in the exercise of his franchise but in everything else.... You might have made the national government so strong that, right or wrong, nobody could resist it." That is "an effective method to keep peace and order.... It is employed with singular success in Russia." But "what has in the meantime become of the liberties and rights of all of us," asked this Forty-Eighter who had left Germany to escape just such tyranny. "If this can be done to Louisiana...how long will it be before it can be done in Massachusetts and in Ohio? How long before the constitutional rights of all the states and the self-government of all the people may be trampled under foot?...How long before a soldier may stalk into the National House of Representatives, and, pointing to the Speaker's mace, say, 'Take away that bauble'?"[23]

A compromise kept the Republican administration in Louisiana afloat for two more years. In 1875 the focus of attention shifted to neighboring Mississippi, where legislative elections took place that year. Of all the Reconstruction state governments, Mississippi's was one of the most honest and efficient. And of all the "carpetbaggers," Governor Adelbert Ames was one of the most able, effective, and idealistic. Few carpetbaggers fit the nefarious stereotype of the genre, and Ames fit it least of all. Having graduated near the top of his class at West Point in 1861, this native of Maine fought in most of the battles of the Eastern theater in the Civil War, was awarded the Medal of Honor, and achieved promotion to brevet major general in the regular U.S. Army in 1865 at the age of twenty-nine. After commanding the military district of Mississippi and Arkansas and shepherding those states back into the Union, Ames was elected senator from Mississippi in 1870 and governor in 1873. His experiences in the Civil War and afterward produced a deep and genuine commitment to education and equal justice for the freedpeople.

To most whites in Mississippi, it mattered little that the state government under Ames was relatively honest and efficient by the standards of the time. It was not *their* government. Whites owned most of the property and thus paid most of the taxes. They resented the portion of those taxes that went to black schools. The black majority sustained Republican county and state governments for which few whites had voted. In 1875 the White Line rifle clubs determined, as they expressed it, to "carry the elections peacefully if we can, forcibly if we must." Their strategy became known as the Mississippi Plan.

Part of this plan involved economic coercion of black sharecroppers and laborers, who were informed that if they voted Republican they could expect no more work. But violence, threatened and actual, was the main component of the Mississippi Plan. White Liners discovered that their best tactic was the "riot." When Republicans held a political rally, several White Liners would attend with concealed weapons, and others would lurk nearby in reserve. Someone would provoke a shoving or heckling incident. Someone else would fire a shot—always attributed to a Republican—whereupon all hell would break loose. When the shooting finally stopped, black and Republican casualties usually outnumbered White Liner casualties by about twenty to one. Then the White Liners would ride out into the country and shoot any black man they suspected of political activism—and sometimes his family as well. Several years later, one White Liner candidly confessed that "the question which presented itself then to the people of Hinds County was whether or not the negroes, under the reconstruction laws, should rule the county.... Throughout the countryside for several days the negro leaders, some white and some black, were hunted down and killed, until the negro population which had dominated the white people for so many years was whipped."[24]

The only way to counter this force was by equal or greater force. Ames was reluctant to mobilize the black militia—who in any case would be outnumbered and out-gunned—because it would play into the hands of white propagandists who spouted endlessly about savage Africans murdering white men and raping their women. The solution seemed to be federal troops. Ames sent an urgent message to Washington requesting military support. Grant meant to comply. He instructed his attorney general to prepare a proclamation ordering lawless persons to cease and desist—a necessary prelude to sending troops—but also urged Ames "to strengthen his position by exhausting his own resources in restoring order before he receives govt. aid."[25]

The new attorney general, a conservative Republican, goaded Ames more than Grant intended. "The whole public are tired out with these annual autumnal outbreaks in the South," wrote the nation's chief law enforcement officer, "and the great majority are now ready to condemn any interference on the part of the government.... Preserve the peace by the forces in your own state, and let the country see that the citizens of Mississippi, who are...largely Republican, have the courage to fight for their rights."[26] No troops came.

Ames did mobilize a few companies of black militia, even though he recognized that to use them in combat against the heavily armed Confederate veterans in the rifle clubs "precipitates a war of races and one to be felt over the entire South."[27] To avoid such a result, Ames negotiated an agreement with Democratic leaders whereby the latter promised peace in return for disarming the militia. "No matter if they are going to carry the State," commented Ames wearily, "let them carry it, and let us be at peace and have no more killing."[28] Not surprisingly, however, violence and intimidation continued under this "peace agreement," and on election day black voters were conspicuous by their absence from the polls. In five counties with large black majorities, Republicans polled twelve, seven, four, two, and zero votes. In this way a Republican majority of thirty thousand at the previous election became a Democratic majority of thirty thousand in 1875.

The Mississippi Plan worked so well that other Southern states carried out their own versions of it in the national election of 1876. The last Republican state governments in the South collapsed when the new president, Rutherford B. Hayes, withdrew all federal troops in 1877. The Democrats had "redeemed" the South, which remained solid for their party and for white supremacy for almost a century.

"Reconstruction, which had wound up producing a lower-intensity continuation of the Civil War, was over," writes a historian of the era. "The South had won."[29]

This did not mean, however, that the loser of the Civil War had garnered the fruits of victory after all. In the war of 1861–65 the North had prevailed and unequivocally achieved the principal goals of that war: preservation of the United States as one nation, indivisible, with liberty for all. A third goal, justice for all, was achieved on paper with the Fourteenth and Fifteenth Amendments. Moreover, it had come tantalizingly close to success on the ground for a few brief years. In the end, justice was sacrificed for the unjust peace ushered in by "redemption" of the South, a peace marred by disfranchisement, Jim Crow, poverty, and lynching. Yet the Fourteenth and Fifteenth Amendments remained in the Constitution. Exactly eighty years after Hayes withdrew federal troops from the South, another Republican president—who also happened to be a famous general—sent them back, to Little Rock, to begin the painful process of winning the final fruits of victory in the larger conflict of which the war of 1861–65 had formed only a part.

NOTES

CHAPTER 1

1   The information in this paragraph is drawn from my personal correspondence and experiences, from the monthly periodical *Civil War News,* and from the newsletters of several Civil War Round Tables.

2   J. David Hacker, "A Census-Based Count of the Civil War Dead," *Civil War History* 57 (Dec. 2011): 307–48.

3   Merrill D. Peterson, *Lincoln in American Memory* (New York, 1994), 355–56.

4   Roy P. Basler, ed., *The Collected Works of Abraham Lincoln,* 9 vols. (New Brunswick, N.J., 1953–55), 2:255.

5   William L. Barney, *The Secessionist Impulse: Alabama and Mississippi in 1860* (Princeton, 1974), 110; Dunbar Rowland, ed., *Jefferson Davis, Constitutionalist: His Letters, Papers, and Speeches,* 10 vols. (Jackson, Miss., 1923), 5:202.

6   Basler, *Collected Works of Lincoln* 2:250; *New York Evening Post,* Feb. 18, 1861.

7   Basler, *Collected Works of Lincoln* 7:301–302.

8   Madison quoted in Gordon S. Wood, *The Creation of the American Republic, 1776–1787* (Chapel Hill, N.C., 1963), 413, and from *Federalist* No. 47 (Modern Library ed.), 312.

9   James D. Richardson, comp., *Messages and Papers of the Presidents,* 20 vols. (Washington, 1897), 7:2780–84.

10 In Isaiah Berlin, *Four Essays on Liberty* (New York, 1970), 118–72.

11 Basler, *Collected Works of Lincoln* 4:438.

CHAPTER 2

1   Amy S. Greenberg, *A Wicked War: Polk, Clay, Lincoln, and the 1846 U.S. Invasion of Mexico* (New York, 2012), 274.

2   Frederick Merk, *Manifest Destiny and Mission in American History: A Reinterpretation* (New York, 1963), 52.

3   Horace Greeley, *Why I Am a Whig* (New York, 1851), 6.

4   Greenberg, *A Wicked War*, 104.

5   Greenberg, *A Wicked War*, 124.

6   Greenberg, *A Wicked War*, 287n13.

7   Greenberg, *A Wicked War* 131, 194.

8   *Congressional Globe*, 29th Congress, 1st Session (Aug. 12, 1846), 1217.

9   Greenberg, *A Wicked War*, 232–33.

10   Roy P. Basler, ed., *The Collected Works of Abraham Lincoln,* 9 vols. (New Brunswick, N.J., 1953–55), 1:420–22, 431–42.

11   Charles W. Ramsdell, "The Natural Limits of Slavery Expansion," *Mississippi Valley Historical Review* 16 (1929): 151–71.

12   The best summary of this "revisionist" school of historians is still Thomas J. Pressly, *Americans Interpret Their Civil War* (Princeton, N.J., 1962), 289–328.

13   James G. Blaine, *Twenty Years of Congress from Lincoln to Garfield*, 2 vols. (Norwich, Conn., 1884), 1:272; Milo Milton Quaife, ed., *The Diary of James K. Polk during His Presidency, 1845 to 1849*, 4 vols. (Chicago, 1910), 2:308.

14   The Webster quotation is from his famous Seventh of March (1850) Speech in the Senate on the Compromise of 1850: *Congressional Globe*, 31st Congress, 1st Session, Appendix, 269–76; Crittenden quoted in Michael Holt, *The Political Crisis of the 1850s* (New York, 1978), 77.

15   Leonard L. Richards, *The California Gold Rush and the Coming of the Civil War* (New York, 2007), x.

16   *Charleston Mercury* quoted in Robert S. Starobin, *Industrial Slavery in the Old South* (New York, 1970), 220; *Southern Quarterly* quoted in William R. Brock, *Parties and Political Conscience: American Dilemmas 1840–1850* (Millwood, N.Y., 1979), 319.

17   Richards, *California Gold Rush and the Coming of the Civil War*, 103.

18   Richards, *California Gold Rush and the Coming of the Civil War* 103, 96.

19   Richards, *California Gold Rush and the Coming of the Civil War* 127.

20   Charles H. Brown, *Agents of Manifest Destiny: The Lives and Times of the Filibusters* (Chapel Hill, N.C., 1980); Robert E. May, *Manifest Destiny's Underworld: Filibustering in Antebellum America* (Chapel Hill, N.C., 2002); Robert E. May, *Slavery, Race, and Conquest in the Tropics* (New York, 2013).

CHAPTER 3

1   Harry S. Stout, *Upon the Altar of the Nation: A Moral History of the Civil War* (New York, 2006), xi, 463.

2   Stout, *Upon the Altar of the Nation*, 13.

3   Roy P. Basler, ed., *The Collected Works of Abraham Lincoln*, 9 vols. (New Brunswick, N.J., 1953–55), 8:332.

4   Jefferson Davis, *The Rise and Fall of the Confederate Government*, 2 vols. (reprint of 1881 ed., New York, 1990), 2:252.

5   Stout, *Upon the Altar of the Nation*, xiv.

6   Basler, *Collected Works of Lincoln* 4:332, 5:48–49.

7   Sherman to Ellen Sherman, July 28, 1861, and undated, probably August 1861, in Mark A. DeWolfe Howe, ed., *Home Letters of General Sherman* (New York, 1909), 209, 214; Stephen W. Sears, ed., *The Civil War Papers of George B. McClellan* (New York, 1989), 344.

8   John Bennett Walters, *Merchant of Terror: General Sherman and Total War* (Indianapolis, 1973), 57–58; Walters, "William T. Sherman and Total War," *Journal of Southern History* 14 (1948), 463.

9   Stout, *Upon the Altar of the Nation*, 139.

10 Stout, *Upon the Altar of the Nation*, 141, 143, 191.

11 Stout, *Upon the Altar of the Nation*, 139.

12 Stout, *Upon the Altar of the Nation*, 137, 304, 389, 459.

13 Stout, *Upon the Altar of the Nation*, xvi.

14 Stout, *Upon the Altar of the Nation*, 185, 187.

15 Stout, *Upon the Altar of the Nation*, xvi.

16 Stout, *Upon the Altar of the Nation*, 244, 317.

17 Stout, *Upon the Altar of the Nation*, 359.

18 Andrew Ward, *River Run Red: The Fort Pillow Massacre in the American Civil War* (New York, 2005); John Cimprich, *Fort Pillow, a Civil War Massacre, and Public Memory* (Baton Rouge, La., 2005).

19 Stout, *Upon the Altar of the Nation*, 319.

20 Stout, *Upon the Altar of the Nation*, 461.

21 Stout, *Upon the Altar of the Nation*, xvi.

22 James M. McPherson, *Battle Cry of Freedom: The Civil War Era* (New York, 1988), 619; J. David Hacker, "A Census-Based Count of the Civil War Dead," *Civil War History* 57 (Dec. 2011), 307–48.

23 James Michael Russell, *Atlanta, 1847–1890* (Baton Rouge, La., 1988), 114–15, 113.

24 Stout, *Upon the Altar of the Nation*, xvi, 34, 37, 377, 396, 401.

25 Stout, *Upon the Altar of the Nation*, 93, 170.

26 Stout, *Upon the Altar of the Nation*, 426–27.

27 Stout, *Upon the Altar of the Nation*, xvii, xxi, 146, 321.

28 Stout, *Upon the Altar of the Nation*, 229, 254.

29 Stout, *Upon the Altar of the Nation*, 183, 268, 455.

30 Stout, *Upon the Altar of the Nation*, 189, 459.

31 David Goldfield, *America Aflame: How the Civil War Created a Nation* (New York, 2011), 268.

32 For a discussion of the revisionists, see Thomas J. Pressly, *Americans Interpret the Civil War*, 2nd ed. (Princeton, N.J., 1962), 291–328. For two examples of revisionist writings, see Avery Craven, *The Repressible Conflict* (Baton Rouge, La., 1939), and James G. Randall, "The Blundering Generation," *Mississippi Valley Historical Review* 27 (1940): 3–28.

33 Goldfield, *America Aflame*, 3.

34 Goldfield, *America Aflame*, 3.

35 Goldfield, *America Aflame*, 8, 156–57.

36 Quoted in the introduction to Robert Johannsen, ed., *The Lincoln-Douglas Debates of 1858* (New York, 1965), 9.

37 Goldfield, *America Aflame*, 158.

38 Goldfield, *America Aflame*, 7, 100.

39 Goldfield, *America Aflame*, 3, 181, 316, 369, 504.

40 George C. Rable, *God's Almost Chosen Peoples: A Religious History of the American Civil War* (Chapel Hill, N.C., 2010), 1.

41 Quoted in Rable, *God's Almost Chosen Peoples*, 370.

42 Basler, *Collected Works of Lincoln* 8:333.

CHAPTER 4

1 *The Fate of Liberty: Abraham Lincoln and Civil Liberties* (New York, 1991).

2 "Was the Civil War a Total War?" *Civil War History* 37 (March 1991): 5–28.

3 James L. Sellers, "The Economic Incidence of the Civil War in the South," *Mississippi Valley Historical Review* 14 (Sept. 1927): 179–91; Stanley Engerman, "Some Economic Factors in Southern Backwardness in the Nineteenth Century," in *Essays in Regional Economics*, ed. John F. Kain and John R. Meyer (Cambridge, Mass., 1971), 300–302.

4 Neely, "Was the Civil War a Total War?" 11, 27.

5 Harry S. Stout, *Upon the Altar of the Nation: A Moral History of the Civil War* (New York, 2006).

6 *Ordeal by Fire: The Civil War and Reconstruction* (New York, 2nd ed. 1992, 3rd ed. 2001).

7 Sherman to Henry W. Halleck, Dec. 24, 1864, *The War of the Rebellion:... Official Records of the Union and Confederate Armies*, 128 vols. (Washington, 1880–1901; hereinafter abbreviated *OR*), ser. 1, vol. 44, p. 799.

8 Mark Grimsley, *The Hard Hand of War: Union Military Policy toward Southern Civilians, 1861–1865* (Cambridge, 1995), 157, 186, 219, 223.

9   Mark Twain and Charles Dudley Warner, *The Gilded Age* (1873; reprint New York, 1969), 137–38.

10 Mark E. Neely Jr., *The Civil War and the Limits of Destruction* (Cambridge, Mass., 2007), 108, 197.

11 Scott quoted in Neely, *The Civil War and the Limits of Destruction*, 9.

12 Neely, *The Civil War and the Limits of Destruction*, 12, 28.

14 Neely, *The Civil War and the Limits of Destruction*, 34.

14 James M. McPherson, *For Cause and Comrades: Why Men Fought in the Civil War* (New York, 1997), 149–50. These and subsequent quotations of Confederate and Union soldiers are from their letters and diaries written during the war.

15 McPherson, *For Cause and Comrades*, 153.

16 Charles Francis Adams Jr. to Charles Francis Adams, June 19, 1864, in Worthington Chauncey Ford, ed., *A Cycle of Adams Letters, 1861–1865*, 2 vols. (Boston, 1920), 2:154.

17 Quoted in McPherson, *For Cause and Comrades*, 154.

18 Neely, *The Civil War and the Limits of Destruction*, 140–41.

19 Neely, *The Civil War and the Limits of Destruction*, 108.

20 Michael Fellman, *Inside War: The Guerrilla Conflict in Missouri during the American Civil War* (New York, 1989); Stephen Z. Starr, *Jennison's Jayhawkers: A Civil War Regiment and Its Commanders* (Baton Rouge, La., 1973); Donald L. Gilmore, *Civil War on the Missouri-Kansas Border* (Gretna, La., 2006).

21 Neely, *The Civil War and the Limits of Destruction*, 70–71.

22 Noel C. Fisher, *War at Every Door: Partisan Politics and Guerrilla Violence in East Tennessee, 1860–1869* (Chapel Hill, N.C., 1997); Robert R. Mackey, *The Uncivil War: Irregular Warfare in the Upper South, 1861–1865* (Norman, Okla., 2004). See also John C. Inscoe and Gordon B. McKinney, *The Heart of Confederate Appalachia: Western North Carolina in the Civil War* (Chapel Hill, N.C., 2000), and Daniel E. Sutherland, *A Savage Conflict: The Decisive Role of Guerrillas in the American Civil War* (Chapel Hill, N.C., 2009).

23 Mackey, *The Uncivil War*, 5.

24 *OR*, ser. 1, vol. 44, pp. 13, 741, 799.

25 Neely, *The Civil War and the Limits of Destruction*, 29.

26 Sheridan to Halleck, Oct. 7, 1864, *OR*, ser. 1, vol. 43, pt. 1, pp. 30–31.

27 Neely, *The Civil War and the Limits of Destruction*, 119.

28 J. David Hacker, "A Census-Based Count of the Civil War Dead," *Civil War History* 57 (Dec. 2011): 307–48.

29 Neely, *The Civil War and the Limits of Destruction*, 211.

30 Neely, *The Civil War and the Limits of Destruction*, 214.

31 Mark S. Schantz, *Awaiting the Heavenly Country: The Civil War and America's Culture of Death* (Ithaca, N.Y., 2008), 98, 4.

32 Schantz, *Awaiting the Heavenly Country*, 38.

33 Drew Gilpin Faust, *This Republic of Suffering: Death and the American Civil War* (New York, 2008), 6–7.

34 Schantz, *Awaiting the Heavenly Country*, 2, 60, 61.

35 McPherson, *For Cause and Comrades*, 68–69.

36 Faust, *This Republic of Suffering*, 174, 187.

37 McPherson, *For Cause and Comrades*, 71.

38 Faust, *This Republic of Suffering*, 60.

39 Faust, *This Republic of Suffering*, 17–18.

40 Faust, *This Republic of Suffering*, 268.

41 Faust, *This Republic of Suffering*, 99, 232.

42 Faust, *This Republic of Suffering*, 236–37.

43 Faust, *This Republic of Suffering*, 248–49.

44 Schantz, *Awaiting the Heavenly Country*, 179.

45 Schantz, *Awaiting the Heavenly Country*, 1; Faust, *This Republic of Suffering*, xiv, xv, 268, 249.

46 Faust, *This Republic of Suffering*, xiii.

47 Faust, *This Republic of Suffering*, xiii.

CHAPTER 5

1 Charles Wilkes to Gideon Welles, Nov. 15, 16, 1861, *Official Records of the Union and Confederate Navies*, 30 vols. (Washington, 1894–1922; hereinafter abbreviated *ORN*), ser. 1, vol. 1, pp. 124–31. See also Craig L. Symonds, *Lincoln and His Admirals* (New York, 2008), 75–78.

2 Welles to Wilkes, Nov. 30, 1861, *ORN*, ser. 1, vol. 1, p. 148; Symonds, *Lincoln and His Admirals*, 80–82.

3 Quoted in Symonds, *Lincoln and His Admirals*, 82.

4 Russell quoted in Symonds, *Lincoln and His Admirals*, 86. For the most recent accounts of the much-studied "Trent Affair," see Howard Jones, *Blue and Gray Diplomacy* (Chapel Hill, N.C., 2010), 83–111, and Amanda Foreman, *A World on Fire: Britain's Crucial Role in the American Civil War* (New York, 2010), 172–98.

5 Symonds, *Lincoln and His Admirals,* 92–94; David Herbert Donald, *Lincoln* (New York, 1995), 323; William H. Seward to Lord Lyons, Dec. 26, 1861, *ORN*, ser. 1, vol. 1, pp. 177–87.

6 Charles Francis Adams to Charles Francis Adams Jr., Jan. 10, 1862, in Worthington C. Ford, ed., *A Cycle of Adams Letters, 1861–1865*, 2 vols. (Boston, 1920), 1:99.

7 Ephraim D. Adams, *Great Britain and the American Civil War*, 2 vols. (New York, 1925), 1:140.

8 *ORN*, ser. 2, vol. 3, pp. 271, 299, 331; Dunbar Rowland, ed., *Jefferson Davis, Constitutionalist: His Letters, Papers and Speeches*, 10 vols. (Jackson, Miss., 1923), 5:401, 403.

9 Lyons to Russell, Nov. 29, 1861, in Adams, *Great Britain and the American Civil War*, 1:254; Slidell in *ORN*, ser. 2, vol. 3, p. 340.

10 *Parliamentary Papers*, 1861, vol. 62, *North America*, no. 8, "Papers Relating to the Blockade of the Ports of the Confederate States," 119–20, quoted in John D. Hayes, ed., *Samuel Francis Du Pont: A Selection from His Civil War Letters*, 3 vols. (Ithaca, N.Y., 1969), 1:326n. Italics added.

11 Quoted in Henry Donaldson Jordan and Edwin J. Pratt, *Europe and the American Civil War* (Boston, 1931), 17.

12 Palmerston to Austen H. Layard, June 19, 1862, in Hubert Du Brulle, "'A War of Wonders': The Battle in Britain over Americanization and the American Civil War" (Ph.D. diss., University of California at Santa Barbara, 1999), 210n.

13 This exchange is conveniently reprinted in James V. Murfin, *The Gleam of Bayonets: The Battle of Antietam and Robert E. Lee's Maryland Campaign, September 1862* (Baton Rouge, La., 1965), 394, 396–97, from the Russell Papers, Public Record Office, London.

14 Palmerston to William Gladstone, Sept. 24, 1862, in Phillip Guedalla, ed., *Gladstone and Palmerston, Being the Correspondence of Lord Palmerston with Mr. Gladstone, 1861–1865* (Covent Garden, 1928), 232–33; Russell to Henry R. C. Wellesley, Earl of Cowley (the British ambassador to France), Sept. 26, 1862, in Frank Merli and Theodore A. Wilson, "The British Cabinet and the Confederacy: Autumn, 1862," *Maryland Historical Magazine* 65 (1970): 247n.; Palmerston to Russell, Sept. 23, 1862, in Murfin, *Gleam of Bayonets*, 400.

15 Charles Francis Adams to Charles Francis Adams Jr., Oct. 17, 1862, in Ford, *Cycle of Adams Letters*, 1:192; Adams to William H. Seward, Oct. 3, 1862, in *Papers Relating to Foreign Affairs, 1861–1862*, pt. 1 (Washington, 1862), 205.

16 Palmerston to Russell, Oct. 2, 22, 1862, in Adams, *Great Britain and the American Civil War* 2:43–44, 54–55.

17 Henry Adams to Charles Francis Adams Jr., Jan. 23, 1863, in Ford, *Cycle of Adams Letters* 1:243; Richard Cobden to Charles Sumner, Feb. 13, 1863, in Belle Becker Sideman and Lillian Friedman, eds., *Europe Looks at the Civil War* (New York, 1960), 222.

18 Foreman, *A World on Fire*, 409–10.

19 John R. Hamilton to James North, April 23, 1863, *ORN*, ser. 2, vol. 2, p. 409. See also Frank J. Merli, *Great Britain and the Confederate Navy, 1861–1865* (Bloomington, Ind., 1970), 160–77.

20 Adams, *Great Britain and the American Civil War*, 2:144. See also Merli, *Great Britain and the Confederate Navy*, 178–217; Bulloch to Stephen R. Mallory, Dec. 2, 1862, and June 30, Sept. 2, and Oct. 20, 1863, *ORN*, ser. 2, vol. 2, pp. 307, 445–46, 488, 507–11.

21 Bulloch to Stephen R. Mallory, Feb. 17, June 10, 1864, *ORN*, ser. 2, vol. 2, pp. 585, 666; Slidell to Judah Benjamin, Aug. 8, 1864, *ORN*, ser. 2, vol. 2, p. 1187.

CHAPTER 6

1 Charles Steedman to Sally Steedman, Sept. 30, 1864, in Amos Lawrence Mason, ed., *Memoir and Correspondence of Charles Steedman, Rear Admiral, United States Navy* (Cambridge, Mass., 1912), 385.

2 *Personal Memoirs of U. S. Grant*, 2 vols. (New York, 1885–86), 1:574.

3 Du Pont to Andrew Hull Foote, Jan. 25, 1861, in James M. Hoppin, *Life of Andrew Hull Foote, Rear-Admiral United States Navy* (New York, 1874), 148.

4 Loyall Farragut, *The Life of David Glasgow Farragut, First Admiral of the United States Navy, Embodying His Journal and Letters* (New York, 1879), 203; Christopher Martin, *Damn the Torpedoes: The Story of America's First Admiral, David Glasgow Farragut* (New York, 1970), 153–54; James P. Duffy, *Lincoln's Admiral: The Civil War Campaigns of David Farragut* (New York, 1997), 40–41 See also Farragut to Richard P. Ashe, April 22, 1861, David G. Farragut Papers, Huntington Library, San Marino, California.

5 Howard K. Beale, ed., *Diary of Gideon Welles*, 3 vols. (New York, 1960), 2:134–35, entry of Sept. 22, 1864.

6 John Sanford Barnes, "The Battle of Port Royal, S.C.," ed. John D. Hayes, *New York Historical Society Quarterly* 45 (1961): 378–79, journal entry of Oct. 30, 1861.

7 Roswell H. Lamson to Flora Lamson, Nov. 4, 1861, in James M. McPherson and Patricia R. McPherson, eds., *Lamson of the Gettysburg: The Civil War Letters of Lieutenant Roswell H. Lamson, U.S. Navy* (New York, 2007), 39.

8 Roswell Lamson to Flora Lamson, Nov. 8, 1861, in McPherson and McPherson, *Lamson of the Gettysburg*, 42–43; Du Pont to John A. Dahlgren, Nov. ?, 1861, in Madeleine V. Dahglren, *Memoir of John A. Dahlgren, Rear Admiral, U.S. Navy* (Boston, 1882), 29.

9 James Grimes to Gustavus Fox, Feb. 3, 1862, in Robert M. Thompson and Richard Wainwright, eds., *Confidential Correspondence of Gustavus Vasa Fox, Assistant Secretary of the Navy, 1861–1865*, 2 vols. (New York, 1918–19), 1:414–15.

10 Samuel Phillips Lee to Elizabeth Blair Lee, April 17, 1862, Blair-Lee Papers, Princeton University Library; Jonathan M. Wainwright to David D. Porter, June 1, 1862, *Official Records of the Union and Confederate Navies*, 30 vols. (Washington, 1894–1922; hereinafter abbreviated *ORN*), ser. 1, vol. 18, pp. 143–44.

11 Charles E. Dufour, *The Night the War Was Lost* (Garden City, N.Y., 1960), 269–70.

12 Farragut to Welles, May 6, 1862, *ORN*, ser. 2, vol. 18, p. 770.

13 George Washington Cable, "New Orleans before the Capture," in *Battles and Leaders of the Civil War*, ed. Robert U. Johnson and Clarence C. Buel, 4 vols. (New York, 1888), 2:20; Dufour, *The Night the War Was Lost*.

14 Farragut to Welles, March 16, 1863, *ORN*, ser. 1, vol. 19, p. 665.

15 Fox to Farragut, April 2, 1863, in Fox, *Confidential Correspondence* 1:331; Farragut to Virginia Farragut, July 15, 1863, in Farragut, *Life of Farragut*, 381.

16 Fox to Du Pont, April 3, May 12, June 3, 1862, in Fox, *Confidential Correspondence* 1:114–15, and John D. Hayes, ed., *Samuel Francis Du Pont: A Selection from His Civil War Letters*, 3 vols. (Ithaca, N.Y., 1969), 2:91n, 96–97.

17 Du Pont to Fox, Sept. 20, 1862, in Fox, *Confidential Correspondence* 1:114–15; Du Pont to Fox, May 31, 1862, in Du Pont, *Civil War Letters* 1:91–92.

18 Du Pont to Commodore Theodorus Bailey, Oct. 30, 1862, and Du Pont to Captain Henry A. Wise, Jan. 16, 1863, *ORN*, ser. 1, vol. 13, pp. 423, 513; Du Pont to Henry Winter Davis, Oct. 25, 1862, in Du Pont, *Civil War Letters* 2:259n.

19 Fox to Du Pont, Feb. 20, 1863, in Du Pont, *Civil War Letters* 2:450.

20 Du Pont to Fox, March 2, 1863, Du Pont to Henry Winter Davis, April 1, 1863, in Du Pont, *Civil War Letters* 2:464, 534.

21 Du Pont to James Biddle, March 26, 1863, in Du Pont, *Civil War Letters* 2:510.

22 Charles Steedman to Sally Steedman, April 3, 1863, in *Memoir and Correspondence of Steedman*, 366–67.

23 Du Pont to Sophie Du Pont, April 4, 1863, in Du Pont *Civil War Letters*, 2:544.

24 *Diary of Gideon Welles* 1:237, 247, entries of Feb. 16 and March 12, 1864.

25 Du Pont to Welles, April 8, 1863, *ORN*, ser. 1, vol. 14, pp. 3–4. The reports and other documentation of the battle are on pp. 3–112.

26 Du Pont to Senator James W. Grimes, Aug. 8, 1863, and Du Pont to Sophie Du Pont, April 8, May 2, 1863, in Du Pont, *Civil War Letters* 3:220, 3, 74.

27 Article in *Baltimore American*, reprinted in *ORN*, ser. 1, vol. 14, pp. 57–59; Du Pont to David Hunter, April 8, 1863, *ORN*, ser. 1, vol. 14, p. 31. For the aftermath of the battle and the criticisms of Du Pont, see Kevin J. Weddle, *Lincoln's Tragic Admiral: The Life of Samuel Francis Du Pont* (Charlottesville, Va., 2005), 195–207.

28 *Diary of Gideon Welles* 1:228, 309, entries of April 30, May 23, 1863; Weddle, *Lincoln's Tragic Admiral*.

29 Drayton to Samuel Francis Du Pont, Sept. 18, 1864, in Du Pont, *Civil War Letters* 3:383.

30 For all of the reports, dispatches, and other documentation of the battle, see *ORN*, ser. 1, vol. 21, pp. 397–600.

CHAPTER 7

1   Gary W. Gallagher, *The Union War* (Cambridge, Mass., 2011), 2.

2   Gallagher, *The Union War*, 1.

3   Gallagher, *The Union War*, 147.

4   Roy P. Basler, ed., *The Collected Works of Abraham Lincoln*, 9 vols. (New Brunswick, N.J., 1953–55), 7:500, 507.

5   Gallagher, *The Union War*, 148.

6   Quoted in Adam Goodheart, *1861: The Civil War Awakening* (New York, 2011), 302, 313–14.

7   Goodheart, *1861: The Civil War Awakening*, 327, 329.

8   Michael Burlingame and John R. Turner Ettlinger, eds., *Inside Lincoln's White House: The Complete Civil War Diary of John Hay* (Carbondale, Ill., 1997), 19, diary entry of May 7, 1861.

9   Goodheart, *1861: The Civil War Awakening*, 298.

10 Vincent Harding, *There Is a River: The Black Struggle for Freedom in America* (New York, 1981), 231, 230, 225, 226, 228, 235.

11 Ira Berlin, chief ed., *Freedom: A Documentary History of Emancipation, 1861–1867*, ser. 1, vol. 1, *The Destruction of Slavery* (Cambridge, 1985), 2, 3.

12 Barbara J. Fields, "Who Freed the Slaves?" in Geoffrey C. Ward with Ric Burns and Ken Burns, *The Civil War: An Illustrated History* (New York, 1990), 181, 179.

13 Lerone Bennett Jr., *Forced into Glory: Abraham Lincoln's White Dream* (Chicago, 2000), 7, 58.

14 David Blight, *A Slave No More: Two Men Who Escaped to Freedom, Including Their Own Narratives of Emancipation* (New York, 2007), 160.

15 See James M. McPherson, "Who Freed the Slaves?" in McPherson, *Drawn with the Sword: Reflections on the American Civil War* (New York, 1996), 192–207; Allen C. Guelzo, *Lincoln's Emancipation Proclamation: The End of Slavery in America* (New York, 2004); and Richard Striner, *Father Abraham: Lincoln's Relentless Struggle to End Slavery* (New York, 2006).

16 Blight, *A Slave No More*, 14.

17 Blight, *A Slave No More*, 172.

18 Blight, *A Slave No More*, 67.

19 Blight, *A Slave No More*, 257.

20 Blight, *A Slave No More*, 15.

21 Blight, *A Slave No More*, 132.

CHAPTER 8

1   Eric Foner, *The Fiery Trial: Abraham Lincoln and American Slavery* (New York, 2010), 25–26.

2 Foner, *The Fiery Trial*, 66.

3 Foner, *The Fiery Trial*, 3, 103.

4 Roy P. Basler, ed., *The Collected Works of Abraham Lincoln* (New Brunswick, N.J., 1953–55), 2:461.

5 Basler, *Collected Works of Lincoln* 2:255–56.

6 Foner, *The Fiery Trial*, 262.

7 Foner, *The Fiery Trial*, 323, 256.

8 Foner, *The Fiery Trial*, xxiii.

9 Basler, *Collected Works of Lincoln* 5:371–72.

10 Foner, *The Fiery Trial*, 225.

11 Foner, *The Fiery Trial*, 244, 253, 256, 258.

12 Basler, *Collected Works of Lincoln* 6:409–10.

13 Basler, *Collected Works of Lincoln* 7:500, 507.

14 Foner, *The Fiery Trial*, 331.

15 William Hanchett, *The Lincoln Murder Conspiracies* (Urbana, Ill., 1983), 37.

16 Foner, *The Fiery Trial*, 334.

17 James Oakes, *The Radical and the Republican: Frederick Douglass, Abraham Lincoln, and the Triumph of Anti-Slavery Politics* (New York, 2007), 256, 269, 271.

18 Oakes, *The Radical and the Republican*, 272.

19 *Douglass' Monthly* 5 (Aug. 1862): 692–94.

20 *Douglass' Monthly* 5 (Oct. 1862): 721.

21 Frederick Douglass to Theodore Tilton, Oct. 15, 1864, Tilton Papers, Buffalo Public Library; *Liberator*, Sept. 23, 1864.

22 Oakes, *The Radical and the Republican*, 170.

23 Oakes, *The Radical and the Republican*, 272.

24 Oakes, *The Radical and the Republican*, 149.

25 Oakes, *The Radical and the Republican*, 152, 154.

26 Basler, *Collected Works of Lincoln* 5:219, 222.

27 Oakes, *The Radical and the Republican*, 184.

28 Basler, *Collected Works of Lincoln* 5:388–89; Oakes, *The Radical and the Republican*, 189.

29 Oakes, *The Radical and the Republican*, 122, 124, 129.

30 Basler, *Collected Works of Lincoln* 2:501.

31 Oakes, *The Radical and the Republican*, 125, 127.

32 Oakes, *The Radical and the Republican*, 194.

33 Republican quoted in V. Jaque Voegeli, *Free but Not Equal: The Midwest and the Negro in the Civil War* (Chicago, 1967), 45; Oakes, *The Radical and the Republican*, 194.

34 Oakes, *The Radical and the Republican*, 213, 232, 259.

35 Oakes, *The Radical and the Republican*, 287.

CHAPTER 9

1   Roy P. Basler, ed., *The Collected Works of Abraham Lincoln*, 9 vols. (New Brunswick, N.J., 1953–55), 1:509–10.

2   T. Harry Williams, *Lincoln and His Generals* (New York, 1952), vii.

3   Colin R. Ballard, *The Military Genius of Abraham Lincoln: An Essay* (London, 1926); T. Harry Williams, *Lincoln and His Generals*; Kenneth P. Williams, *Lincoln Finds a General: A Military Study of the Civil War*, 5 vols. (New York, 1949–59); Allan Nevins, *The War for the Union*, 4 vols. (New York, 1959–71).

4   Mark E. Neely Jr., *The Abraham Lincoln Encyclopedia* (New York, 1982); Don E. Fehrenbacher, *Lincoln in Text and Context: Collected Essays* (Stanford, Calif., 1987); Gabor S. Boritt, ed., *The Historian's Lincoln: Pseudohistory, Psychohistory, and History* (Urbana, Ill., 1988); Merrill D. Peterson, *Lincoln in American Memory* (New York, 1994).

5   Basler, *Collected Works of Lincoln* 8:332.

6   Michael Burlingame and John R. Turner Ettlinger, eds., *Inside Lincoln's White House: The Complete Civil War Diary of John Hay* (Carbondale, Ill., 1997), 20, diary entry of May 7, 1861.

7   Basler, *Collected Works of Lincoln* 3:268; 7:23, 8:151.

8   Carl von Clausewitz, *On War*, trans. and ed. Michael Howard and Peter Paret (Princeton, N.J., 1976), 87–88.

9   *The War of the Rebellion . . . Official Records of the Union and Confederate Armies*, 128 vols. (Washington, 1880–1901; hereinafter abbreviated *OR*), ser. 1, vol. 34, pt. 3, pp. 332–33.

10 Allen Thorndike Rice, ed., *Reminiscences of Abraham Lincoln by Distinguished Men of His Time* (New York, 1888), 391–92.

11 *Chicago Tribune*, Sept. 16, 1961, quoted in Thomas J. Goss, *The War within the Union High Command: Politics and Generalship during the Civil War* (Lawrence, Kans., 2003), 42.

12 *OR*, ser. 3, vol. 2, pp. 401–2; Abraham Lincoln to Edwin M. Stanton, Jan. 12, 1863, in Basler, *Collected Works of Lincoln* 6:55.

13 Goss, *The War within the Union High Command*, xv.

14 Lincoln to Frémont, Sept. 2, 1862, Lincoln to Orville H. Browning, Sept. 22, 1861, in Basler, *Collected Works of Lincoln* 4:506, 532.

15 Gideon Welles, "The History of Emancipation," *Galaxy* 14 (Dec. 1872): 842–43.

16 For the platform, see Edward McPherson, *The Political History of the United States during the Great Rebellion*, 2nd ed. (Washington, 1865), 406–7.

17 Basler, *Collected Works of Lincoln* 5:357.

18 Lincoln to Andrew Johnson, March 26, 1863, in Basler, *Collected Works of Lincoln* 6:149–50.

19 Basler, *Collected Works of Lincoln* 6:410, 7:500, 507.

20 *Personal Memoirs of U. S. Grant*, 2 vols. (New York, 1885-86), 2:122.

21 Basler, *Collected Works of Lincoln* 5:34-35.

22 Lincoln to McClellan, Feb. 3, 1862, Basler, *Collected Works of Lincoln* 5:118-19. For Johnston's apprehension of just such a campaign plan as Lincoln proposed, see Johnston to Jefferson Davis, Nov. 22, 1861, *OR*, ser. 1, vol. 5, pp. 1072-73.

23 Basler, *Collected Works of Lincoln* 5:182; Stephen W. Sears, ed., *The Civil War Papers of George B. McClellan* (New York, 1989), 234.

24 Lincoln to McClellan, April 9, 1862, in Basler, *Collected Works of Lincoln* 5:185.

25 Lincoln to McClellan, April 9, 1862, in Basler, *Collected Works of Lincoln* 5:185.

26 Lincoln to Sherman, Dec. 26, 1864, in Basler, *Collected Works of Lincoln* 8:181.

27 Lincoln to McClellan, Oct. 13, 1862, in Basler, *Collected Works of Lincoln* 5:461; Francis P. Blair to Montgomery Blair, Nov. 7, 1862, in William F. Smith, *The Francis Preston Blair Family in Politics*, 2 vols. (New York, 1933), 2:144.

28 Basler, *Collected Works of Lincoln* 4:95.

29 Basler, *Collected Works of Lincoln* 5:85n.; Lincoln to Buell (copy to Halleck), Jan. 13, 1862, Basler, *Collected Works of Lincoln* 5:98.

30 *OR*, ser. 1, vol. 46, pt. 1, p. 11; Burlingame and Ettlinger, *Inside Lincoln's White House*, 193, diary entry of April 30, 1864.

31 Lincoln to Hooker, June 10, 16, in Basler, *Collected Works of Lincoln* 6:257, 281.

32 Lincoln to Halleck, July 7, 1863, in Basler, *Collected Works of Lincoln* 6:319.

33 *OR*, ser. 1, vol. 27, pt. 3, p. 519; Howard K. Beale, ed., *Diary of Gideon Welles*, 3 vols. (New York, 1960), 1:370, entry of July 14, 1863; Burlingame and Ettlinger, *Inside Lincoln's White House*, 62, diary entry of July 14, 1863.

34 Lincoln to Meade, July 14, 1863, in Basler, *Collected Works of Lincoln* 6:328. Endorsed by Lincoln: "never sent, or signed."

35 Lincoln to Henry W. Halleck, Sept. 19, 1863, in Basler, *Collected Works of Lincoln* 6:467.

36 Quoted in Shelby Foote, *The Civil War: A Narrative: Fort Sumter to Perryville* (New York, 1958), 430.

37 Lincoln to McDowell, May 25, 28, 1862, in Basler, *Collected Works of Lincoln*, 5:235, 246.

38 Henry W. Halleck to Buell, Oct. 19, 1862, *OR*, ser. 1, vol. 16, pt. 2, p. 627. See also Lincoln to McClellan, Oct. 13, 1862, in Basler, *Collected Works of Lincoln* 5:460-61.

39 Rufus Ingalls to Montgomery Meigs, Oct. 26, 1862, *OR*, ser. 1, vol. 19, pt. 2, pp. 492-93; Lincoln to Nathaniel Banks, Nov. 22, 1862, in Basler, *Collected Works of Lincoln* 5:505-6.

40 James S. Rusling, *Men and Things I Saw in Civil War Days* (New York, 1899), 16-17; Washburne to Lincoln, May 1, 1863, Abraham Lincoln Papers, Robert Todd Lincoln Collection, Library of Congress.

41 Lincoln to Flag Officer Louis M. Goldsborough, May 7, 10, 1862, in Basler, *Collected Works of Lincoln* 5:207, 209; William Keeler to his wife, May 9, 1862, in Robert W. Daly, ed., *Aboard the USS "Monitor," 1862: The Letters of Acting Paymaster William Frederick Keeler* (Annapolis, Md., 1964), 113, 115; Salmon P. Chase to Janet Chase, May 11, 1862, in John Niven, ed., *The Salmon P. Chase Papers*, vol. 3, *Correspondence, 1858–March 1863* (Kent, Ohio, 1996), 193–97, quotation from 197.

CHAPTER 10

1 George B. McClellan to Mary Ellen Marcy McClellan, (hereinafter Ellen), Sept. 7, 1862, Feb. 26, 1863, McClellan Papers, Library of Congress (repository hereinafter cited as LC). All citations of McClellan's letters and reports will be to the original sources. These documents are also published in a superbly edited collection by Stephen W. Sears, *The Civil War Papers of George B. McClellan* (New York, 1989), and can be found there by the appropriate date.

2 Francis Preston Blair to Montgomery Blair, Nov. 7, 1862, in William E. Smith, *The Francis Preston Blair Family in Politics*, 2 vols. (New York, 1933), 2:144; Theodore Calvin Pease and James G. Randall, eds., *The Diary of Orville Hickman Browning*, 2 vols. (Springfield, Ill., 1925), 1:563, entry of July 25, 1862.

3 McClellan to Samuel L. M. Barlow, July 25, 1862, Barlow Papers, Huntington Library, San Marino, Calif. (repository hereinafter cited as HL); McClellan to Ellen, July 31, 1862, Oct. 11, 1861, McClellan Papers, LC.

4 McClellan to Ellen, Aug. 8, Oct. 11, Nov. 17, 1861, McClellan Papers, LC.

5 McClellan to Ellen, Oct. 11, 1861, McClellan Papers, LC.

6 McClellan to Ellen, July 13, 22, 1862, McClellan Papers, LC.

7 Chandler to his wife, July 11, 6, 1862, quoted in Bruce Tap, *Over Lincoln's Shoulder: The Committee on the Conduct of the War* (Lawrence, Kans., 1998), 124, 122.

8 Howard K. Beale, ed., *The Diary of Gideon Welles*, 3 vols. (New York, 1960), 1:93–102, entries of Aug. 31, Sept. 1, 1862; John Niven, ed., *The Salmon P. Chase Papers*, 5 vols. (Kent, Ohio, 1993), 1:366–68, diary entries of Aug. 29, 30, 31, Sept. 1, 1862.

9 William Howard Russell, *My Diary North and South*, ed. Fletcher Pratt (New York, 1954), 240, entry of July 27, 1861; Allan Nevins, *The War for the Union: The Improvised War, 1861–1862* (New York, 1959), 269.

10 McClellan to Ellen, July 27, 30, Aug. 9, Oct. 31, 1861, McClellan Papers, LC.

11 *The War of the Rebellion: A Compilation of the Official Records of the Union and Confederate Armies*, 128 vols. (Washington, 1880–1901; hereinafter abbreviated as *OR*), ser. 1, vol. 11, pt. 3, pp. 3–4.

12 McClellan to Ellen, Aug. 8, 1861, McClellan Papers, LC; Scott to Cameron, Aug. 9, 1861, *OR*, ser. 1, vol. 11, pt. 3, p. 4.

13 McClellan to Lincoln, Aug. 10, 1861, Abraham Lincoln Papers, Robert Todd Lincoln Collection, LC.

14 McClellan to Ellen, Aug. 8, 9, 14, 16, 19, 1861, McClellan Papers, LC.

15 U. S. Congress, *Joint Committee on the Conduct of the War, Report of the Joint Committee on the Conduct of the War*, 8 vols. (Washington, 1863–1866), vol. 2, pt. 1 (the Army of the Potomac), 241 (hereafter cited as *JCCW*).

16 Wade to Chandler, Oct. 8, 1861, in Russel H. Beatie, *Army of the Potomac: McClellan Takes Command, September 1861–February 1862* (New York, 2004), 25–26.

17 McClellan to Ellen, Oct. 26, 1861, McClellan Papers, LC; Scott to Simon Cameron, Oct. 31, 1861, *OR*, ser. 3, vol. 1, pp. 538–39.

18 McClellan to Ellen, Oct. 19, 1861, McClellan Papers, LC.

19 Michael Burlingame and John R. Turner Ettlinger, eds., *Inside Lincoln's White House: The Complete Civil War Diary of John Hay* (Carbondale, Ill., 1997), 30, entry dated November 1861.

20 Burlingame and Ettlinger, *Inside Lincoln's White House,* 25, 29, entries of Oct. 10, 26, 1861.

21 McClellan to Simon Cameron, undated but probably Oct. 31, 1861, *OR*, ser. 1, vol. 5, pp. 9–11.

22 McClellan to Ellen, Oct. 31, 1861, McClellan Papers, LC.

23 Burlingame and Ettlinger, *Inside Lincoln's White House*, 32, entry of Nov. 13, 1861; McClellan to Ellen, Nov. 17, 1861, McClellan Papers, LC.

24 "Memorandum to George B. McClellan on Potomac Campaign," circa Dec. 1, 1861, in Roy P. Basler, ed., *The Collected Works of Abraham Lincoln*, 9 vols. (New Brunswick, N.J., 1953–55), 5:34–35.

25 "General M. C. Meigs on the Conduct of the Civil War," *American Historical Review* 26 (1921): 292.

26 Howard K. Beale, ed., *The Diary of Edward Bates, 1859–1866* (Washington, 1933), 218, 220, entries of Dec. 31, 1861, Jan. 3, 1862.

27 Minutes of the meeting written by McDowell, quoted in William Swinton, *Campaigns of the Army of the Potomac* (New York, 1866), 80.

28 Swinton, *Campaigns of the Army of the Potomac*, 79–85.

29 Randall, *Diary of Browning* 1:525, entry of Jan. 18, 1862; Basler, *Collected Works of Lincoln* 5:115.

30 McClellan to Edwin M. Stanton, Feb. 3, 1862, in *OR*, ser. 1, vol. 5, pp. 42–45.

31 McClellan to Samuel L. M. Barlow, Nov. 8, 1861, Barlow Papers, HL.

32 Several versions of this anecdote exist; this one from Helen Nicolay, *Lincoln's Secretary: A Biography of John G. Nicolay* (New York, 1949), 149, is evidently based on recollections by her father, who may have been present at the meeting. See also Tap, *Over Lincoln's Shoulder*, 113.

33 James H. Campbell to his wife, March 4, 1862, in Don E. Fehrenbacher and Virginia Fehrenbacher, eds., *Recollected Words of Abraham Lincoln* (Stanford, Calif., 1996), 76.

34 Stephen W. Sears, *To the Gates of Richmond: The Peninsula Campaign* (New York, 1992), 3–9; *JCCW*, vol. 2, pt. 1, pp. 270, 360, 387.

35 Basler, *Collected Works of Lincoln* 5:149–50, 155.

36 *OR*, ser. 1, vol. 11, pt. 1, p. 61.

37 McClellan to Samuel L. M. Barlow, March 16, 1862, Barlow Papers, HL; McClellan to Ellen, June 22, 1862, McClellan Papers, LC.

38 McClellan to Ellen, Aug. 10, 1862, McClellan Papers, LC.

39 Burlingame and Ettlinger, *Inside Lincoln's White House*, 37, entry of Sept. 1, 1862.

40 Beale, *Diary of Welles* 1:113, entry of Sept. 7, 1862; Burlingame and Ettlinger, *Inside Lincoln's White House*, 38–39, entry of Sept. 5, 1862.

41 Lincoln to McClellan, Sept. 15, 1862, Basler, *Collected Works of Lincoln* 5:426.

42 Halleck to McClellan, Oct. 6, 1862, *OR*, ser. 1, vol. 19, pt. 1, p. 72; Halleck to Hamilton R. Gamble, Oct. 30, 1862, *OR*, ser. 3, vol. 2, pp. 703–4.

43 Burlingame and Ettlinger, *Inside Lincoln's White House*, 232, entry of Sept. 25, 1864.

44 James H. Wilson, *Under the Old Flag*, 2 vols. (New York, 1912), 1:400.

45 For a recent exploration of McClellan's military leadership that emphasizes the importance of the general's political beliefs, see Ethan S. Rafuse, *McClellan's War: The Failure of Moderation in the Struggle for the Union* (Bloomington, Ind., 2005). Two other recent studies largely agree with the approach taken in the present essay: John C. Waugh, *Lincoln and McClellan: The Troubled Partnership between a President and His General* (New York, 2010), and Chester G. Hearn, *Lincoln and McClellan at War* (Baton Rouge, La., 2012).

CHAPTER 11

1 All quoted in Merrill D. Peterson, *Lincoln and American Memory* (New York, 1994), 185, 342n.

2 Roy P. Basler, ed., *The Collected Works of Abraham Lincoln*, 9 vols. (New Brunswick, N.J., 1953–55), 5:53.

3 Basler, *Collected Works of Lincoln* 4:235–36.

4 Basler, *Collected Works of Lincoln* 4:236.

5 Basler, *Collected Works of Lincoln* 4:240.

6 Basler, *Collected Works of Lincoln* 2:255.

7 Basler, *Collected Works of Lincoln* 2:405–6.

8 Basler, *Collected Works of Lincoln* 3:376.

9   Basler, *Collected Works of Lincoln* 4:268; Michael Burlingame and John R. Turner
     Ettlinger, eds., *Inside Lincoln's White House: The Complete Civil War Diary of
     John Hay* (Carbondale, Ill., 1997), 20, entry of May 7, 1861.

10   Basler, *Collected Works of Lincoln* 4:439.

11   *Indianapolis Daily Journal*, April 27, 1861.

12   Josiah Perry to Phebe Perry, Oct. 3, 1862, Josiah P. Perry Papers, Illinois State
     Historical Library, Springfield; Robert T. McMahan diary, entry of Sept. 3, 1863,
     State Historical Society of Missouri, Columbia.

13   Titus Crenshaw to father, Nov. 10, 1861, in Charlotte Erickson, *Invisible
     Immigrants: The Adaptation of English and Scottish Immigrants in Nineteenth-
     Century America* (Coral Gables, Fla., 1972), 348; George H. Cadman to Esther
     Cadman, March 6, 1864, Cadman Papers, Southern Historical Collection,
     University of North Carolina, Chapel Hill; Peter Welsh to Mary Welsh, Feb. 1, 1863,
     and to Patrick Prendergast, June 1, 1863, in Laurence Frederick Kohl and Margaret
     Cosee Richard, eds., *Irish Green and Union Blue: The Civil War Letters of Peter
     Welsh* (New York, 1986), 65–66, 102.

14   Quoted in G. D. Lillibridge, *Beacon of Freedom: The Impact of American
     Democracy upon Great Britain, 1830–1870* (Philadelphia, 1955), 5, 28.

15   Alexis de Tocqueville, *Democracy in America*, 12th ed., trans. George Lawrence,
     ed. J. P. Mayer (New York, 1966), xiii; Serge Gavronsky, *The French Liberal
     Opposition and the American Civil War* (New York, 1968), 11; Lillibridge, *Beacon
     of Freedom*, 80.

16   *Times* quoted in Frank L. Owsley, *King Cotton Diplomacy: Foreign Relations of the
     Confederate States of America*, 2nd ed., rev. by Harriet C. Owsley (Chicago, 1959),
     186; Earl of Shrewsbury quoted in Ephraim D. Adams, *Great Britain and the
     American Civil War*, 2 vols. (New York, 1925), 2:282.

17   *Pensamiento Español*, Sept. 1862, quoted in Belle Becker Sideman and Lillian
     Friedman, eds., *Europe Looks at the Civil War* (New York, 1960), 173–74; Eduard
     de Stoeckl quoted in Albert A. Woldman, *Lincoln and the Russians* (Cleveland,
     1952), 216–17.

18   *Revue des Deux Mondes*, Aug. 15, 1862, and John Stuart Mill, *Autobiography*, both
     quoted in Sideman and Friedman, *Europe Looks at the Civil War*, 81, 117–18.

19   Lincoln quoted in *The Reminiscences of Carl Schurz*, 3 vols. (New York, 1907–8),
     2:309; *Saturday Review*, Sept. 14, 1861, quoted in Adams, *Great Britain and the
     American Civil War* 1:181; *Economist*, Sept. 1861, quoted in Karl Marx and
     Friedrich Engels, *The Civil War in the United States*, ed. Richard Enmale (New
     York, 1937), 12.

20   Basler, *Collected Works of Lincoln* 5:423, 6:30.

21 Quoted in Frederick W. Seward, *Seward at Washington as Senator and Secretary of State* (New York, 1891), 151, and Francis B. Carpenter, *Six Months at the White House with Abraham Lincoln* (New York, 1866), 269.

22 Basler, *Collected Works of Lincoln* 5: 537.

23 Basler, *Collected Works of Lincoln* 8:333.

24 Sir Edward Bulwer-Lytton to John Bigelow, April 2, 1865, quoted in Sideman and Friedman, *Europe Looks at the Civil War*, 282; Beesly quoted in Harold M. Hyman, ed., *Heard Round the World: The Impact Abroad of the Civil War* (New York, xi, 73.

25 Quoted in Hyman, *Heard Round the World*, 323.

26 Reena Mathew, "One Set of Footprints," essay in the author's possession.

27 Basler, *Collected Works of Lincoln* 4:426.

CHAPTER 12

1 John Y. Simon, et al., eds., *Papers of Ulysses S. Grant*, 31 vols. to date (Carbondale, Ill., 1967–), 18:264.

2 Quoted in Don E. Fehrenbacher, *The South and Three Sectional Crises* (Baton Rouge, La., 1980), 40.

3 *New York Weekly Tribune*, Feb. 13, 1859; the representative is quoted in James A. Rawley, *Race and Politics: "Bleeding Kansas" and the Coming of the Civil War* (Philadelphia, 1969), 239–40.

4 Quotations from Allan Nevins, *The Emergence of Lincoln*, vol. 2, *Prologue to Civil War, 1859–1861* (New York, 1950), 121–22.

5 *Boston Commonwealth*, June 24, 1865.

6 Whitelaw Reid, *After the War: A Tour of the Southern States 1865–1866* (Cincinnati, 1866), 296; Sidney Andrews, *The South since the War* (Boston, 1866), 68.

7 Quoted in Hans L. Trefousse, *Andrew Johnson: A Biography* (New York, 1989), 197, and Brooks D. Simpson, *The Reconstruction Presidents* (Lawrence, Kans., 1998), 68.

8 *Chicago Tribune*, Dec. 1, 1865.

9 Michael Perman, *Reunion without Compromise: The South and Reconstruction, 1865–1868* (Cambridge, 1973), 82; Andrews, *The South since the War*, 391.

10 Quoted in Richard Zuczek, *State of Rebellion: Reconstruction in South Carolina* (Columbia, S.C., 1996), 47.

11 Gilles Vandall, *Rethinking Southern Violence: Homicides in Post–Civil War Louisiana, 1866–1884* (Columbus, Ohio, 2000). The author classifies an estimated 4,986 homicides in Louisiana from 1866 to 1884, with peaks in 1868 and 1873–74. Many of these were ordinary murders rather than politically motivated killings, but the latter constituted at least half of the total. See especially pp. 13 and 22.

12 Quoted in Allen W. Trelease, *White Terror: The Ku Klux Klan Conspiracy and Southern Reconstruction* (New York, 1971), 268–69.

13 Trelease, *White Terror*, 189–225.

14 Frederic Bancroft, ed., *Speeches, Correspondence, and Political Papers of Carl Schurz*, 6 vols. (New York, 1913), 2:487, 488, 489, 490, 495, 502.

15 Everette Swinney, "Enforcing the Fifteenth Amendment," *Journal of Southern History* 27 (1962): 202–18; Robert J. Kaczorowski, *The Politics of Judicial Interpretation: The Federal Courts, Department of Justice and Civil Rights, 1866–1876* (New York, 1985), 79–99; Lou Falkner Williams, *The Great South Carolina Ku Klux Klan Trials, 1871–1872* (Athens, Ga., 1996).

16 James K. Hogue, *Uncivil War: Five New Orleans Street Battles and the Rise and Fall of Radical Reconstruction* (Baton Rouge, La., 2006), 130.

17 *25 Fed. Cas.* 707, p. 210; *U.S. Reports*, p. 542.

18 Ted Tunnell, *Crucible of Reconstruction: War, Radicalism, and Race in Louisiana, 1862–1877* (Baton Rouge, La., 1984), 196–202.

19 Nicholas Lemann, *Redemption: The Last Battle of the Civil War* (New York, 2006), 28.

20 Hogue, *Uncivil War*, 145.

21 Quoted in Lemann, *Redemption*, 93–94.

22 *Washington National Republican*, Jan. 24, 1874; William B. Hesseltine, *Ulysses S. Grant, Politician* (New York, 1935), 358.

23 Bancroft, *Speeches . . . and Political Papers of Schurz*, Vol. 3, pp. 111, 121, 144, 151–52, 141, 130–31, 125.

24 Lemann, *Redemption*, 114.

25 Lemann, *Redemption*, 122–23.

26 Richard N. Current, *Three Carpetbag Governors* (Baton Rouge, La., 1967), 88.

27 Lemann, *Redemption*, 120.

28 *Mississippi in 1875: Report of the Select Committee to Inquire into the Mississippi Election of 1875*, Senate Report no. 527, 44th Congress, 1st Session (Washington, 1876), p. 1807.

29 Lemann, *Redemption*, 179–80.

INDEX